CLOSE ENCOUNTERS WITH MY LORD

*To Kay and Jim,
dear friends
The Lord is my Shepherd
and Protector.
Nancy L. Hurley*

Close Encounters with My Lord

Conversations with God

Nancy Lee Hurley

Tate Publishing & *Enterprises*

Close Encounters with My Lord
Copyright © 2010 by Nancy Lee Hurley. All rights reserved.

No part of this publication may be reproduced, stored in a retrieval system or transmitted in any way by any means, electronic, mechanical, photocopy, recording or otherwise without the prior permission of the author except as provided by USA copyright law.

Scriptures taken from the *Holy Bible, New International Version*®, niv®. Copyright © 1973, 1978, 1984 by Biblica, Inc.™ Used by permission of Zondervan. All rights reserved worldwide. www.zondervan.com

The opinions expressed by the author are not necessarily those of Tate Publishing, LLC.

Published by Tate Publishing & Enterprises, LLC
127 E. Trade Center Terrace | Mustang, Oklahoma 73064 USA
1.888.361.9473 | www.tatepublishing.com

Tate Publishing is committed to excellence in the publishing industry. The company reflects the philosophy established by the founders, based on Psalm 68:11,
"The Lord gave the word and great was the company of those who published it."

Book design copyright © 2010 by Tate Publishing, LLC. All rights reserved.
Cover design by Jeff Fisher
Interior design by Joel Uber

Published in the United States of America

ISBN: 978-1-61663-851-1
1. Religion / Christian Life / Personal Growth
2. Religion/ Christian Life / Spiritual Growth
10.08.16

Dedication

I dedicate this book to my husband, Ron; my sons, Ron II and John; their wives, Nancy and Laura; and my four grandchildren, Jennifer, Christopher, Patrick, and Ron III; and my great-granddaughter, Sarina. I thank them for their loving support of me all through their lives as well as mine. Without them and my Lord, I would be nothing. I am truly blessed!

Acknowledgments

I want to thank Ashley Luckett, my editor, for her patience and loving care she gave me and especially to my book. Without her guidance this book wouldn't be what it is: the true essence of my life. Thank you, Ashley!

I thank Virginia Olsen, my dear friend, for her time and dedication in checking out all the contents of this book.
Thank you, Virginia!

> "Almighty God, you know that we have no power in ourselves to help ourselves. Keep us both outwardly in our bodies and inwardly in our souls, that we may be defended from all adversities which may happen to the body and from all evil thoughts which may assault and hurt the soul; through Jesus Christ our Lord, who lives and reigns with you and the Holy Spirit, one God, forever and ever. Amen."
>
> —February 24, 2004, *Collect–The Book of Common Prayer*

Table of Contents

Prologue: A Time to Think	11
God's Remnant in My Family	15
A Frightening Night Alone	21
My Time as a Guinea Pig	25
What Went Wrong?	27
Wrongly Accused	33
Someone I Trusted	39
Being Left Alone Again with Strangers	43
Praising God from the Choir Loft	51
Tragedy Hits	55
A View of God's Plan for Me	63
My Balloon Bursts	71
The Lord's Rays Come through the Clouds	79
Preparing for our Life in New Mexico	89
We Begin Our Married Life	93
My World Shatters on Two Levels	97
Joy Comes into My Life	105
Wonderful Visits	115
Another Gift from God	121
A New Beginning for Our Family	131
Summers in God's Garden	137

Our New Life in Michigan Begins	145
Reconciliation with Mother	149
My Life Changes	163
Dealing with Dad's Sad Situation	175
The Battle Lines Are Drawn	189
Life Changes Come Swiftly	203
Beginning Again	217
Good Times Abound for Our Family	229
Merry Ol' England	245
Onto a New Life: Retirement	263
Looking Back	271

Prologue

A Time to Think

Since my birth sixty-eight years ago, I have lived and seen a lot. One day two years ago I sat in a bistro, having a steak sandwich, listening to three women discussing their lives and how God had been an integral part of them. As I continued to sit there, partly in my own daydreams and getting more oblivious to their conversation, I heard my Lord say, "It's time for you to put to paper all we have done together and what you have learned from my presence in your life." Shock waves shot through me as I wrestled with this news. I shook in my boots with the magnitude of this venture.

As I drove home from the bistro I thought about what I had heard the Lord tell me. How was I going to do this? This was a monumental task. What I needed was a plan of action. As I sat later that day at my computer, I began creating an outline. Doing so, another shock wave ran through my body. As I laid my life and experiences out in front of me, I saw all the times I hadn't seen, heard, or known he was at work in my life. "How can that be?" I asked myself. "That isn't possible." When I really looked at myself and my outline, I realized it was true. He had been with me through the good as well as the not-so-good times. Many times I was blind to his intervention in my life. The pain of that and the realization that he had protected me many more times than I ever suspected and the regret of never seeing or thanking him made me weep. How was it that I never saw the numerous times of his grace and intervention in my life? I loved him then but even more with each passing day of my life. How could I have been so blind to the beauty of his love and caring for me? The whole idea overwhelmed me!

Now, looking back over my life, I don't see how I missed those times he was there for me. How could I have missed his presence? I must have been looking at earthly things (the anger and guilt I felt with people and situations in my life). As I shut him out at these times of frustration, I missed out on feeling and knowing his presence and love. Many times I had failed to learn the lessons he had placed in my path for my growth, while I only grew bitter in the process. One question I repeatedly asked of him was, "How could you let this happen to me if you love me as you say you do?" All I saw was my abusive, alcoholic family and their rejection of me. In my immaturity, I didn't see or hear his call to me to come closer to him and lean on him for strength and love. All I focused on were the things wrong with my life. What he was attempting to teach me or what we could do together weren't on my radar screen. Many times, I blamed him for not helping me when, in essence, he was trying to get my attention to see that his way was better, but I refused to see it his way. What a better life I could have had if I had only surrendered myself to him and his way of life. I refused to relinquish myself to him. As I sat glued to my outline, what sadness gripped me! Even now I am more aware of what I missed out on for not having him closer to me.

I kept, and still keep, asking myself, "How could I not have seen or felt him? Why wasn't I aware of him? I knew he was out there but refused to accept his reality in my life."

In this book, I will address these probing questions as I open my life up to you, relating how much I missed by not always being aware of him and his plan for me. Maybe you will see yourself in some of these dark moments, as well as the joyful ones when I was aware of his presence. I hope this will lead you to do your own assessment of his presence in your life. Walk with me along my path and become aware of our heavenly Father in your life. I will explore my feelings of rejection and being unwanted into how he taught me about Himself and how he cared and loved me so I could ultimately find him and eventually submit my life to him. Now, knowing him has become the greatest gift in my life. My wish is that in my sharing myself with you, you will find him and his presence in your life as well.

God's Remnant in My Family

"Flesh gives birth to flesh,
but the Spirit give birth to Spirit."
(John 3:6)

One afternoon, sixty-eight plus years ago, Mother sat on our front porch talking with three of her closest friends. While sipping tea and munching some of Mother's freshly baked snicker doodle cookies, they talked about all the problems in their lives and the world. Although they couldn't solve them, they debated how to change them.

All of a sudden, their discussion turned to their concerns about Mother's health, since she seemed to be gaining weight around the middle, was tired all the time, and just didn't seem herself. What was the problem? They started quizzing her. Elaine Meadows, Mother's closest friend, said, "I am very concerned about you, Eloise. Your abdomen seems to have a swelling, and I am afraid you might have a tumor." Minnie Short and Sue Barker agreed in unison. They persisted until Mother promised she would see her doctor just to stop their talk.

I know I'm too old to be pregnant, but I am gaining in my stomach area, so I will see Dr. Blackwell just to appease them, Mother thought, although she had become worried by their concerns.

The appointment and her discussion with Dr. Henry Blackwell proved more disconcerting than she had ever expected. She thought she had gone through her change of life, but he wanted her to check in with Dr. Lawrence Nixon, an obstetrician-gynecologist to get his opinion. Dr. Nixon's assessment sent shockwaves through her. He told her she was six months pregnant!

I can only imagine the thoughts going through her mind. I can just imagine her saying, "Dr. Nixon, that just can't be possible. I have gone through the change!" Well, he assured her that she definitely was pregnant and due to deliver in approximately three months. With that, Dr. Nixon scheduled her next maternity checkup. She couldn't deny my reality anymore. I was on the way, and nothing she could do would stop what was about to happen to her and the family: me!

The shock to my parents, James and Eloise, must have been monumental. They were in their late thirties and had two older children—an eighteen-year-old daughter, Ruth, ready for high school graduation in late May, and a thirteen-year-old son, Jim, a high school football hunk and academic. Wanted or not, I was to become part of their family.

My sister angrily denounced my impending arrival with, "How could you do this to me? I will be the laughing stock at Uniontown High School. When I graduate from high school in a month, your baby will be born two months later. What will all my friends say or think?"

Jim took a more practical approach to this news; there would be a baby sister or brother in the house within the next few months. He would be the big brother to whomever. What a twist of fate.

In hopes of easing Ruth and Jim into my coming, Mother and Dad decided my sister and brother could name me. Ruth chose Nancy Lee: Nancy after her best friend, and Lee, for General Robert E. Lee, her favorite Civil War hero. She loved his strength of conviction and fighting through to the bitter end. Jim put together the names of his two closest friends to make Richard Edmond.

Whatever the atmosphere was within our family home for the next three months, it stopped the afternoon of July thirtieth. Mother had ironed all day, which was her Tuesday routine. As her pains became more pronounced, she called Dad at work, telling him he needed to come and take her to Uniontown General Hospital. Deliverance was at hand for both Mother and me. Dad, a mine foreman for Bethlehem Steel, came home as quickly as possible and drove us to the hospital. By the time Ruth and Jim got home from school, our "Gram," my mother's mother, was in attendance at our house, had dinner started, and was waiting with them for the news from the hospital.

In those days, husbands and fathers were relegated to the maternity waiting room. As soon as the baby arrived, he could see his wife and baby and then call home, telling the family the news of the baby's arrival and his or her statistics. Toward late evening, my cries could be heard by all in the immediate birthing area. I wanted people to know I had arrived.

That fall, Ruth enrolled in Hood College and began her studies in history and English. Her goal was to be a high school history and English teacher. Oh, I am sure she wanted to study another subject as well: boys. She was a beautiful, tall, hourglass-figured redhead. She had her admirers, not only at high school but also at college. I am sure she was glad to be away from her squawking baby sister, who took Mom's attention and time away from her. She didn't appreciate sharing Mother or the limelight with me. She was the firstborn, and I was just an interloper along the way. I was an inconvenience and embarrassment for her.

Playing high school football, Jim had to keep up with his college prep courses to remain on the team. He planned to graduate from Uniontown High School and then enroll in engineering at Duke University.

Not long after my arrival, my mother slipped on the basement steps and broke her ankle, which put her out of commission for taking care of me. She did the best she could for me during the day, but when Jim came home, he had to take me in my buggy to football practices and face the embarrassing questions from his teammates. Oh, how he must have hated that, but he did it.

As I grew up, he took care of me like a big brother should. He would play ball with me or sit and read to me. His caring and sensitivity made me feel wonderful. He was like God watching over me and beaming down on me. I felt wonderful and loved. Ruth, on the other hand, treated me like her selfish, spoiled, little sister. In a way, I was. I was in her way, an intrusion into her life. I wanted to be just like her: all grownup and doing all the things she did. She didn't like that idea. She let Mother and me know it right from the start. I was the baby, and that was all there was to it.

As I grew, I loved being outside in the sunshine. I loved lying on the grass and looking up at the clouds, seeing the various animals or other shapes in their fluffy interiors. Just running barefoot in the grass, sitting under the big tree in our front yard, or listening to the birds singing their beautiful warbles filled me with amazement and joy.

One day, I remember just lying in the grass looking up at all the cloud formations. I saw giraffes, lions, horses, and people's faces. I loved deciding what each cloud looked like. I felt wonderful just being a part of all that surrounded me. I learned that God's world filled me with happiness. I could feel my Lord and heavenly Father looking look down at me. What a sunshiny day it was. All felt good in my world. With the sunrays shining down on me, I felt him smiling on me.

Another of those great afternoons, when I was five, Mother shattered my daydreaming into a thousand pieces. She noticed I was outside in the yard and had taken Ruth's art case with me. I didn't see any problem with "borrowing" her paint set; I wanted to paint, just like her. I had just opened up the case when Mother found me with it. She scolded me, telling me those were Ruth's painting things and I was never to touch anything of hers again without permission.

With my soaring euphoria crushed, she grabbed the case from me, closed and locked it up, then rushed it back into the house. I don't know if Ruth ever knew what I had done or not, but I knew I wouldn't touch anything of Ruth's again.

After Mother left, tears rolled down my cheeks. I sobbed, and then I turned my head skyward. The sunrays reminded me that God was up there and that he loved me, even if she didn't. Since my birth, her attention and praise went to Ruth; nothing I did was good enough for her. Her critical nature found its nature in comparing me to Ruth. "Your sister could read by now; why aren't you?" She never took the time to read with me or take interest in my education. She was busy with her ladies' groups, housework, or doing what pleased herself. My needs were last on her list of priorities. I questioned God, "Why doesn't she want to spend time with me? She doesn't seem to want me around." As I grew, I knew God was with me, making me feel loved and happy. "Thank you, Lord. I love you, too. I love feeling you with me and loving me in a way no one else can ever make me feel."

A Frightening Night Alone

"The Lord is my shepherd... Even though I walk
through the valley of the shadow of death,
I will fear no evil for you are with me."

(Psalm 23:14)

The summer between first and second grade, I learned that my tonsils needed to be taken out. After an overnight stay in the hospital, the surgery would occur the following morning. At that time, I would be taken into a large room and then a bag would be put over my nose. As I breathed into this bag, I would go to sleep so the doctor could take out my tonsils. Later that morning, I would wake up back in my hospital bed and soon after would be driven home.

I carried on merrily with my friends until the afternoon Mother drove me to the hospital. I don't remember much about the admission process, as I kept looking around at all the nurses dressed in stiff, white clothes with white, starched caps on their heads, bustling around with important things to do. I didn't like this place; it scared me, as I didn't know what would happen to me in the morning when they took my tonsils out. The question on my mind was, "Will it hurt?"

As Mother and I walked out of the elevator on my floor, fear filled me as I realized I didn't want to be there or have my tonsils out. The nurse overseeing the children's ward showed me to my bed and told me to put on a hospital gown. This only added to my fear. Mother stayed with me for a little while, trying to calm me. I kept saying, "I want to go home with you. I don't want to stay here. I don't like this place—it scares me."

She told me, "I can't take you home. Your tonsils must come out, as they are making you sick too often." She reminded me, "Remember, Rosie Mullens, Ruth's close nurse friend, will sit with you until you go to sleep so you won't be afraid." I didn't care. I didn't want to be left here. My thoughts led to, *Mom, why are you leaving me? Can't you stay here until I am asleep or Rosie comes?*

Fear enveloped me, knowing I had to stay in this horrible place where I didn't know anyone. This was the place where a doctor would remove my tonsils. All I had been told was I would go to sleep then wake up with my throat being sore. I could eat all the ice cream and Jell-O I wanted. What a treat that would be! I was told I must not talk, as that would only make my throat sore. A couple days later, my throat wouldn't hurt and I could eat anything I wanted and could play outside again.

About six o'clock, Mother left. I was on my own and alone. Looking around the ward, I saw five beds, including mine, lined up along my side of the room, with another five across from me. Each bed held an ill child or one awaiting surgery. My room companions talked to the child next to them, read, or colored pictures for their parents. I just lay there wanting to cry, but I didn't want to let people know I was scared.

The boy across from me seemed quite ill, as the head nurse kept close tabs on him. She frequently put a long, silver instrument against his chest and then placed its tube ends into her ears to listen to him. After finishing her task, she wrote something about him in her big, black book. I didn't like that book; I felt it contained bad things about him.

About eight o'clock, the burly, no-nonsense nurse told us, "Lights out, kids. Time for sleep." With that, she turned off all the ceiling and side lights, except for the one on her desk.

I asked her, "Could you have Rosie come and sit with me now?"

She said, "I don't know anyone by that name." I just remained still, watching the ceiling and praying that Rosie would come. With the realization of how alone and afraid I was, the tears finally came.

Miss Burly, as I thought of her, told me, "Stop crying, and just go to sleep."

I called out to God in my prayers. "Oh, Lord, I am so scared. Be with me tonight and keep me safe. Help me sleep. Help me tomorrow to not be afraid or show my fear. Protect me tomorrow." I just kept thinking of him as the only one who cared enough about me to be with me all through the night. Later, I did fall asleep with my pillowcase wet with my heard cries and unheard whimpers.

With the dawn, things began perking again. Soon, a long bed on wheels pulled up to my bed. The young attendant told me to scoot on it because he was taking me for a ride. I began to cry, as I didn't want to go to wherever he was taking me.

The new ward nurse came over and tried to calm me, but it just made things worse. All of a sudden, she said, "If you are good little girl and stop crying, I will make sure he takes you past the newborn nursery. You'd like that, wouldn't you? You can see all the new babies there."

I wanted to see the babies, so I stopped crying. Everyone knew that would take my mind off what lay ahead for me. Passing the nursery, the young man let me sit up and take a long look at all the little ones, some crying and some sleeping. What a wonderful sight!

All too soon, we were on the move again. I moved through two heavy, wide doors into a room filled with all kinds of scary-looking things. Within seconds, the doctors and nurses whisked me onto the operating table. A kindly man in a white overcoat and a white thing over his mouth said, "I am going to put this mask over your nose. See, it's just like mine. I want you to breathe in deeply; there is nothing to be scared of. It will help you go to sleep, and when you wake up, your tonsils will be out." As I began breathing in the white square, all I could smell were overly ripe bananas.

I asked him, "Did you put bananas in here?" Before he could answer me, I had fallen asleep.

Before long, the nurses had me back in my bed. Mother and Dad kept trying to wake me up from my anesthetic-induced sleep. All I could think about was my throbbing throat and how everyone had lied to me. This wasn't just any old sore throat; it seemed that it would never stop hurting.

An hour later, my doctor came in and checked on me. He told me, "You can go home and eat all the ice cream and popsicles you want. The more ice cream you eat, the better your throat will feel; it will stop the pain. Remember, do not talk; that will only make your sore throat worse and you don't want that, do you?"

Mother replied, "I have the freezer stocked with ice cream and popsicles for her."

After arriving home, Grandma and Grandpa Hamilton, Dad's parents, came to see me, bringing lots of coloring books and crayons. I wasn't a good hostess, as I slept through most of their visit. All I knew was my surgery was over and my tonsils were out. All I wanted was for my throat to stop hurting. But I loved eating one of my favorite foods: ice cream. I couldn't have the other one, spaghetti, but I would have some after my throat healed.

As I recuperated, I kept thanking the Lord for staying with me through the night at the hospital, my surgery, and now that I was recovering. "Thank you, thank you, God, for being with me through the last two scary days. I love you. You certainly were my shepherd as I walked through my valley of fear. Amen."

My Time as a Guinea Pig

"Will I recover from this?"
(2 Kings 8:9)

When I was seven, I spent the summer of 1948 with Gram, my mother's mother, in Detroit, Michigan.

In the evenings, after cleaning up the dinner dishes, she and I would sit on her wide, open front porch. On many of those hot, muggy summer nights we would eat her homemade cookies and drink cold glasses of lemonade. Occasionally, she let me walk to the corner grocery store alone to purchase needed milk, eggs, and bread. Along with the grocery money, sometimes she gave me a penny so I could buy a paper strip of yellow, pink, and green dot candy. Oh, what a treat! I felt so grown up when she allowed me to go there all by myself.

About a month into my stay, I started feeling sick and didn't know what was wrong with me. I had a fever, no energy, and just felt plain sick. Gram put me to bed and kept hoping I would get better. After a few days, my temperature remained. She called Doc Sargent, a dear friend and doctor. After some tests, he determined I had a kidney infection. He gave Gram some medicine and told her, "If that doesn't help in a day or so, call me, and I will come and check her again."

A few days later, I wasn't any better; in fact, I was worse. Doc Sargent said, "I see Nancy isn't any better. We need to get this taken care of right now; she can't go on like this. I brought with me a new experimental drug for her. I haven't used it on any of my other patients, but I have heard it is a wonder drug. I don't know what the effects will be on her or her condition, but we have to do something. This might be just what she needs."

"What is it?" Gram asked.

Doc said, "Penicillin. We should see improvement in her in a day or so."

The very next day I sat up and wanted to be out of bed. I felt the best I had in more than a week. Gram told me to stay in bed until Doc saw me. The following day, I saw him again. He was amazed at how quickly I had recovered. I remember him saying penicillin was a miracle drug. It certainly was for me. He told me I was his guinea pig. I proved that the drug definitely did cure infections and quickly. I thought of myself as a modern wonder.

After Doc examined me thoroughly, he told me I could go outside and play quietly. Again and again, I thanked God for coming to my aid by bringing Doc and the miracle drug. When I went outside in the sunshine, I felt my Lord shining down on me, making me feel wonderful all over. "Thank you, Lord; thank you!"

During the time I was so sick, I wondered why Mother never came to see me or check on me. "Lord, why didn't she come? Why doesn't she care about me and my welfare? What is so wrong with me? I wish you could tell me or change things so she would like or even love me. Could you do that for me? Once again, thank you for healing me and making me healthy again. I love being in your sunlight and caring ways. Amen."

About two weeks later, Jim came to drive Gram and me home. He told us Dad had taken a job as the new vice president of Island Creek Coal Company. They had already moved to Holden, West Virginia, a little mining town.

What Went Wrong?

―――

"Do not be terrified by them, because the Lord your God, who brought you out of Egypt, will be with you."

(Deuteronomy 20:3)

Our first Easter in our new home approached. A real treat for Mother, Dad, and especially me was the arrival of Dad's mother, Grandma Hamilton. While getting our little town ready for Easter, our small local theater was showing a film on the life of Christ. I so wanted to see it. Grandma, being a minister's widow, said she would like to see it also. On the second day of her visit, Grandma and I discussed going to see the movie one night while she was with us.

The following evening before dinner, I asked her if we could go that night. She told me I had to talk to Dad when he came home from work. She didn't think he would agree to it since we hadn't had dinner; but if he did, she would like to go with me.

A little later, when I heard him come through the front door, I left my bedroom and ran to talk to him. Since he had never refused me anything before, I didn't think this would be any different. Oh, was I to learn and see him differently with my request!

This particular evening he came home in a foul mood. I was oblivious to this and waited for him to take off his coat and have his usual couple of drinks with Mother before dinner. I waited until they came out of their sitting room before approaching him.

I was in total denial that he would refuse my idea. I didn't notice he was in no mood to listen to or deal with his precocious eight-year-old daughter. He had always been so gentle and loving to me. I just knew I could work out going to the movie with Grandmother without any problem. Oh, was I about to learn a very hard lesson!

I began by telling him Grandmother and I wanted to go to the movie. He immediately said, "What is the movie, and when is it playing?"

I told him, "It's the story of Jesus's life, and it's on tonight."

He thought about it a moment and said, "No, it's too late to go tonight." I reminded him Grandmother was going to go with me.

This time his demeanor and tone took a sharp turn. "No, I said and I mean it, Nancy!" shouted Dad. Shocked, I stepped back. I had the blind tenacity to ask why.

He said, "There are bad people out there who might want to kidnap you, and I won't let that happen."

I said, "But Dad, I really want to see it, and I will be with Grandmother."

At that point, his anger at my belligerence became a volcano of anger the likes of which I had never seen before. He took off his belt, folded it, and said, "Either you do as I say, or else I will use this on you. If you don't like the rules here, there is the door; you can just leave. I don't want you here unless you're willing to obey me."

I stood there immobile for a minute until he started toward me with his leather belt in his hand. As I fled upstairs to my bedroom, I could hear him behind me. Terror filled me, as I didn't know what he would do if he caught me. In his mood, I feared if he caught me he might not stop whipping me until I was dead. His size and the ferocity of his anger resembled a very angry father bear. I had never seen this side of my dad before.

I ran into my room and quickly hid under my bed, fearing for my life. I kept asking myself, "What happened?" I didn't accept that my impudence in this matter was the catalyst for his outburst. What happened to my loving, caring dad? This angry man wasn't the father I knew and loved.

After a few minutes of attempting to find me, he returned downstairs for an additional drink to calm down. I wondered what I had done to enrage him so, especially in front of his mother. "Lord, help me understand this. I can't believe he would do this. Why didn't you protect me? I am so frightened now of him. I needed you. Where were you in all this? What is it with Mother? Why didn't she help me? Why doesn't she care about me? Lord, please help me!"

Later that evening, after they had had dinner, Mother found me. She said, "You need to go downstairs and apologize to your father for your behavior that made him so angry." Fearing his anger and what he would do to me if I got close to him, I refused. I needed to keep my distance from him until he cooled down. From that moment on, I felt a wall between us that I would never breach for fear this angry father would come out to get me. I felt I had lost my dad and his love because I persisted in my demands to him. I should have remembered how irritated and angry he became when Ruth or Jim didn't listen to him. I was his little girl; I didn't believe this would happen to me. I had felt special. Now I knew better. I learned not to demand and persist in what I wanted, or this other father would come out. I was really afraid of his anger. Being a tall and muscular man, he was formidable to anyone, especially to me now.

Again, my problem with my mother came out. Since I was born, she made it clear to me that I was the bane of her life. Whenever I got in her way of doing something she wanted or I wanted her attention or didn't do what she wanted, she became angry or frustrated, telling me, "If it wasn't for you, I would have a wonderful life." This only added to this night for me. As angry and fearful as I was with Dad, I became angry with Mother because she blamed me for everything that happened that night. I was to blame for what he did. If I hadn't been so rebellious, selfish, and obstinate, he would never have gotten that mad. This was the beginning of my lifelong feeling that I was so horrible no one could love me. I felt not only did I not have her love but now Dad's as well. My dream was that he would come to me and talk over what had happened earlier that evening. My fear sat inside me like a dead elephant. Neither they nor I won that night—we all lost.

Today, I realize I should have gone and talked it out with Dad, but my fear of him at the time kept me closed up and scared of the one man I adored. Satan worked on me, saying it wasn't my fault. He was the adult and I was the child; therefore, I didn't have anything to do with what happened that night. I should have prayed and asked for God's help and protection to go to Dad and work it out with him. All I knew was that I was too afraid of his anger and what might happen to me if he became angry again with me. I wouldn't let that happen again. From that moment I began to hide from him.

Because of that night, my anger with Mother only intensified. I knew she had never wanted me, and this only made the situation between us even more untenable. Years later, a therapist friend of mine told me I was not the responsible one, as Dad was the adult and should have been able to control himself. What I did was normal for a spoiled, precocious daughter whose father loved her immensely until that night. I had believed Dad would never deny me anything until that event. Oh, how spoiled and naïve I was. I never expected this fury in him. I asked myself over and over, "What did I open up in him that he would treat me this way. I loved him and I thought he loved me. How could this happen to me?"

"Oh, Lord, I am so scared. Help me feel safe in this house with parents who seem so indifferent to me. I know Mother has never wanted me around, but to allow him to treat me this way with such anger tells me she must not love me at all. She never even tried to help me; she just let him rant and rave about total obedience or to leave his home. To me this proved that she really didn't want me around or love me, or she would have tried to circumvent the situation. She didn't; therefore, in my mind, she didn't care for me a bit. This was her way to get rid of me.

"Oh, Lord, I am so little and they are so big and angry with me. Help me live in this house in safety, as I can't go out on my own. I know I can't live by myself without someone taking care of me. I wish I was with you, as I know only you can take care of me. What did I ever do to her so she can't or won't love me? Lord, help me build some kind of relationship with her and Dad. I am too young to go out on my own in the world. I am only nine years old, not eighteen. I can't survive out there on my own. Lord, be my protector and guide. Help me get through this. Amen."

Wrongly Accused

"The trouble he causes recoils on himself..."
(Psalm 7:16)

Life in Holden slowly fell into place for me during the next few years. Since Dad oversaw the operations of Island Creek Coal Company there, many of my classmates steered clear of me. I was the head honcho's daughter, and they were afraid to play with me. I, however, did forge friendships with two girls whose families didn't seem to have time to care who I was or what power my dad had over their fathers. Both worked long hours and drank away their paychecks while the mothers were overworked or neglectful to their daughters. Their mothers were just happy to have me come and play with them, keeping the girls out of their hair for a couple hours. Helena and Brenda were my salvation in the cold world that surrounded me.

My mother was too busy keeping up with the executive house and making sure all that was expected of her was done perfectly. I was on my own, fending for myself. Mother always said I shouldn't be with Helena and Brenda, as they were beneath my social level. No one was on my social level; Dad was the boss over everyone. Even with that, she wanted me out of her hair as much as Helena and Brenda's mothers, so we created our own bond. Mother's whole life was based on getting Dad to succeed in his position so he could advance up the corporate ladder. She wasn't around for me, but they were.

Mother and Gram had changed the third floor into a large sewing room for Gram and her projects, although they set aside a portion for my dolls and playthings. Days on end, I watched Gram's fingers pin materials and linings together and then use her old trundle sewing machine to create new images to decorate our home. When she had time for me, she attempted to teach me how to sew like her, but my mind and fingers didn't work like hers. At those times, her frustration with me got the better of her and she just ripped out what I had done and finished the project herself. At these times, I felt like a total failure.

One of the rules Mother and Gram impressed on me was not to use the iron unless someone watched what I was doing. Many times, I had to wait my turn to iron my dolls' dresses. One day, I broke that rule; doing that would haunt me forever.

Helena and Brenda came to play dolls with me. After all the times I had played dolls, their dresses looked crumpled, so I wanted to make them look pretty again. I knew how to use the iron and how Gram plugged it into the dangling cord above her wood ironing board. I drug her chair over to the ironing board, climbed up on it, and then plugged the cord into the overhead socket. Oh, how grownup I felt.

I heard Mother rumbling around downstairs, going from one room to another, putting newly washed and folded clothes into closets or dresser drawers. Being aware of the no-iron rule, I quickly finished ironing the dress I was working on, pulled the cord out of its socket, and put Gram's chair back. I just hoped the iron would be cold before Mother or Gram might come upstairs to see what I was doing.

Helena, Brenda, and I continued to play until they had to go home for dinner. After saying good-bye to them, I went to my room to wait dinner. Mother never asked me if I had used the iron. I was safe, or so I thought.

Just before dawn the following morning, Gram woke and thought she smelled wood burning. Thinking Mother had gotten up early to start breakfast on the kitchen's wood stove, she decided to go downstairs to check. The house was frigid since the furnace couldn't keep up with the freezing outside temperature from the overnight's snowfall.

She didn't find Mother and found the stove ice cold, telling herself she was wrong about the smell. She returned to the warmth of her bed, still wondering about the smell. After a short catnap, she again woke to the wood burning smell still hanging around.

Once again she returned to the kitchen; she didn't find Mother, and the stove was still ice cold. This time she decided to investigate the odor. What she found would shock all of us! She found a smoldering fire in the sewing room. Her iron had burnt through the wood ironing board and then onto the wood floor beneath. She yelled to Mother and Dad, telling them she had found fire and smoke beginning to engulf the sewing room and to call the fire department.

Until the cause of the smell had been found, Mother and Dad hadn't woken me. After remembering Helena, Brenda, and I had been in the sewing room the afternoon before, Mother surmised we had used the iron. When she woke me she asked briskly, "You and the girls had the iron on yesterday, didn't you?"

I didn't answer her because I was too much in shock.

"You had been told not to use that iron, and you did. You forgot to turn it off, and now it has burned through the ironing board and into the floor over the only escape stairwell. You could have killed us if your grandmother hadn't found the fire. Go downstairs and then outside and stay there while we get what we can of our things out of the house," Mother said.

By this time, I heard the sirens blaring from atop the Holden Fire Department trucks. Mother kept retrieving as much family memorabilia and clothes as possible while the house became more engulfed.

As the fire trucks approached our steep incline, the fire department faced two major problems. First, could all the trucks and their equipment make it up the steep incline with the new blanket of snow? Second, could they save the house because of the age and wood construction of the house? The fire seemed to be winning the battle for the house. Little could be done to stop the fire's speed. The fire chief ordered Mother, Gram, and Dad to stop making trips back into the house, as the house had become a firetrap. The fire would soon eat through the roof and walls, making them implode, trapping everything and everyone in its wake. The house couldn't be saved. Nothing more could be done or saved. The house was a total loss.

After her first trip outside, Mother sent me to a neighbor's home, where I would be safe and out of the way. As the morning and fire progressed, I watched through their windows as our house burned to the ground. The only thought running through my head was, *How could this have happened*? I worked it over and over in my head. I remembered pulling the iron plug out of its light socket. I made sure of it so Mother would never know I had used the iron. The iron was disconnected, so it couldn't burn through the ironing board or spark the fire. I knew that for a fact. My question remained unsolved: What happened?

Oh, how scared I was of Mother finding out that I had used the iron. I knew I had disobeyed using it but I also knew without a shadow of a doubt I had pulled its plug out of the light socket before the girls and I left the sewing room. I was positive about that. I knew how angry Mother would be even if I pleaded with her that the iron was off; the fire really wasn't my fault.

On top of her anger, I was fearful of Dad's reaction and fury as well, especially when he learned of my disobedience. I had seen his anger before and didn't want to see it again.

"Oh, Lord, I know I did wrong by disobeying Mother and Gram, and I know I should be punished for it. My prayer is that you will protect me from Dad's anger. Please, please protect me. I am so scared of him when he is angry. Please forgive me for what I have done and help me through this. I am counting on you. I love you, God. Amen."

I couldn't believe it. I knew I hadn't done it. Oh, what had happened? My guilt and fear were so raw that I began questioning myself after Mother's words to me. Had I left it on? No, I knew I had pulled the plug out! Why had she told me the fire was my fault and that I had almost killed all of us? I knew I hadn't started the fire.

I had made sure the iron was off and cold before the girls went home so Mother wouldn't find out I had used it. Oh, how I wished I hadn't had the girls over or used the iron. I wanted to hide my disobedience. I was angry at being accused of doing something I hadn't done. The fire wasn't my doing. I was innocent of the fire but not of my disobedience. Still, I couldn't rectify this whole situation in my head, especially Mother's words and anger.

After the fire had been put out, Dad questioned the fire chief about the fire's cause. The chief believed that with the house's age, construction materials, and the age of the electrical wires, this was an accident waiting to happen. With the frigid overnight temperatures, he believed the furnace had been on all night with no cooling-off times. One of the wires must have overheated and sparked the fire. He didn't know about the iron or its ironing board being burned, so that didn't enter his evaluation.

Later that day, we found accommodations in the company's clubhouse. Mother and Dad planned to stay there until we could find a new place to live. About the same time, I realized how distraught and angry Mother and Dad were about the fire. They were embarrassed by its happening. They wanted to be seen as perfect, making no mistakes. The fire they felt was a blemish on their reputation. Nothing like this had ever happened to them. What would the townsfolk think, especially if they knew the girls and I were playing with the iron upstairs the night before? Mother made it perfectly clear to those who asked about the fire it wasn't their fault or Gram's, but mine. Again, I was the one she blamed, innocent or not. She refused to believe the fire chief; she wanted me to be the embarrassment, not them.

Soon after settling into our new housing, Mother once again bore into me about how bad and disobedient I was. In front of Dad,

Mother asked me if I had been ironing against her rule. Fear struck me as I noticed how angry and upset Dad was. I feared what he would do to me for disobeying her. Unfortunately, my fear of Dad led me to lie to protect myself. At that moment, my whole world fell apart. Not only had I lied to my parents, but God knew it also. My parents knew I was lying, but they couldn't do anything because they had no proof. Although they were angry about this, they were more disappointed in me for lying to them. Adding to my guilt, I knew God knew I had lied and he would punish me in his own way. I felt like the worst little girl in the world. Who would ever love me now? I was so bad, no one would. I didn't like me either. How could I get over this? I was caught in my lie like a fly in a spider's web.

Soon, Helena and Brenda told everyone we had been in the attic and I had ironed the dolls' clothes. The news spread quickly throughout our little coal-mining town. From then on—and even today—people referred to me as the little girl who started the Holden fire. Oh, how this has haunted me!

Looking back now, all this could possibly have been resolved if I had told the truth and made a new start with them. I have carried this burden all my life. The guilt still hangs over me.

Then and even times today I pray to my Lord and Master, "O Lord, forgive me of my sin of disobedience and the sin of lying. Both of these are abhorrent to you. Please release me of these and cleanse me of all the sin I carry because of this event. Thank you Lord for listening to me and helping me with all I have done against my parents and especially you. Amen."

As Gram tried to make things right with family members before she died, she told Mother and Dad the truth of that night. After dinner the night before the fire was discovered, she had gone back to the sewing room to finish up the lining to the living room drapes so they would be finished before Christmas. She didn't remember turning off the iron before going to bed for the night. It was easier for her to let me take the blame, as Mother would have sent her home to Detroit. She wanted Mother and Dad to forgive her and hoped that when they told me I would forgive her. I didn't learn of this until many years later.

Someone I Trusted

> "The prudent see danger and take refuge but
> the simple keep going and suffer for it."
> (Proverbs 27:12)

Once in every child's life, he or she meets a person he or she trusts instinctively without really looking into who that person really is. The person seems like a true friend, when in reality, that person is a fox in sheep's clothing. A child doesn't see this and at times instinctively goes to the fox without seeing the threat to him or her.

After the fire and its ugliness, Helena and Brenda left me like a hot potato, refusing to play with me or invite me into their homes. My family moved into temporary housing until the company decided whether it would build a new house for us or not. Mother and Dad buried themselves into his emerging company career in order to cover their embarrassment about the fire and my "involvement" in it. With the stress of dealing with both these issues, Mother and Dad's drinking increased. I never knew what to expect from them or their nightly behaviors, so I found myself hiding in my room from them more and more.

At the same time, Gram began sewing new drapes and furniture coverings for our new home; thereby, she was unavailable to me as well. With no one to play with, I retreated more into my room or watched television. I felt like a child no one had time for. For the most part, I was on my own—a lonely little girl in search of a friend or someone to take an interest in me.

Saturdays, I walked to the neighborhood movie house, where for a quarter (ten cents for admission, ten cents for a bag of popcorn, and five cents for a bar of candy) I could be whisked away for the afternoon by my western heroes: Roy Rogers and Dale Evans, Gene Autry, Tom Mix, Lash La Rue, and Hopalong Cassidy. Oh, in between the two featured films were the appropriate *Tom and Jerry* cartoons and news films. About five o'clock, Mother would telephone the theater, telling them to send me home for dinner.

As I walked home, I always passed the company drugstore. Sometimes I even looked in the front window to see the wall rack of comic books full of action, fantasy, comedy, and sports. I loved checking out what was new, even though I didn't have any money left to buy any of them.

Mr. Reynolds, a short, stout, loveable older man, was the drugstore's proprietor. The store not only had the basic medicines, magazines, comic books, and beauty supplies, but an extended soda fountain and sandwich bar with five revolving, metal barstools as well as a couple of booths for those who didn't want to sit at the counter. He made wonderful-looking sandwiches. I loved watching him create his masterpieces. He first laid two slices of bread on his cutting board, spreading both with mayonnaise. Onto the first slice of bread he scooped egg, chicken, or ham salad and then topped that with lettuce and tomato slices and finished it off with the second bread slice. After cutting the sandwich diagonally, he added potato chips and a pickle to a paper plate. The customer usually ordered a fountain cherry coke to wash it all down with. At times, he would make chocolate shakes, sundaes, and fizzy drinks for people. Oh, how I wanted to learn how to pull the fizzy drink handle that made sodas, push down the plungers that poured out the luscious chocolate or strawberry sauces over the ice cream sundaes, or ladle out the chopped nuts, whipped cream, and stemmed maraschino cherries to finalize the delicacy. He told me he would get in trouble if he let me "work" with him. At ten, I was too young. When I got older, maybe fifteen or sixteen, he said he would let me.

As the time passed, I spent more and more time with Mr. Reynolds. He began teaching me various craft projects, such as how to make key chains and necklaces. I loved spending time with him, as he gave me the attention I so desperately wanted. This went on for a several months. It never occurred to me how overly involved he was with me or I with him. I just loved his attention. Mother had said she didn't like me spending time with him; it didn't look good. I felt she wanted to take the only person away from me who paid me any attention. I became angry with her.

One day after I had finished a new key chain braiding project, he asked me into his storeroom. After saying yes, I found myself in his formerly off-limits area. What a wondrous cavern filled with all kinds of medicines, medical supplies, perfumes, beauty products, and cigarettes all sitting on wall shelves just waiting to be sold to some willing or needy customer. He had never before invited me back into his storeroom. He stood in the back of the room so he could look out into the drugstore proper. This way he could see or hear anyone entering his store.

I didn't understand what he had planned for me in this inner sanctum. Before I knew it, he had me pinned against the wood cabinet on the faraway wall where no one could see either of us. He kept looking back over his shoulders to make sure no one coming through the front door could see us. Within moments, I realized what he was doing. He ran his hand over my body then slipped his hand into my blouse, then onto my breast. He made me promise never tell anyone about this or we would get in trouble. I sensed that what he was doing wasn't right. In shock, I forced his hands and body away from me and fled from his presence. I left him in shock or frustration. I just knew I wanted out of there as quickly as possible. I must have flown home, as Mother was shocked to see me. She asked what was wrong and I said, "Nothing." I didn't want to discuss this scary, embarrassing moment with her or anyone.

A couple of nights later at the dinner table, Dad asked me if I had seen Mr. Reynolds lately. I said no, as I hadn't. I never wanted to see him again. I wondered why Dad had asked me.

The next thing he said was, "Has he ever taken you into backroom of the store?" Embarrassed by what had happened there, remembering my promise, and fearful of what would happen to him or me if I did, I said no. Once again I lied to my parents because I didn't know what would happen to me.

Someone had told Dad that Mr. Reynolds had taken other girls back there. Dad said, "If Mr. Reynolds had done that, I would see he was put in jail." My first fear was that if Mr. Reynolds could be put into jail, so could I. My second thought was what would Dad do to me if he knew? So once again, I lied to keep my "friend" and me out of jail.

The only ones who knew the truth were my Lord and I. I was so upset with myself for not listening to Mother or allowing myself to be taken in by his "attention." She had told me it didn't look good for me to spend time with him. Had she seen his true potential? No one will ever know. I thought he was a nice man who enjoyed having me around and teaching me things. In my loneliness, I needed a friend, but looking back, I picked the wrong one.

"Thank you, Lord, for making me aware that what Mr. Reynolds was doing was very wrong and getting me to flee from him and his store. You were the only one who saved and protected me from something that could have proved to be very dangerous to me. Again, I confess my lying to Mother and Dad. Help me not to do that again. I was too embarrassed to admit I should have listened to her but too afraid to admit my need for someone to pay attention to me. All my loneliness had dictated my actions, not my thinking. I promise I will never go back there again. Lord, I need you to be with me as my friend and protector, as no one else seems to be. Always be with me, as I can't do this myself. I need you. Thank you, Father, for getting me away from harm and back into the safety of my home! Help me to know who to trust and not. I have had someone inside the family as well as someone outside the family who have frightened me. I need you with me, Lord, more than ever. Amen."

Being Left Alone Again with Strangers

"All my longings lie open before you, O, Lord, my sighing is not hidden from you. My heart pounds, my strength fails me, even the light has gone from my eyes."

(Psalm 38:9–10)

After finishing my first year in junior high school, Mother told me I would be going to a new school that fall. West Virginia schools didn't have a good educational system; therefore, my education would not get me into a proper college. She had enrolled me in an all-girls' parochial college-prep school: St. Anne's School in Charlottesville, Virginia, which had an excellent reputation. Its graduates went on to prestigious colleges and married into the right families.

"You will love it there," she said. Dummy me! I thought the whole family was moving there. Later, I found out that no, the family wasn't moving there; only I was moving there. I rebelled, saying, "I'm not going there, and you can't make me."

Mother said, "You'll be with girls your own age and learn lots of new things. You'll learn how to take care of your room and clothes as well as learn social skills to help you succeed in life and marry into a good family. You also will receive a good education." With the tone of her voice and determination to make this happen, I knew she wouldn't change her mind no matter what I said.

As the time came closer, shopping for new clothes and the nametags to be put into my underwear, blouses, skirts, shoes, liners, and books became the priority. I felt like I was going to prison. I felt as though Mother had finally come up with a way to punish me for all my wrongdoings, especially being born. Wanting to be rid of me, she had found the way. As upset as Gram was, no amount of her haranguing could change Mother's mind about sending me to St. Anne's. I was going and that was that.

All too quickly, that Friday in September came when all my treasures and clothing were packed into a large steamer trunk and then moved into the trunk of Mother's car. The following morning, while Mother and Gram sat in the car, I sobbed as I said, good-bye to Dad in our driveway. I had hoped he could stop this, but that didn't happen. Once in the car, Mother told me to stop crying; I would see him at Thanksgiving or Christmas. That only made me cry all the harder. I was leaving all I knew and loved.

After driving all day to Charlottesville, Mother found a nice motel about twenty miles from the school. Later, she took us to a nearby restaurant for dinner, but that didn't make me or Gram feel any better about what would happen the next day. That night, I cried myself to sleep. I wanted time to stop so I wouldn't have to go to this place.

Sunday, D-Day for me, came much too fast. After dressing, we had a late breakfast at the motel's little café. Then, we drove the last miles to St. Anne's School. We arrived at St. Anne's about noon. After signing in at the administration building, I learned where I would be living for the next nine months. My room was on the second floor of the underclass dormitory where all the boarding freshmen—three eighth graders, a sixth grader, and myself—would live. My roommate was another eighth grader from Charleston, West Virginia, while the other two eighth-grade girls were from Richmond, Virginia, and from Bogalusa, Louisiana. The lone sixth grader was devastated at being left there by her father who had just remarried. As bad as I felt about being here, I felt even worse for her. Being two years younger and being left alone here where she didn't know anyone had to be harder on her than it did me. She just couldn't stop crying. After putting my things into my closet and dresser then making my bed, I knew Mother and Gram would be leaving soon. I tried to hold back the tears, but they just flowed down my face.

At five o'clock, the Sunday vesper bell rang. All the students began filing into the main house for the service. Just as we arrived there, Mother said it was time for her and Gram to leave. I kept saying, "Please don't leave me here. I am afraid. I want to go home with you. Don't leave me. I'll do whatever you say if you will just take me home."

Mother said, "You will be all right in a couple of days when you make some friends and begin your school work." No way could I convince her to take me home. I was here for the duration. Panic, anger, and fear overwhelmed me as I sobbed, watching them drive away. I wanted to run away but didn't know how or where to go. I was stuck. Once again, I felt alone and unwanted.

As I entered the room for vespers, Miss Williams, my dormitory head, began playing "Now the Day is Over." I was so overcome knowing that night had come and I was alone; sobs just flowed out of me. I hid in the back corner of the room so no one could see or hear me. I just wanted to be left alone.

How can you leave me here? How am I going to survive here? Don't you love me at all? shot through my head and soul. I felt alone and abandoned. I was only thirteen years old and on my own. What was I supposed to do in this place? Mother had told me to grow up. Nothing could contain the pain I was in.

My classes included ancient history, Old Testament studies, English, French I, algebra, and choir. The homework overwhelmed me since I had no background for these classes or their homework. God sent an angel to comfort me. Miss Allis, my floor monitor, whose room was next to mine, taught my ancient history as well as Old Testament Study classes. She took me under her wing and helped me through the traumatic months that lay ahead. While teaching me to knit argyle socks, she and I talked out my feelings. What a savior she was for me! I loved her and her subjects. Mrs. Del Greco, a loving grandmother-type teacher, taught me how to diagram sentences, learn vocabulary, read literature, and write essays. Gruff and disciplined Mrs. Stocker taught me about how a plus b equals c and all the stuff that went along with it. French-born Miss Le Grande worked with me through elementary French. Choir let me praise the Lord with my voice and soul. After school, I played either goalie or fullback for our field hockey team. I enjoyed smacking the ball as far as I could against our opponents. It felt good to hit something.

Because of my homesickness, lack of study skills, and the lack of background for my classes, my grades were atrocious. During this first year, the question of why I was here lingered. What had I done to deserve this punishment? Didn't Mother love me at all, or did she just want to get rid of me? What was so wrong with me that she didn't want me? What was wrong with her that she didn't see the good potential in me like God did? He was the only one who I felt loved me.

With failing grades, I had to repeat eighth grade. The second fall there, I felt the need to be more connected to my Lord. I took inquirers' classes. Miss Coleman, the school's principal and religious chairman, taught this class. After weeks of training, I felt so excited about my decision and my upcoming confirmation. I asked Mother and Dad to come for my confirmation service. Unfortunately, she said they were too busy to come.

On the crisp mid-November Sunday morning of my confirmation, the sun shone for all to see. Bundled up in my navy, double-breasted wool coat, I made my way into the church to have a word with the Lord before the service began. While kneeling, pouring out my fervent prayer. "Oh, Lord, be with me today especially when I ask you to come into my life and lead me in your ways and paths. Forgive me for all my wrongdoings. Make me worthy to be called one of your own. Let me make you proud of me. I love you, Lord." When I finished my prayer, I felt the warmth of the sun and the Lord coming in on me through the large stained-glass window next to me. He told me, "I am with you always." What an exhilarating moment for me! My Lord loved me even with all my mistakes and lies of the past. I was his, and he loved me! What more could I want or ask for?

The service itself made me realize even more that I was his. As I knelt before Bishop Goodwin, he put his huge hands on my head and prayed over me as I took my confirmation vows. What joy that brought me! I had become one of God's own. I knew I could always come to him and he would help me through every facet of my life.

He helped me through the next year and a half of school. I made some friends, studied hard, and became the goalie on the St. Anne's field hockey team. My life wasn't as grim as before, but scholastically I was a failure.

Before coming home for Christmas during my ninth grade year, Mother mentioned the possibility that our family was moving to Huntington, West Virginia, seventy miles north of Holden. Dad had taken on the vice presidency of his company and needed to move near its corporate offices. By Christmas break, Mother and Dad had moved us lock, stock, and barrel into our new home; a real home, not a company house.

In addition, another change was in store for me. That fall, Mother had quietly made an application to a private high school in Huntington for me. On Christmas she told me I had been accepted at Marshall High School and could begin there after Christmas break. What a Christmas gift for me! A new beginning! Somehow I knew this would change my life. I would make it here, whereas at St. Anne's I knew I would never make it.

With this wonderful news, fear and insecurity shot through me. I was returning home. I would be with new classmates, which made me uneasy. My childhood had been spent on a farm in rural Pennsylvania with no children to play with. Before I was to start kindergarten, Gram convinced Mother to keep me home and she would teach me reading and arithmetic. Unfortunately, Gram only wanted me to be around her to take care of her needs and didn't teach me anything I needed for first grade. By the time I did enter first grade, my lack of educational and social skills put me at a distinct disadvantage. On top of that, I felt like a dummy. Why Mother never challenged Gram on this was and is beyond me.

During my first seven years of school, I changed schools five times, making it hard to make friends or to learn, as each school had different learning and teaching strategies. Making and keeping friends became an impossibility. My life had been filled with adults and isolation, so when I went to St. Anne's I realized I didn't know how to socialize or study with girls my own age. My fear just heightened my insecurities of being different and unwanted. Some girls made friends easily, while I stood back, not knowing what to do. I was afraid to trust their friendships or feel they really cared about me.

At the beginning of January and the start of the second semester, I entered Marshall High School. Now I had two new concerns. I was new to the school, classes, teachers, and students. My second concern: my classes now contained boys, which only accentuated my social anxieties. All this was scary, uncharted, new territory for me. The girls buzzed around each other as well as flirted with the boys and vice versa. I felt hopelessly lost in this new environment. Because of Mr. Reynolds, I didn't want to be close enough to any of the boys so they could touch me. My plan was to do my studies while remaining aloof and isolated from any of them. My need to protect myself from boys, friends, and life made me lonelier than I ever expected.

Adding to my own feelings of insecurity, Gram warned me that friends would only get me in trouble. I had seen that in my "friendships" with Helena, Brenda, and Mr. Reynolds. What I didn't realize was that she wanted to keep me in a cocoon so she could dictate who I could see and what I could do but most importantly, to have me all to herself so I'd take care of her. She didn't care if I was lonely for friendships; my needs were secondary to hers. Her guilt trips only reinforced my insecurities. To her surprise, as well as mine, Marshall would change all that.

It was there that I began to blossom into a happy young lady; even my grades became honor roll status. I started feeling good about myself. My biggest problem now was my social skills, which

I didn't have, especially with my male counterparts. I wanted to be like all the other girls but just couldn't bring myself to get close to the boys in my class.

"Thank you, Lord, for bringing me home and putting me in a position where I can grow and become all I can be. You are a gracious, loving Lord who heard my sobs and upheaval, took pity on me, and changed my life for the best. How can I ever thank you enough for being there for and with me? You are the only one who loves me for me and not for what they want to see lacking in me or for what they want out of me. You are so great and loving to me! Thank you, thank you, Lord. I love you. Amen."

Praising God from the Choir Loft

"I will praise God's name in song."
(Psalm 69:30)

One Sunday while a junior at Marshall High School, I noticed in our church bulletin a call for new choir members. Being in my school's small elite choir, I decided to try my luck at becoming a soprano in our prestigious Trinity Episcopal Church choir.

With knees knocking under my skirt, I auditioned not only before the choirmaster, Dr. Creighton, a vocal music professor at Marshall College, but the whole church choir as I sang some of my favorite hymns. He asked me to sit and take part in the evening's practice so he could see if I could hold my own in the first soprano section and be able to blend in with the rest of the twenty-one other choir voices. I knew I could not screw this up or I would be gone. I had to be good during this final evaluation. After listening to the other members (all adults), I thought I would never make the choir.

It took the entire practice before Dr. Creighton invited me into the choir. I rejoiced inside, trying not to show my exuberance at my acceptance into this most illustrious group. I loved singing with them and to the Lord.

As we entered the church each Sunday morning service, singing praises to our Lord, I felt incredibly full of God's love for me and my love for him. I felt as though he was looking down on me and smiling like a proud father when his daughter did something pleasing to him. Oh, how wonderful I felt from the top of my head to the ends of my toes.

"Yes, Lord, I sing to you with all the love in my heart, as you have blessed me with your love. I just want you to know how grateful I am for all you have done for me. You have always been there for and with me through the good times as well as the very bad times. Thank you, Father, for everything!"

I sometimes felt tears of joy creep down my cheeks as I became overwhelmed with the feeling that he was with me, loving me all through my songs. I didn't care if anyone noticed. I was singing to my Lord and Father. What greater compliment could I give one so wonderful?

I loved singing the anthems, as I was able to show the congregation the gift God had given me along with the feeling of joy I received as I sang to him. I loved praising him for all his love for me. At times I wondered how he could love me so much when I was so unworthy of his love.

One evening after driving home from choir practice, filled with the joy of the Lord, Mother just had to burst my bubble once again. She said she had talked to Dr. Creighton after service on Sunday and asked him how I fit into his choir. He told her, "Nancy has a sweet little voice, but she will never be a soloist."

Crushed, I ran to my bedroom, holding my tears and emotions in check. After closing my door, I fell on my bed, crying my heart out to the Lord. "How can she be so hurtful, Lord? I know I don't have the range and fullness of Mary Ann Johnson, but I love what I am doing. Lord, why does Mother have to find ways to destroy the things that mean so much to me? Lord, I know I am not special, but when, for a moment, I feel so good, why does she have to tear me down? Why, Lord? Why?"

When the tears subsided, I asked, "Lord, where are you when I need you? Why didn't you protect me or punish her for hurting me once again? Why does she need to take the things that make me feel good and tear them and me down? Lord, help me! Come to my defense! I need you to tell me I'm okay. Lord, what can I do to get Mother and Dad to love me? I am crying out to you from the depths of my being—one in total pain. Where are you, Lord, when I need and call out to you?"

Other than the night Mother left me at St. Anne's, I had ever felt so alone and unwanted. What could I do to bring myself out of this depth again? I needed the Lord to once again to be with me and walk me out of this. He was the only one I trusted who knew and loved me for who I was. Mother never would. Why did she have to tear me down every time I felt good about myself?

Tragedy Hits

"Though he brings grief, he will show
compassion so great in his unfailing love."
(Luke 3:32)

After losing thirty-five pounds (my "baby fat," as Mother and Gram called it), being elected vice-president of my senior class, and becoming the photography editor of my high school's yearbook, my confidence level helped me fend off Mother's barbs and insults. She was still a thorn in my side, but I was too happy and focused on me to allow her barbs do a lot of damage. "Thank you, Lord, for helping me grow into the person you see me as!"

The summer between my junior and senior years in high school, my parents decided to go to England to visit some aging relatives of Dad's. We flew to London to begin a three-week tour of England, Scotland, and Wales. As an added bonus, we flew to Paris for the first weekend of our trip. "Oh, Paris! How glorious are your sights, sounds, and fashions." We sat at sidewalk cafes and drank their thick, overwhelming coffee and ate fluffy, buttery croissants.

We toured the famous sights: the impressive Eiffel Tower, the Louvre Museum, Place de Concord, at one end of the Champs Elysee, Notre Dame along the River Seine, the hilltop Sacre Coeur, and the artists' area of Montmartre. Oh, so breathtaking! My head spun from all we did and saw. I even used what little French I had learned from Mrs. Matthew's French class.

I remember coming up to an older French gentleman and asking, "Ou est le tour Eiffel?" He looked at me indignantly, as my French was atrocious, and pointed to the tower, telling me how to get there in English. Mother and Dad watched and thought how good I was to understand him, thinking he was speaking French to me. I never let on that he had spoken English. I felt so proud of myself for going up to him and trying my elementary French. Later I told them what really happened. I was not lying anymore by commission or omission. I was filled with excitement and hope.

We flew back to London, a magical city where one might think he or she would see Mary Poppins floating above, holding on to her umbrella. We spent the next two days touring the city atop one of London's famous red double-decker tour buses. The tour guide related all the history about each of the major sights: Buckingham Palace, Parliament, Westminster Abbey, Harrods, Fortnum and Mason, Piccadilly Circus, the Tower of London, and St. Paul's Cathedral.

Mother, Dad, and I got off the bus a couple of times to personally tour certain places. We took time to tour both Houses of Parliament. The House of Parliament's splendor made me think of all the years the House of Lords (whose chairs bore the regality of red leather) and the House of Commons (whose chairs of the lesser chamber bode of green leather) had spent days and months arguing out the business of the nation and world.

Around the corner stood the incredible Westminster Abbey. We walked the aisles, viewing the statues of historical military men, crypts of past royalty, and the Poet's Corner. The cathedral I loved most was St. Paul's. Westminster reminded me of a large church where royal functions took place, while St. Paul's felt like home. St. Paul's dome made me want to reach skyward to touch heaven. The joy there encompassed me, and I knew the Lord looked over it and me.

When our bus passed by Buckingham Palace, our guide joked with us that we couldn't stop in for tea and scones, as Queen Elizabeth

II wasn't home. "When she is in residence, her flag is hoisted up on the Palace flagpole. When she is away, her flag is absent," he told us. What an experience that would have been. In reality, no commoner would ever be asked to tea there.

After too few days in London, we boarded a Thomas Cook tour bus for the beginning of our two-week tour. Our driver enjoyed driving his bus and cracking jokes with us like a true Irishman. Our crusty British tour coordinator gave lots of information about the sights. On our first day we drove across the bottom of England and into Wales. We stopped at Canaveron Castle, which years later served as the setting for Prince Charles' installation as Prince of Wales by his Mother, Queen Elizabeth II.

With a little time on our hands, Mother, Dad, and I strolled through the town until the smell of fish and chips caught us. We went into the shop and purchased three take-aways (take-outs) of this delicacy. What surprised us was that the proprietor wrapped the fish and chips in white butcher paper and then shook a bit of malt vinegar over the top. Oh, how good that tasted! We finished our walk while munching on the last bites of our snack before boarding our bus again.

After a good night's sleep, we drove on to St. Andrews, where Dad viewed the golf course, wishing he could play there. That evening, we spent the evening away from our tour group having dinner with a British business acquaintance of Dad's, Mr. John Barclay. His two-story stone home felt cold and damp. While in his study drinking our before-dinner libations, we were warmed by a massive fire in the fireplace. The fire warmed me like God's blanket of love. We ate the traditional English meal of roast beef, Yorkshire pudding, roasted potatoes, carrots, onions, and for dessert, an apple crumble. It was a wonderful, filling English dinner.

Reconnecting with our tour group, we moved onto the Urquhart Castle, where we hoped to see Nessie, but to no avail. A couple of hours later, we learned she had showed her head just minutes after our bus pulled away. Oh well, maybe the next time.

A few more stops along our tour route, we arrived in Blackpool, the prestigious UK vacation spot. Mother, Dad, and I walked along the coastline shops and tents where vendors sold all kinds of jewelry, trinkets, pottery, and Aryan wool, hand-knitted sweaters. Mother and Dad even tried some cockles seafood vendors were selling; I didn't want any part of this "delicacy."

The following morning, we left the tour to visit Dad's relatives living in the Midlands. After renting a car, Dad began the drive. Oh, how different it seemed for him to be driving on the left side of the road while the steering wheel and pedals were on the right side. I wanted to try it, so I asked if I could. After some begging and pleading, Dad relented. Behind the wheel, I realized how different and difficult this procedure was and quickly gave it back to him. At least I had the courage to try.

We visited Aunt Maude and her local coal business in Birmingham and then drove on to see her son, Ben, and his family in Leeds. He took us on a walk to Dad's old home and Grandpa Hamilton's church, where he preached for many years before bringing the family to the States in 1909. I loved reliving Dad's life with him. From there, we visited cousins Barry and Vernon, along with their families.

Too soon, the time came to go to Liverpool to board *The Media* for home. We all needed a bit of rest after our long, involved vacation.

On arrival in New York, my brother, Jim, met us. I loved seeing him, as it had been a year since I had seen him. The previous summer, I had spent two weeks taking care of his son, Jimmy III, while he and his wife, Eileen, moved into their new home in Winnetka, Illinois. He had been promoted to Western Manager for MacKiernan and Terry, a large pier/dock construction company based in Chicago that forced their move from Pittsburgh to the Chicago area.

After dinner that night, I had a surprise—my bed pulled out of the wall. I had never seen anything like that. As I tried to sleep, I saw the stars and moon outside my window. Slowly, I drifted off. It was morning before I knew it.

We all took a cab to the airport. Mother, Dad, and I said good-bye to him as we boarded our plane for home; his flight home left a couple hours later. What we didn't know was what was about to happen.

One evening, a little more than a month later, Eileen called, telling Dad that Jim had flown to Dubuque, Iowa, that morning to inspect a new dock construction there. He hadn't returned. He had told the company he would fly up, circle the plant three times, and then land at the little landing strip near their plant. With this signal, they were to send a car to pick him up. After Jim circled the plant three times, the men drove to pick him up. When they got there, Jim wasn't anywhere to be found. Thinking it was a fluke, they didn't report the incident when they returned to their offices.

When he didn't return home for dinner that night, Eileen became concerned and called the airport where he had rented the Piper Cub plane. He had filed his flight plan before taking off. The airport began checking airports along his route and found nothing. There hadn't been any reported maydays or small-craft touchdowns along his flight path. He was listed as missing.

After talking to Eileen, Dad called Jack Huth, the company's chief pilot, and asked him to check into this as fully as he could. A little later, Jack called saying no one knew anything about Jim or his whereabouts. There had been no distress calls, downed airplanes, or refueling along his flight path. Dad told Jack they would fly up there in the morning. I said I would go as well to help Eileen with young Jim.

All night long and through the next day I prayed. "Lord, please let Jim be all right. He is the best brother anyone could have. He is too young to die. He has a child to raise. Please let Dad find him alive. I don't care if he is hurt as long as he is alive. Please, Lord, help us find him."

After flying into O'Hare and picking up a rental car, Jack and Dad drove me to Eileen and Jim's. "No more news," she cried when we arrived.

I kept saying, "Lord, no news is good news. Right?"

Once back at O'Hare, Dad and Jack flew to Dubuque. After flying into the airstrip where Jim was scheduled to fly into, they contacted the company to talk to the men who were to pick him up. Talking to them, Dad learned the men hadn't reported him missing. Because of this, no search was instituted for him or his plane.

Back in the company plane, Dad and Jack began their own aerial search. Later that afternoon, they found Jim's plane nose down in the Mississippi River. A few minutes later they saw what looked like a body in the water. After returning to the nearby airstrip, they notified the authorities of their findings. Police and other search groups followed them back to the site and began rescue operations.

Within minutes, Jim's body was retrieved from the water. Jack and the other rescue people realized that Jim had known he was in trouble because he had taken off his shoes, gotten out of the plane, and attached to his leg was his logbook with all his travel times and mileage.

The irony of his death came from an old football injury, not the plane crash. While playing high school football he had suffered a separated shoulder, which gave him problems every so often. Again, his shoulder came out of socket again and never let him swim the short distance to shore. With no one reporting him missing, he must have treaded water for hours; with no rescue, his shoulder and legs gave out on him and he drowned.

Late that evening, Dad and Jack came to Eileen's and told us the devastating news. The next day, Eileen, Jimmy, Dad, Jack, and I flew to our home in West Virginia. Jim would be buried in a beautiful nearby cemetery there. The grief was unbearable for our family. We just held each other up as best we could. Dad wouldn't let any of us show any emotion, as that was the English way. From his upbringing, emotions were not allowed. The night Dad became so angry with me about the movie scared me more because of his emotion than the possibility of physical punishment. His anger really frightened me. He had kept his emotions inside himself or in his drinking glass. "Stiff upper lip and all." Whenever I was in Mother and Dad's presence, I held my grief and pain inside. When I was alone in my bedroom, I cried and cried into my pillow until I was exhausted enough to fall asleep.

During those times I cried to the Lord, "Why, Lord? Why him and not me? He has a family, and I am only me. I loved him so, and he was so good to me. My heart is breaking. If you needed someone in my family, why didn't you take me? No one would care if I died. I would be happy to be at home with you; you could take care of me like Mother and Dad haven't. I know you love me. Lord, help me through all this pain and grief. Let me feel your peace and love at this time. I need you more than I ever have. Come to me, dear and loving Father."

Then I heard the Lord say, "I am here. It's not time for you to return home to me. I have work for you to do." With that, I begrudgingly accepted his word and realized I needed to move past this tragedy, knowing the Lord was watching over me. I knew he'd help me. I didn't know how or when, but I knew he would. "Oh, Lord, help me to accept your plan. I don't understand, but I know you do."

A View of God's Plan for Me

"God had planned something better for us so that only together with us would they be made perfect"

(Hebrews 11:40)

As I threw myself into many school activities my senior year at Marshall High School, I made sure I left time for study. I had to make excellent grades to be accepted into the University of Southern California. Another reason was to not have to think of Jim and his death. I couldn't let the pain overwhelm me, even though I felt devastated and very much alone. I wasn't Jesus, so I couldn't raise him, like Lazarus, from the dead. I had to make peace with what had happened. My big brother was gone, and I needed to get past that.

Since this was my last year in high school, I wanted it to be the best. As photography editor of the school's yearbook, I attended all the basketball practices and games, cheerleader tryouts, school club activities, and school dances, taking candid shots showing our students in action. I loved doing it.

What I didn't know in all this turmoil was that God had a gift for me. His plan involved one young man, and a very special one at that. The first Saturday in December, I drove into town as I sometimes did on Saturdays to window shop and maybe find a new dress or pair of shoes. Saturdays had become my day of doing something fun for myself.

I pulled into the Kresge parking structure, where I always parked. As I turned in, I saw John Pack, the college student/parking attendant, who motioned to me to pull over. I had known him for two years. Since no one was behind me, I pulled over and chatted with him. He said I looked sad, and he tried to cheer me up with some of his corny jokes. It didn't work. He knew about Jim's death and how upset I was about that.

This particular morning he shocked me with a question. "Nancy, how would you like to double date with me and my fiancée? I have a fraternity brother I think you would like to meet and possibly date." This flustered me, to say the least. I tried not to let my shock show. I couldn't believe he thought one of his fraternity brothers would consider taking a high school senior out. That seemed unheard of, but he was making it possible. None of the boys in my class were interested in me, so I thought, *Why not?* Before I knew it, I said, "Yes, but I want to meet him first; don't want a dud!"

With a laugh, he said, "If that's the only way I can entice you, then I'll make it happen." My spirit soared. A college guy!

During my lunch hour the following Friday, I snuck out of school and walked over to the college cafeteria. When John saw me, he waved me over. As I neared the table, I noticed a nice-looking and well-dressed young man. He stood up as I came close. John introduced me to Ron Hurley. I sat down, and we discussed the plans for a movie and a sandwich afterward that Sunday night.

Sunday night, precisely at six o'clock, the doorbell rang. I answered the door and introduced Ron to my parents. We talked for a couple of minutes before we headed to John's old jalopy. There John introduced me to his fiancée, Nancy.

After finding a parking place, the four of us walked down the street to the Keith-Albee Theater. The movie for the evening was *The Man Who Understood Women*. What a title! It was a fast movie, a clone of an Alfred Hitchcock venue. Later, we got back in the car and drove to one of the college hangouts, Wiggins. Being as nervous as I was, and knowing college guys had little money, I only ordered a coke, as did John's Nancy. The guys, not having eaten since breakfast, ordered barbecued pork sandwiches and big mugs filled with frosty root beer, both Wiggins specialties. While the guys ate, we talked about the movie and who had figured out the plot and killer first. At about ten, Ron walked me to the door and thanked me for a lovely evening. He told me that tomorrow started final exam week and then he would be going home for Christmas. He would call me after he returned to school in January. I said I would look forward to his call, as I had had a wonderful evening with him.

In January, our senior class began tryouts for its production of *Oklahoma*. What a huge undertaking. Our high school was a private laboratory school for Marshall College's student teachers. Our student numbers from freshmen to seniors consisted of 150 students.

Mr. Duncan, our speech and debate teacher, accepted the directorship of it, and Miss Galperin, our vocal and choir instructor, took on its musical direction. One day after speech class, Mr. Duncan asked if I would be interested in being his assistant, as I was so organized and got the job done. I couldn't get the "yes" out fast enough. What a position of importance that was! Now I had to prioritize my time to be able to be his assistant and photography editor of the yearbook while staying on top of the honor roll. A lot to handle!

After dating a few times in January, Ron asked me to his fraternity's annual Sweethearts' Ball. I searched for the perfect dress, finding a beautiful black, chiffon, cocktail-length dress with an embroidered rhinestone and lace cummerbund.

As I finished dressing for this special evening, I felt beautiful. I didn't look like the "creampuff" my classmates had called me before losing my "baby fat." I was a different Nancy. Looking in the mirror at myself in my new black dress and accessories, I saw the new, sophisticated Nancy.

After meeting his fraternity brothers and their dates, Ron and I danced the night away, listening to songs like Nat King Cole's "When I Fall in Love." I felt so in love. My first true love! I was going to relish every moment, even if his fraternity brothers frowned on our budding relationship. I was a high schooler, not a college girl, and that made a huge difference to them, but not to us. Ron and I didn't care what they thought. It was all about how we felt for each other that mattered.

A couple weekends later, he asked me to go steady, giving me his class ring, which he had only received a couple of weeks before. I truly was in love, and I knew how he felt about me. Oh, did I feel important. I was so in love, I couldn't think of us ever being apart.

As winter turned into spring, my time became even more precious. By March, the yearbook had been sent to the publisher. My thoughts centered on the play, prom night, graduation, and college decisions. I had been accepted at Marshall College, the University of Cincinnati, and Trinity College in San Antonio, Texas. My true hope of the University of Southern California had blown away, as I wasn't a California resident, a prerequisite for admission there. Along with these thoughts, my real attention centered on Ron and how much I loved him. How could I leave him for college? Mother and Dad wanted me to go to college, but my relationship with Ron might ruin my college career. I would put him first not school.

Days flew by. Before I knew it, opening night for *Oklahoma* was upon us. My self-confidence and self-esteem had risen to greater heights than ever before, as I had accomplished so much: overseeing the completion of scenery and backdrops, rehearsing lines with various cast members, making sure the cast wardrobe was finished and complete, and listening to all the songs and orchestration. Things were great, and I couldn't be happier.

Each of the two weekend performances (four performances in all), the college auditorium was filled to capacity. After each performance, we received standing ovations and shouts of "Bravo."

With the play completed, my high school days flew past at lightning speed. I scrambled to find a prom dress, wanting something special for that night with Ron. After searching and trying on a myriad of dresses, I finally found a beautiful strapless, full-length, tiered, yellow, chiffon dress.

At six o'clock on prom night, Ron called for me in his black tuxedo and bowtie. What a striking figure he made! He helped me and my bounteous dress in the car; how he got me into it was beyond me. He drove us to the Frederick Hotel, where the junior-senior dinner and later the prom were to be held. Oh, how I didn't want the evening to end!

After the last dance, all the juniors and seniors returned to their cars and homes to change for a night full of after-prom parties that parents were hosting. Ron drove me home and then went to change at his dorm before returning to my house, where the first party would be.

By the time I arrived home, Mother and Dad had all the fixings for hamburgers and hot dogs, chips, baked beans, and all kinds of sodas ready for us. I ran upstairs and changed quickly. After two hours of eating and dancing to Chubby Checkers, Paul Anka, Johnny Mathis, and a host of other entertainers, the group moved on to the next of two parties planned for us. Ron and I stayed to help Mother and Dad clean up the leftovers from my once-hungry classmates. The next two parties would be repeats of ours, with the final one starting at five a.m. at Gus Von Stroh's home, where his parents would serve breakfast.

Before moving onto the next party, Ron and I took a few quiet moments for ourselves. Mother and Dad had gone to bed, as we had worn them out from all the cooking and blaring music. We drank cokes and munched on potato chips still not returned to their bags. We cuddled up on the sofa, unaware of whatever was on the television.

Ron really wasn't into watching television, as he had something important to ask me. Pulling me onto his lap, he told me how much he loved me and hoped I felt the same. I said I did. He became more serious and nervous than I had ever seen him before. A few weeks before, he had mentioned to me to think about what kind of future we might have together or if we even had one. Even though I had been thinking about it I wasn't prepared for what came. Slowly and softly, he asked, "Will you marry me?"

My answer instinctively was yes. He gave me his fraternity pin, meaning we were engaged, but that fact had to be concealed from my parents, as that wouldn't go over well with them. I returned his class ring, since we had passed that stage in our relationship.

I would be Mrs. Ronald Hurley, Mrs. Nancy Hurley, after I finished college. I couldn't contain my feelings.

I knew God had sent Ron to me as his gift. All I could do was praise him for sending me the most wonderful man to be my husband, soul mate, and lifetime partner. I prayed God would soften my parents' hearts to our relationship and be happy for us. I knew he could do the impossible. This was an insurmountable feat for me to do alone. I needed his help.

"Lord, let me keep this a secret. Help me know this is what you have planned for me. Let me know you are with us and for us. Lord, I believe you sent Ron to me as my life partner. I love him so much and want us to be a family. You have brought so much love into my life I am bursting with joy. Thank you, Lord. I praise and thank you from the bottom of my heart and soul. Amen."

With that I heard the Lord say, "Nancy, you are young and will have problems with your parents, especially your mother, but I will be here to listen to your pain and help you through this. Ron is the one I planned for you. Just trust in my love for you and what I have ahead for you. Believe I am with you in all things."

When I came home after the last party, Mother and Dad had just finished breakfast. I told them Ron and I had had a wonderful evening and we had just finished breakfast at Gus's. Mother asked where Ron's ring was. I told her Ron had exchanged it for his fraternity pin, to which she asked me what that meant. I said it was just a step up from going steady. I didn't want them to know how significant this step was, as I knew from their faces they weren't at all pleased. My dream of going to Marshall College with Ron hung in the balance if she knew the totality of my relationship with Ron. She had other plans, greater plans for my future—plans that didn't include Ron. When she made up her mind to something, it usually came about. I was fearful of her knowing about us. I needed to keep the meaning secret until Ron and I could work to change their minds about our relationship.

Days flew now. Graduation was closer and closer. Senior Week arrived, and we had to take our final exams so our teachers could tabulate our grades, making sure we were able to graduate. Another activity for our school came. *The Brigadier* (our school yearbook) was distributed to all paying students. The centerfold of the yearbook announced the senior girl of the year; this year there was a first, the senior boy. Those titles were bestowed on the students who exemplified the best in the senior class. All the seniors, as well as our teachers, voted on these distinctions. This was a coveted prize to get.

I remember distribution morning. I had arrived late at school. In the main hall, I passed G.G. Varnum, the yearbook editor, the head cheerleader, and the girl I knew would be named Miss Brigadier. Instead of saying hi to me, she seemed quite upset and avoided me.

What's the matter with her? I thought. *Being Miss Brigadier should make her ecstatic, as she worked so hard for it; she deserves it.* As I walked into the main office, classmates and teachers said, "Congratulations!" This puzzled me!

Mrs. Hanes, our school secretary, smiled at me when she handed me my yearbook. I felt spooked by everyone's attention. As I leafed through the book, I found out what all the smiles and congratulations were about. I had been chosen as Miss Brigadier. I about fainted. I never believed in a thousand years that I would get that distinction. No wonder G.G. was upset when she saw me. She expected that distinction for herself, and rightly so. When I saw her again, I told her I didn't expect to get this and she should have gotten it for all the work she had done to get it. Although inside me I felt I too deserved it. I was class vice president for two years, assistant to the director of *Oklahoma*, photography editor for the yearbook, and honor student. I did deserve it. She wasn't the only one.

The real shock to me was that Ron Bowen took Mr. Brigadier status. I had expected Tom Melton, all-star basketball player, student council president, Boy's State representative, and all-around nice guy to get it. Ron was an intellectual, shy, unassuming, and a loner. How did that happen?

When I showed Mother the honor, she mumbled, "That's nice. What did that mean?" I tried to explain the honor, but she wasn't impressed. Once again, she didn't care about the honors I received—being vice-president, photography editor, honor student. Nothing I did received praise from her. "Lord, why doesn't she want to see the good in me, only the things she can criticize me for? Am I so bad to want her attention?" I flew up the stairs, sobbing with each step. Fortunately, when Dad came home that night, Dad realized the specialness of the honor and told me so. It was the first time in a long time he told me how proud he was of me. He couldn't do that when Mother was around, as she didn't like him paying me any attention.

"Thank you, Dad." I felt so good and special, at least for the moment, hoping Mother wouldn't find a way of taking that moment away from me too.

The last days of school filled us with graduation practices. On graduation night, all twenty-four of us were nervous as we donned our gowns, mortarboard caps, and tassels. When "Pomp and Circumstance" began, we went into our practiced routine. The ceremony and diploma presentations proceeded without a hitch or faint. After all was said and done, we proudly walked back out the front door where our families congratulated us.

"Thank you, Lord, for all the help you have given me these past years. You have been with me throughout these three-and-a-half years. You saw to it that these years here were filled with activities that would raise my level of confidence and self-esteem so I would know I could succeed in life. You even made sure I met my life partner. Please soften Mother and Dad's hardness to Ron and me and our love and future marriage. Please bless us in whatever lays ahead. Without you at my side, I would never have become the person I am today. You are the one, the only one, who tells me how special I am and that you love me. I get it sometimes from Dad, but for whatever reason, Mother can never tell me that. I know you are with me in all I do. Thank you, Lord. Thank you so much for being there for me and making me feel so loved. Amen."

My Balloon Bursts

Hear, O Lord, my righteous plea; listen to my cry.
Give ear to my prayer.

(Psalm 17:1)

I should have known I was sailing too high. My attempts to keep our relationship off the radar screen hadn't been successful. Mother lowered the boom, telling me she and Dad wouldn't agree to my attending Marshall College with Ron. How ironic since she and Dad had eloped right after high school but she wouldn't have any part of my relationship with Ron. I knew I wanted to get married and have a happy life with him. College wasn't my main priority.

She reminded me, "You have been accepted at two other colleges. You need to visit them and then choose which one you want to attend. Marshall is no longer an option." Separating us was her main goal. She was having no part of Ron becoming her son-in-law. Once again I realized her resolve for my future would win out. There was nothing I could do but cry it out on my bed. How could she do this?

She always made life decisions for me, as well as Ruth and Jim, even if they were married. She continuously reminded us, "You don't know what is best for yourselves; I have the experience to know what is best." I had no rights about how my life would be, who I was, or who I would become.

She planned for me to marry into a wealthy, social-class family no matter if I loved him or not. I couldn't count the times she said, "Money is better than love. You can love a rich man just as you can love a poor man. You will learn to love him after you marry him."

After graduation, Mother and I drove to San Antonio, Texas, to see Trinity College. Both of us decided this southwest school wasn't for me. The environment, the lack of my curriculum choices, and the distance from home didn't sit well with either Mother or me. For once I said, "Hooray! We agree on something."

Without telling me until we arrived in San Antonio, Mother explained that she and Dad had planned a two-week vacation at Paradise Inn Dude Ranch in Colorado Springs, Colorado. Dad would meet us in San Antonio, take a look at Trinity College himself, and then we would drive to the dude ranch the next day. Again, I felt the crush of her demands on me. This was the start of her plan to break us up. After seeing Trinity, Dad agreed Trinity wasn't the college for me.

Now, with Marshall College and Trinity College out for my college years, the University of Cincinnati remained as my school of choice.

The following morning, we piled our luggage and ourselves into Mother's car and headed off to the dude ranch, which lay beneath the snowcapped Pike's Peak. The only thing this area had was uninhabitable countryside filled with brown soil, some juniper shrubs, and colorful wildflowers along with the usual western shops selling their western shirts, skirts, boots, jeans, cowboy hats and some riding equipment. I didn't want any part of this. I hadn't signed up for this. This wasn't my cup of tea. I wanted Ron, not this "wonderful graduation gift."

After two weeks of horseback riding, campfire meals, and rodeo training, we packed for the drive home. I wanted to see Ron and have him hold me. The few calls I could make left me lonelier and emptier than the one before. I was more than ready for the trip home. As I began driving home, Mother and Dad said more than once, "Slow down. We're not on a race track going for the checkered flag." But for me it became a race to get home.

Once home, seeing Ron on the weekends invigorated me. To help pay for his college expenses, he had taken a full-time summer job doing chemical testing on various types of coals at a nearby coal company. We only saw each other on the weekends, but I loved every minute we had together.

Before I knew it, college approached. With that I knew Ron and I would have to say good-bye again. Too soon, my things were solidly packed into Dad's car. Mother, Dad, and I drove off to the University of Cincinnati. Ron and I were only a three-hour drive apart, but it seemed like a vast ocean between us.

When our car pulled up to the freshman orientation center, the director shocked us by saying the university had overbooked the dormitories. About a month before the fall semester was to begin, it realized that fifty some freshmen and sophomores, including myself, had no dorm accommodations. To fix this problem, the university had purchased a hotel down the street from the campus. I would be living there. My parents, especially Mother, ranted and raved about this, but the university's decision was final. I could go along with the decision or not attend the university. I almost thought for a minute that they'd take me home and allow me to attend Marshall in spite of themselves, as angry as they were about not being told of this situation and its solution. Even with this, Mother was stoic in her resolve to have me remain here. Nothing would change her mind.

After getting directions to Ludlow Hall, we jumped into the car to see this facility. The decrepit, three-story, brick building overshadowed the rest of the buildings on Ludlow Avenue. Across the street was the infamous Burnett Woods, a local park known for rapes and other crimes. The university supplied us boarders here with bus passes so we didn't have to walk to class. With this, Mother and Dad decided I would be safe here.

My room was the last rear room on the third floor. As I entered the room, I put down my suitcases and began unpacking. I noticed my roommate had already moved in but was nowhere in sight. After eating a late lunch at the Hitching Post Deli down the street, Mother and Dad left for home.

Reentering my new home, I found a petite girl rummaging through my closet. She introduced herself as Sue Richmond, my roommate. Seeing how surprised I was at her being in my closet, she apologized but said she just wanted to see if we were the same size so we could trade clothes at times. That wouldn't work, as she was a petite and I was a missy.

We got along from the start. We both had steady boyfriends and weren't looking for anyone new. She'd go home on the weekends to see Dave, and I longed for any weekends when Ron could get away to see me. He had a friend, Pete Shamus, whose fiancée, Anne, was a nursing student at the university. On weekends he could get away, Ron bummed a ride with him. Ron shared the gas costs. They slept in the car Friday and Saturday nights to save money. Pete left early on Sunday afternoon, while Ron rode the midnight train home. His train got into the outskirts of Huntington at three o'clock in the morning, so he usually found a ride back to his dorm with the local newspaper deliveryman.

During the first semester my grades took a beating, as I was angry and really wanted to be with Ron. With the winter semester, I knew I needed to put more time into my studies. One class I loved was Education 102, which required me to help out weekly at a nearby inner-city day-care facility. What a rough neighborhood, but I loved the kids!

The director, Mrs. Wheeler, watched me as I played various games with the kids. I even invented some new competitions for them. About a month later, she asked me if I would take on a group of seven sixth grade girls and teach them personal hygiene and nutrition. I felt great that she was pleased with my work.

I loved working with these girls. Most of the girls lived in poverty-level, broken homes. Wanting to know them better, I sat with them the first day and talked about their families, what they did to take care of their bodies, and what kinds of food they ate. Most of them bathed only two or three times a week because water was expensive.

With that information, I realized clothes washing was probably a weekly or every two week chore. Finally, I asked what they might eat for dinner that evening. Almost in unison came, "Greens, boiled potatoes, and cornbread."

At that moment I embarrassed myself by asking, "Is that all? No meat." From the looks on their faces, I knew I had not only embarrassed myself, but also them. From my perspective, meat was always part of the meal.

They said, "That's too expensive. We only have meat on Sundays." What a jolt to my mind and soul! It never occurred to me they wouldn't have a full meal like I did.

At that moment, I said, "Thank you, Lord, for all the blessings you have bestowed on me: my family, a roof over my head, clothes, and good food to eat. Lord, help me teach these girls how to make their lives more fulfilled and successful. You wanted me to learn the lesson that not everyone has it as good as I do. I believe I have learned the lesson. Thank you, Lord." I knew I desperately wanted to help them in any way I could.

After my second time to the center, I stood at the nearby bus stop for my ride home. Mrs. Wheeler noticed me and offered to drive me home, as the university was on her way home. She didn't want me waiting for a bus home in this bad area of the city. Oh, what a blessing that was!

During our drives, Mrs. Wheeler asked how the girls were and what I was doing with them. I explained our discussions about hygiene, family life, and nutrition. She told me how pleased she was with my work. After dropping me off in front of the campus, I walked toward the cafeteria thinking about how little my girls would eat that night while I had a smorgasbord to choose from.

Halfway through the semester, I began talking about low-cost and wise choices in fresh fruits and vegetables, and school lunch ideas they could discuss with their mothers. I taught them simple ways to add protein to their meals. Since they had never cooked or baked, I taught them recipe measurements when cooking. We made and ate pancakes and different kinds of cookies while we created menus and shopping lists for the needed items. Tackling one step at a time, I saw their eagerness to learn ways to eat better.

One evening on the way home, I broached the question of a final project with them. I reminded Mrs. Wheeler that Mother's Day was approaching. Wanting to show the mothers how much they had learned, I suggested a mother's dinner. Her concern was the money to fund such a project. If she could come up with the money, she would approve it.

A simple meal definitely was in order, as their skills were still basic. I asked the girls if they would like to do something special for their mothers for Mother's Day. Their eyes lit up with excitement and eagerness for the task. We discussed a simple dinner to show their skills as well as keep the costs to a minimum. They decided on meatloaf, mashed potatoes, green beans, and chocolate ice cream sundaes. We presented our shopping list and costs to Mrs. Wheeler, who said she would get back to us the following week. She sounded impressed and willing if she could fit it into her budget.

The following Tuesday, she informed me that the mothers' dinner was a go. One of her staff would purchase the needed food items and put the food in the refrigerator for us.

To see the joy, excitement, and glow on their faces was fantastic. A light bulb turned on inside of them. They knew they could show their mothers how much they had learned and how much they loved them. Isn't that the same way God turned on the light bulb in me when I needed it? I thought I would explode with energy just knowing he was with me to show me the way. I wished I could have done this with my Mother, but her own agenda of emotional turmoil didn't let her accept that from me.

The afternoon of the event arrived, along with my girls. We set up two rectangular tables, placing white paper tablecloths on each. The girls found two tall glasses for the bunch of fresh white daisies I had brought just to add to the festiveness for this evening. Next, they placed the silverware, napkins, and water glasses on the tables. Oh, how pretty the tables looked! The girls were thrilled with the way things looked.

When we started dinner preparation, the girls worked together in organized groups to make the meat loaf, peel, cook, and mash the potatoes, clip and cook the green beans, and finally assemble the chocolate sundaes. As always, there were the usual time glitches, but everything smoothed out before the mothers arrived. Even as skeptical as they were about their daughters' abilities, the mothers sat down, waiting to see what would happen. How excited each girl was seeing her mother there and wanting to show her how much she had learned! Each girl filled her own mother's plate and then served her.

The girls were pleased to see Mrs. Wheeler sharing this meal with their mothers. Instead of the water we planned to serve, Mrs. Wheeler provided milk for an additional plus for our meal. The pride and praise the mothers showered on their daughters made me feel wonderful inside, although sad, as my Mother and I didn't have that kind of relationship. I kept my tears of joy and sadness inside so I didn't dampen the beauty, excitement, and joy of what was happening on this special night.

"Thank you, Lord, for showing these mothers and daughters your love and joy as they gave each other gifts of love and admiration. Thank you, Lord, for allowing me to help these budding young ladies on their next step into adolescence. Help them think better of themselves and be joyful in their lives. Show them like you did me the love to help them become all they can be just as you did with me. Praises go to you for all that has been accomplished here tonight. Thank you, Lord, for loving me and showing me how to show your love to these young girls and their mothers, hopefully brightening their paths. Thank you, Lord, for being in my life. I love you for the joy you bring into my life. Amen."

The Lord replied, "Nancy, you have done a great work in these girls. You showed them what it is to be loved and how to begin taking care of themselves. Thank you for your work with them."

I hated leaving those girls at the end of the semester. They wanted me to come back, but I said that was not possible. "Just remember all you learned. When you remember the things we talked about, just know I am with you in spirit. You will make yourselves and me happy doing those things we learned together."

I learned more about life from them than they learned from me. I still wonder what became of them. When I remember our times together, I never forget the glow and confidence I saw on their faces that night. What a thrill that was! I pray they will never forget that night either. Again, I thank God for his presence in their lives and mine.

The Lord's Rays Come through the Clouds

"The Lord turns my darkness into light"

(2 Samuel 22:29)

The end of my first college year came swiftly, along with my return home and my renewal with Ron. As my thoughts were more on Ron than on my studies, my grades, as I suspected, put me on the probation list for the beginning of my sophomore year. At the same time, Ron found out his advisor had forgotten to tell him and six other seniors under his guidance that they needed to take an inorganic chemistry class in order to graduate. If those seniors planned to graduate, they had to take an additional year to complete this course before they could graduate. Fortunately, three of them, along with Ron, had families who could give them the money to finish their schooling, while the other three didn't have that luxury and had to quit. What a tragedy, not only for them but for their families as well.

    I decided to stay home and be with Ron instead of returning to Cincinnati in the fall. With my grades in hand and all the courage I could muster, I told Mother and Dad I wouldn't return to Cincinnati in the fall.

Their first question was, "Well, what do you plan to do? You've made a mess of your grades, so you can't return there or anywhere else." Mother was definitely agitated.

Defiantly, I replied, "I will go to Marshall." That was only a hope because my grades might keep me out. I would need to find something to do if that didn't pan out. As Ron had an additional year at Marshall, we discussed our plans to be married after his graduation in May. With that decided, we needed to broach the subject with my parents. He would talk to his after talking to mine. I told him we would do this together since it involved both of us. Relieved, he agreed to it.

Quickly, the night of this discussion came. We sat with my parents, who listened unhappily to us and refused to give us their answer until they talked about it alone. They asked us to leave for an hour or so in order to talk about this turn of events. We agreed and left for a campus eatery, Stewart's. As we pulled into a space in its drive-in, we ordered hot dogs and frosty mugs of root beer just to have something to do. Neither of us really ate much, as we were too nervous awaiting their answer to our question.

After an hour passed, we returned home to face Mother and Dad and their decision. They reluctantly agreed to our engagement but asked that we wait to announce our engagement until they returned from their planned October Caribbean cruise. We agreed. I couldn't believe it—they had agreed. *Oh, joy abounds!*

The subject of my education came up, and Mother said, "Nancy, Ron has an additional year at Marshall, and you need some kind of skill or education in order to support yourself if anything happens to Ron. (What did she mean by that?) What about taking a year's secretarial course?" I agreed to look into that with her. After investigating the Century College of Business, I enrolled in its yearlong executive secretarial course.

The weekend after our talk with Mother and Dad, Ron went home to tell his parents. He wanted to do this alone, so I stayed behind, waiting for their comments and hopefully their approval. When Ron returned, he told me they thought we were a bit young and he needed to have a job before getting married. I felt sure he would have one by graduation.

Both Ron and I began school the first of September. When Mother and Dad returned from their cruise, they formally announced our engagement with a party, inviting many of their friends. After the party and the public announcement of our engagement in the local papers, plans for our wedding began in earnest. With Vietnam blazing and the possibility of Ron being drafted after graduation, we decided to get married May fifth, almost a month before graduation. Since May fifth was Kentucky Derby day, many of the places we wanted for the reception were already booked. Finally, we found that the Prichard Hotel had a large reception room that hadn't been booked.

In the ensuing months, we all sat down to discuss the size of our wedding. If we had a large wedding with all Mother and Dad's friends and business associates, Ron's family wouldn't come, as they were private people and would be uncomfortable with a large crowd of people they didn't know. Mother then discussed wedding finances, saying a large wedding with all the bells and whistles would keep Ron's family away, as well as being a huge expense. On the other hand, if we decided on a small, intimate wedding, the monies saved could go to purchasing a much-needed VW Beetle for us. Ron and I chose the small, intimate, family wedding in our church chapel. This way, Ron's family would come and we would have a car to boot.

One of the biggest battlegrounds with Mother came over my attendants. Since the wedding was to be small, I wanted Sue, my college roommate and close friend, to be my maid of honor. That wouldn't do for Mother. She heatedly refused, saying Ruth should be my matron of honor and Ron's sister Judy should be my maid of honor. Her thinking centered on this being a family wedding, so only family should be in the wedding party. After more heated disagreements, I finally bowed to her. I had had enough friction and wanted some peace between us.

With February, the other major dispute surfaced: my wedding dress and those of the attendants. "Lord, where are you when I need your help me to get some of the things I want for my own wedding?

I need your strength to hold up under Mother's barrage of demands! She is planning this the way she wants it and not how I want it.

"Help me, Lord, rid myself of my anger at her deciding everything. I want to enjoy getting married. This is the most special day in my life! With her control, I can't enjoy it. She is making it difficult for me. Lord, help me put aside this anger and move on with my wedding and life. Thank you, Lord, for listening to my complaining once again. I am sorry. Please forgive me. Amen."

With all the wedding flowers, luncheon menu and table seating charts completed, champagne ordered, and the invitations sent out, our wedding was finally becoming a reality. It was really going to happen. I would soon be Mrs. Ronald Gene Hurley! I floated through the days.

My secretarial classes went well, although the accounting class kept me up nights trying to figure out debits and credits for my final business accounting project. Ron's classes progressed as well. Since he only needed the one inorganic chemistry class for graduation, he decided to add three graduate classes toward his master's degree, which he planned to complete later.

As time drew near, we needed to take our pre-wedding sessions with my rector. Each session proved more and more we were right for each other. The night we finished our classes, Reverend Atkinson said, "You know you two have a problem."

Ron and I searched each other for what could be our problem. Telling him we had no idea what he was talking about, he said, "You two are of two different religious denominations." That was true. Knowing that, we had been searching various churches to find one we both felt comfortable in.

Before I could say anything, Ron shocked me by saying, "There won't be a problem, as I plan to take your Inquirer's classes to become an Episcopalian." I almost fell off my chair.

Noting my shock, Reverend Atkinson asked, "You didn't know anything about this?"

I said, "No." I asked Ron how his father would feel about this since he was a Southern Baptist minister.

He said, "I believe he will accept it." I hoped he would but wasn't sure of it.

Two weeks later, Reverend Atkinson baptized Ron in a private service with only the three of us in attendance. I became his sponsor. What a wonderful day. I knew God was in our midst, as the sun shone through the church's large stained-glass window near the altar. Ron and I attended the customary confirmation classes together. He would be confirmed along with six other people on May twenty-seventh.

Before we knew it, our wedding was upon us. We checked and rechecked our to-do list, making sure that everything was covered. We didn't want any hitches; we knew we were prepared for our big day.

May fourth came so fast my head spun. That afternoon, I drove to the airport to pick up Sue, who was flying in for the wedding.

At five o'clock, the bridal party and some family members met in the Bethlehem Chapel at our church. Since the chapel was small, we had to take notice of what and when we were to do everything. Reverend Atkinson had us rehearse things twice to make sure all was ready. After the rehearsal, Reverend Atkinson reminded Ron and me that he expected us in the chapel at eight o'clock sharp in the morning for communion. He wanted us to start our marriage the right way. Since our families were of different denominations, we had decided not to have communion with the wedding service so Ron's family wouldn't feel uncomfortable. He also didn't believe in the old wives' tale about the groom not seeing the bride either; he wanted to stamp that out. All I cared about was that the Lord would be there blessing us and watching over us as we began our life together. We told Reverend Atkinson we would be there. Mother didn't like any part of this, but we said Reverend Atkinson required it and we were doing it. She had nothing to say then. Both Ron and I felt so good about starting our day and wedding off this way—it felt so right.

We drove to the Frederick Hotel, where the rehearsal dinner was held. Ron's parents, his sister Judy, my sister Ruth, and her three daughters—Shelley, Beth, and Dawn—Eileen and Jimmy, along with my parents, Sue, and the two of us attended the festive evening. The dinner table was decorated with white and pink carnations, baby's breath, and ferns. Dinner consisted of small steaks, baked potatoes, tossed salad, and ice cream sundaes. The evening flew by. Everyone said good night and then left for their hotels. With each of us hating to say good night to the other, Ron gave me the most wonderful loving kiss, telling me he loved me and couldn't wait for tomorrow.

Mother and Dad drove Sue and me home. I said good night to them, and then Sue and I sat in our pajamas talking about what was going on in our lives: our hopes, my wedding, and her future one. It was like being back at Ludlow Hall; it was so good to be with her. We didn't realize how late it had gotten until Mother came in and said, "It's time for the bride to get some sleep; you can talk in the morning." I laid there for a few excited moments before drifting off to sleep with visions of the wedding flowing through my head.

Before I knew it, the alarm clock struck seven o'clock, meaning I needed to rise and shine. It was my wedding day! Quickly I dressed and drove to the church. The sun was shining brightly when I arrived. Reverend Atkinson and Ron were waiting for me inside the chapel, where in just four hours we would be saying our vows. Just as the sun shone outside, the communion inside made us feel God's presence as well as his giving us his blessing and joy. I felt his reassurance that Ron was the man he planned for my husband, love, and lifetime partner. In these moments, the warmth I felt flowed out of me. I was radiant in his love as well as Ron's.

After arriving home a little after nine, Mother was flustered, as I returned much later than she expected. By eleven o'clock, Mother and Sue were dressed for the ceremony. I would dress at the church so not to crinkle my dress. With my gown, hoop, veil, shoes, and gloves in Mother's car, we drove to the church. Dad and Gram would follow later. Once at the church, Mother took my things upstairs to the bridal suite, where I would dress. All of a sudden, nerves hit me. My stomach felt like it was being bombarded by dive-bombers doing loop de loops in it. Suddenly, Ruth and her daughters appeared. Mother directed the girls to find their grandpa and great-grandmother and then wait with them until the Hurleys arrived. Shelley, the oldest daughter, was designated to bring Mrs. Hurley and Judy up to the bridal suite. Ron and his father would proceed to Reverend Atkinson's office until the service. Mother Hurley told us how nervous and white Dad Hurley was, and she was concerned he would faint during the service. That couldn't happen, as he was Ron's best man. We wanted him to help officiate with the ceremony, but he refused. He just wanted to be part of the attendees, but Ron asked him to be his best man, and he couldn't refuse.

As the music began, Gram, my three nieces, Eileen, and Jimmy, and Ron's grandmother took their places in the chapel. With them in place, Ron, Dad Hurley, and Reverend Atkinson took their places at the altar. Ruth, Judy, both mothers, and I walked from the bridal suite to outside the chapel. Dad beamed when he saw me. I felt so special! Ron's cousin escorted Mom Hurley down the aisle, while George Davidson, Ron's closest friend, escorted my Mother to her place.

The processional music began, and Ruth and Judy made their way to the altar. Dad and I waited at the chapel door for Mrs. Thomas to begin the wedding march. For a moment, fear struck me; my feet seemed cemented to the floor. With a gentle nudge and a reassuring smile from Dad, we began our walk down the aisle. My nerves settled down when I saw Ron waiting for me at the altar. I was stunning in my full-length, white, taffeta gown with miniature pearls embedded along the scooped, lace neckline. My headpiece was a tiara of pearls and white netting. I carried Gram's white Bible that was covered with stephanotis, cymbidium orchids, and thin flowing, white ribbons. Ron wore a navy blue suit, white shirt, and cranberry tie. He looked wonderful to me.

Before I knew it, Ron and I had said our vows, exchanged rings, and had our first kiss (Reverend Atkinson said only perfunctory, not a long, drawn-out kiss). The joy in me flowed out in tears and smiles to everyone as Ron and I walked out of the chapel and into the hall for our first extended kiss as husband and wife. As we came out of the church we were greeted with God's rays of sun and love. What a wonderful feeling!

Oh, how special God made our day. "Thank you, Lord, for being there with and for us."

About three o'clock, I went with Mother and Ruth to a room reserved for us so I could change into my traveling, navy blue two-piece suit with white blouse, navy pillbox hat, and matching handbag and heels. After changing, Ron's parents, Judy, Ruth, and the girls came to the room. I said good-bye to them and thanked them for all they did for us.

All of a sudden, I realized Ron was nowhere to be seen. I asked where he was. Dad said, "I didn't think he should be here right now and told him to wait with the remaining guests." I said, "Oh, Dad, he needs to say his good-byes to everyone here before we leave. Please find him." A few minutes later, Dad brought Ron in so he could say his good-byes as well. We then moved to the stairwell overlooking the first-floor entrance area, where everyone was waiting for us. I threw my bouquet toward Sue, as I wanted her to catch it, but Eileen jumped in front of her and caught it. Oh well, those things happen.

We hurried out the entrance door with people showering us and our car with tons of rice before we could get away. Three hours later, we arrived at the Greenbrier Hotel, where we could only spend two days, as we had to be home Monday, for finals for both of us started in a week. Pulling up to the entrance, we noticed that our little Volkswagen Beetle didn't fit into the scenario of Mercedes, Cadillacs, and other expensive cars. The valet rushed out, opened my door, and then retrieved our suitcases. He couldn't help noticing the "Just Married" signs and tin cans attached to our car's bumper. He asked Ron if he wanted anything done to the car. Ron replied, "Just get all that blasted rice out of it and then park it." The valet smiled as he drove away in our little car.

After entering the hotel, Ron registered for us. Looking like the newlyweds we were, I felt everyone's eyes centered on us. I felt embarrassed by the recognition we were getting along with their unspoken thoughts: *We know what you will be doing tonight*!

As Ron returned to me with our room key, the receptionist called him back. Our wedding gift from Dad was the two days at the hotel.

His secretary had made the reservations for him and us. What could be wrong with our reservation, we wondered. The receptionist, after giving Ron our room key, realized we were honeymooners. He explained our room had two twin beds in it and asked if we would rather have a room with a double bed in it. Embarrassed, Ron said, "Yes. Thank you." He switched the keys and we were on our way. As we got to our room, we saw two maids finishing their nightly rounds. Ron fidgeted with the key until it finally opened our door. Smiling at the women, he picked me up and carried me over the threshold. The women smiled back and giggled a bit.

We couldn't have had two more special days if we had prayed for them. We hated leaving the Greenbrier, but we had to get back to reality. Our final exams and graduations awaited us.

Before his graduation, Ron had accepted a position with the Atomic Energy Commission in Los Alamos, New Mexico. We would be moving there as soon as the FBI finished his all-encompassing security clearance. With our move to Los Alamos imminent, we decided not to rent an apartment. We would live with Mother and Dad until we moved to our new home in the west.

My graduation was shockingly simple. No fanfare or ceremonial rite. With each student on his or her own program timetable, graduations were run of the mill. With all my class work in and graded, I entered Mrs. Carson's office to find out when I would graduate. She said, "Congratulations, you have completed all your work well, and you are ready to graduate." With that, she took me out into the large classroom at break time, announced a graduation, and then handed me my diploma in front of the other students. I thought a little fanfare was warranted, but that wouldn't be the case. Mother, Dad, and Ron didn't know about my graduation until I presented them with my executive secretarial diploma.

Ron's graduation held all the traditional bells and whistles, caps and gowns, orchestra sounds of "Pomp and Circumstance," and family all around. The sun shone in all its glory. The ceremony filled us with awe as we saw Ron walk across the stage to receive his handshake and diploma. I couldn't have been more proud of him. I knew his mom and dad's hearts were bursting with pride and happiness to see their only son graduate from college.

After graduation, Mother and Dad invited the Hurleys to come for a late lunch before returning home. Now it was time for us to ready ourselves for our new life in New Mexico. A new home, possibly a family of our own, and service to God for bestowing all these many blessings on us.

"Thank you, God, for being there with and for us. Only you could have made this happen."

Preparing for our Life in New Mexico

"Those who through faith and patience
inherit what has been promised"
(1 Peter 6:12b)

Life became fast paced for us. Since accepting his position, Ron had kept in touch weekly with Robert Albertson, his personnel contact at Los Alamos, to check whether his security clearance had been completed. Without successful completion of this, his job would be non-existent and Ron would have to find work elsewhere. When the completed clearance paperwork reached his desk, Mr. Albertson would set up an apartment for us. At that point, we would be given his start-up date as well as a move-in date.

The two questions swirled around in our heads: *When will we hear and what do we do until the clearance comes through?* Discussing this dilemma with Mother and Dad, they suggested we go on a real honeymoon trip, since the initial one was only two days. That sounded great, but we needed to be ready for our move to Los Alamos when the clearance telegram came. Mother said to just keep in touch with them, as the telegram would come to the house. A real honeymoon sounded like a great diversion to our worry. That settled it.

We put a few things in our little VW Beetle and took off to Niagara Falls, the honeymoon Mecca for newlyweds. Being our first time alone since our wedding trip, I felt as nervous as I had when we left for our first honeymoon. Driving to Niagara Falls took only a day.

For the next two days, we toured both the American and Canadian sides of the falls, along with their respective novelty shops, for some remembrance of our trip. On our last night, Ron and I phoned home. "No, the telegram hasn't arrived," Dad told us. We began wondering why. "Lord, why isn't the clearance coming through? Is there something in Ron's past the FBI is concerned about? Can you do something to help this along? I know I am to be patient and wait upon you although my patience is waning. Please help us. Amen."

The following morning, Ron called Mr. Albertson about our concerns, and he said this kind of security clearance could take up to eight weeks to be completed. This alleviated our fears. "Thank you, Lord, for helping us even with our patience dwindling when our faith and trust should be in you and your work to and for us." Since we had time, Mother and Dad suggested we stop and visit Ruth on our way home. Sounded like a good idea.

The next day we drove to Uniontown, Pennsylvania, where almost twenty-one years before I had been born and later had my tonsils taken out at Uniontown General Hospital. After driving past the hospital we drove to my first home there. Sitting in our car outside the house, I remembered the fun times.

I had Ron drive past Beeson Street, where Mother, Dad, Gram, and I lived for a year before we moved to Holden. The old place hadn't changed much on the outside, but it looked it was being used as an apartment house for college students. That made me sad.

That evening I took Ron to the Venetian restaurant where my parents and I dined almost weekly on its most wonderful spaghetti and meatballs. Remembering its wood picnic tables and benches topped with red and white checked oilcloth tablecloths, I was stunned when we entered the restaurant. Everything had changed! Instead of the oilcloth tablecloths of the past, the walls were covered with red velvet and black embroidered wallpaper, the now round dining tables were covered with white linen tablecloths, and the chair seats bore red velvet material outlined with brass tacks. The menu and prices had become upscale, serving things like veal Marsalis and veal or chicken scaloppini, pastas with a myriad of sauces and meatballs, and desserts like spumoni and tiramisu. Ron and I chose the spaghetti and meatballs; I hoped the restaurant hadn't changed my beloved recipe. Although it tasted similar, it was not the same. What's the old saying, "You can never go home again." Nothing compared with my memories.

The following day, we drove to Ruth's Wilkinsburg home, outside Pittsburgh. About four thirty, we pulled in, and she and the girls greeted us warmly. Shelley took us up to Ruth's bedroom, where we were to sleep. Ruth and her husband, Bill, were in the throes of a divorce. She planned to sleep on Shelley's other twin bed.

We had a wonderful four days with them. The Lord watched over this time and brought healing to our once-strained relationship—the usual big sister/little sister rivalry. My last problem with her began when she and the girls visited us the Easter before my wedding. Ron and I had gotten our new little Beetle. Oh, how proud we were of it. The previous year, Mother and Dad had bought her a new Beetle to replace her old station wagon. I had asked her if I could drive it, and she said no. Now she wanted to drive our little Beetle. This time I decided turnabout was fair play, and so I told her no.

From the moment I said no I felt terribly guilty and couldn't get my vindictiveness out of my mind and being. I wanted to talk to her about it before she and the girls returned home, but with all the wedding preparations, dress fittings, writing out invitations, and just busy work, I never made the time to discuss it.

What I didn't know was that the Lord knew we both needed healing for this and fixed it so we had the time to do it.

On the second evening of our visit, as afraid, embarrassed, and guilty I felt about the "no," I decided to broach the subject. With all the courage I could muster, I apologized for my behavior and my nasty remark. I told her I had been her spoiled brat sister who wanted to return her "no" for mine. She said she understood and apologized as well. She had always been jealous of me for having a better life than hers. She had lived through the Depression years with little to eat, few clothes to wear, or any of the fineries I had had. Being born after the Depression years, our family finances afforded me a better life. I said I felt guilty about that as well but there was nothing I could do about that. Both of us laid much on the table that night, clearing the air between us and truly becoming loving sisters.

What a wonderful time! I had my sister in a way I never had before and loved every minute of our time together.

The following evening, Mother called, saying a Western Union telegram had come. Ron told her to open it. Robert Albertson informed us that Ron's security clearance had come through. We were to wire him with our moving plans so he could contract with Mayflower to pick up our furniture and goods. Ron's start date was July sixteenth, a little less than three weeks away.

The next morning, after many hugs and tears, Ron and I packed up our little green Beetle. During our long, eight-hour drive home we began taking stock of what we would need for our apartment—furniture, kitchen items, and clothing. Our efficiency apartment resembled a square box with a center storage island that would serve as our closet. The closet divided the room into sections: kitchenette, living/bedroom, and the bathroom. All we really needed were the basics. Knowing we had no money, Dad agreed to loan us five hundred dollars to get us some of the things we needed. We made a contract with him to pay him fifty dollars a month until the loan was paid off. That was manna from heaven. "Thank you, Dad. Thank you, Lord, for blessing us with this provision. Lord, you are always looking out for me and now Ron and me. Once again you have saved us providing for our needs. Thank you, thank you for your providence and care for us. We can never thank you enough."

We Begin Our Married Life

"Wherever you go, I will go."
(Ruth 1:16)

On July ninth, moving day, the Mayflower truck containing the few pieces of furniture we had purchased pulled up to Mother and Dad's. It didn't take them long to load our fifteen book boxes and two wardrobes. Just the bare necessities!

The following morning, we piled our two small suitcases and a bag full of sandwiches, potato chips, sodas, and cookies into our car. After saying our good-byes we pulled out of the driveway. Once on the road, we realized how excited we were to start our new life together. We decided to take it easy since we had five days before Ron had to report in with Mr. Albertson. Ron would check in with him on the sixteenth, sign all the work papers, then pick up the keys to our new "home." We hoped we had coordinated the delivery of our things with our move-in time. Time would tell.

We made Indianapolis the first night. All was going well. Following the famous Route 66, we made Joplin, Missouri, the next night. By the time we pulled into Amarillo, Texas, on the third afternoon, all we wanted was a good, hot meal and a comfy bed. That wouldn't be the case.

That night, we had a ferocious thunderstorm. The following morning as we drove through the city, we were confronted by a problem that could thwart our continuing on our way. The main artery out of the city had been flooded by the previous night's thunderstorm. Now we had to make a decision: go through the high water, hoping our little car wouldn't flood out, or stay until the water subsided. We didn't have a choice; we had to plow through it. Again, the Lord helped. Our little Beetle actually floated through the water like a motor boat. We had heard this could happen with Beetles but never expected to experience it ourselves. Within a half hour, we were through the deluge and on our way to New Mexico. We had made it.

"Thank you, Lord, for seeing us through the flooding. Once again you pulled us out of possible catastrophe."

After driving through miles of desert-like scenes, we finally arrived in Santa Fe. Our drive had been long but we were excited to be so close to our new life. "What would the next day bring?" we asked ourselves.

Monday morning came quickly. We dressed, ate a bit of breakfast next door, and then began our forty-five minute drive to Los Alamos. I couldn't get over all the arroyos, dry riverbeds, the long stretches of juniper bushes growing out of the brown soil, and the seemingly endless tumbleweeds rolling along the uninhabited areas of land.

Turning onto the winding, hilly road to Los Alamos, we felt we were back on mountainous West Virginia roads. The views from my car window were breathtaking. I watched as we passed miles of nothing but bushes and dry, brown soil. The sky was as blue as could be with the sun shining for all to see, and in its midst roamed fluffy white clouds. Oh, how perfect.

As we neared Los Alamos, we passed the little airfield where Ron had flown into for his job interview in April. Next, an ominous sight: a tall, chain-link fence with a gatehouse and two armed guards in attendance. Ron pulled up to one of the guards, who asked why we were there. Ron explained that he was a new hire and had a meeting with Robert Albertson. The guard proceeded to verify the information. Once he confirmed the information with Mr. Albertson, the guard gave us directions to his office then opened the gate so we could drive through. I wondered what kind of place this was: high fences, gates, and armed guards.

Ron found the personnel building among a row of similar office fronts in "downtown" Los Alamos. I sat in the car while Ron went in to fill out his paperwork, have his security photo badge made, and get the keys to our new home. Mr. Albertson called Mayflower in Santa Fe to find out if our furniture had arrived and when it could be delivered. They could deliver it that afternoon.

From there we drove to the three-story apartment building that contained our apartment. After taking out our suitcases, we climbed three flights of stairs. Ron opened the door and once again carried me over the threshold. Mr. Albertson said the apartment had been cleaned for us, but I questioned that. As the previous tenants had only left the Friday before, I doubted house cleaning had had time to clean.

Needing to clean before the furniture came, we drove to the grocery store near our apartment. Before I knew it, we had bought groceries, cleaning supplies, a mop, and a broom to the tune of fifty dollars. I couldn't believe how expensive things were. I would have to watch whatever I bought from there on. We were only earning $590 a month before taxes. After he deposited me and our purchases in our apartment, he left, needing to check in with his boss, meet his coworkers, and see his lab area.

An hour later, I had cleaned the two big front windows overlooking the main street leading into town, mopped the linoleum floor, cleaned out the kitchen cabinets, refrigerator, and stove, the bathroom, and our rectangular closet and storage box.

Two hours later, I heard a rap on the door. Not knowing who might be on the other side of the door, I asked, "Who's there?" Through the door came the answer, "Mayflower!" I opened the door to find a hunky sort of man with a clipboard and pen in hand. He told me to check off each box and furniture label number when he and his buddy brought them in. They hated climbing up three flights

95

of stairs, but a half hour later we were moved in. This was home. My first home as a married woman!

I started unboxing our things and finding places for the household goods, our clothes, and toiletries. I gleefully moved around our little space of heaven. I thought., *I am a married woman with a wonderful husband and my own place to take care of.* Then "Thank you, God, for the joys I feel today. You are wonderful to give me such joy," sang through my thoughts and mouth. "Thank you; thank you, Lord. You have made me so happy. You found my husband and now a home of my own."

My World Shatters on Two Levels

*"See, O Lord, how distressed I am!
I am in torment within."*

(Lamentations 1: 20)

As the weeks passed, Ruth and I grew closer and closer through letters and calls to each other. I had the sister I never really knew. Oh, how joyful I was!

"Thank you, Lord, for reuniting me with my loving, understanding sister, one I didn't know before, but now my life is so blessed with her in it. My big sister—the one I will look up to and learn from." I rejoiced with this newfound start. I couldn't have been happier! The tides of change were moving toward a crash worse than the stock market crash in 1929. Oh, how I was going to grieve. The hit to my stomach and psyche would knock me off my feet.

With her divorce from Bill in full swing, Ruth's ulcer problem had erupted again. The girls lived with her, while Bill lived in an apartment near his work. During this time Mother invited Ruth and the girls to come for a long weekend. Hearing of the ulcer problem, she took Ruth to see Doc Coffee, a dear family friend as well as an excellent surgeon, about her ulcers. He strongly advised her to have two-thirds of her stomach where the ulcers lived removed. If she didn't, the ulcers could perforate and she could die before getting to the hospital for the necessary surgery. Mother convinced her that surgery was her only way to health. Ruth reluctantly succumbed, agreeing to the surgery. Mother said they would pay for the girls to be in camp while she had her surgery and made her recovery. Before returning to Mother's, Ruth dropped the girls off for their summer camp. Two days later, she entered St. Mary's Hospital and Doc Coffee successfully performed her surgery. The first week, I kept in touch with Mother and all seemed to be going well.

The second week, things weren't progressing as well as they had. My prayers went to heaven. "Dear Lord, I know you can heal my sister and bring her back to health. She is wonderful, and I need her as I know her daughters do. Come to her and heal her. She is the best thing to me other than Ron. I love her. Thank you in advance for what you will do for her. In Jesus' name I ask this. Amen."

With July thirtieth came my twenty-first birthday. I turned an adult, no longer a minor. Happiness enveloped me. That evening after Ron got home from work, he took me out to eat at the only restaurant in town. I ordered my favorite food: spaghetti and meatballs. Ron even ordered a small bottle of wine to celebrate. After dinner, we strolled home arm in arm in the moonlight. After some television, we pulled out our bed then snuggled in for the night. What a wonderful night it had been!

We had been asleep for an hour or so when the telephone rang. Who would be calling us at this time of night? At first, we thought it must be a wrong number, but Ron got up and ran into the kitchen to answer the phone.

I heard him say, "Mom, will you repeat that for me?" I knew in an instant it wasn't a Happy Birthday call. If it was about his heart attack-prone mother, he wouldn't be talking to her. I realized he must be talking to my mother. I knew something definitely was wrong. Ron said, "Nancy, I think you need to talk to your mother."

She told me that that morning she had called Doc Coffee, as she was concerned about Ruth's mental state; she was revisiting things from her childhood. Doc came to the hospital but could not find anything wrong. Her incision was healing, her blood work and bodily functions were normal, and she had been walking in the halls. With everything normal, he couldn't figure out what was wrong. Things continued to deteriorate during the afternoon and evening. About ten o'clock Mother's time, Ruth went into convulsions and died in her arms. After telling me Ruth had died, Mother stunned me by asking, "Why weren't you here? You could have saved her."

I questioned myself. How could I have saved her? How could she think that? What was she thinking? Did Mother think I was to be the savior of my family? Did she think since God gifted me with so many blessings that I could use my influence on him to save my sister? I couldn't believe she was once again laying guilt on me. How could I ever have saved her? Ruth was in God's hands and plans, not mine. Why didn't she understand that? Maybe she was so angry with God for taking Ruth that she needed to take her frustrations out on someone and chose me once again. My frustration with her lashed out inside me: Mother always told us "I am the only one who knows what is best for everyone," and now Ruth is dead because of her "knowledge."

Ruth was gone and nothing could bring her back. Mother didn't deal well with the responsibility or consequences of her own decisions for herself or others. I had always been her scapegoat for any family problem, so instinctively she laid this on me as well.

"Oh, Lord, my God, I am crying out to you from the depths of my despair and grief. Please help me deal with these crushing blows: Ruth's death and Mother's accusations. It isn't my fault Ruth died. Yes, I wasn't there, but only you could have saved her. Why didn't you? She had become my support, my loving sister, the one I had just found. Now, she is gone. I am spinning in a whirlpool not of my own making, and I don't know if I can get out. Only you can pull me out of this. Please, please hear me and rescue me from this pain."

With that the Lord came to me. "Nancy, just remember I am always here for you. This is a grievous time for you. You are hurting on many sides. Just trust me and in my love for you. Hold onto me; I am here for you."

I felt guilty, as my life lately had been so fully alive and joyful while Ruth's had been mainly unhappy. Now she was dead. She was Mother's glowing star; I was the ingrate. I was nothing to her—a failure in school and in life and especially in my choice of marriage partner. I had always been her easy mark for her frustrations, and she used it on me. Once again, she reverted into this role.

Now my grief and anger began to surface. *How could she be so cruel? How could she do that to me? She wasn't going to lay this one on me; Ruth's death wasn't my fault. To blame me was unforgiveable.*

She said she couldn't talk anymore, as she needed to make the funeral arrangements; she would call me in the morning. That was so final. *This can't be happening! This is just some kind of horrible nightmare.*

"Lord, make this go away. Tell me this isn't happening! Please don't let this be real in the morning. I love her so. Let this be a huge mistake. This can't be true. I know you know what is best, but this is hard for me to swallow." I couldn't process all that I had heard in the last few minutes.

After replacing the phone, Mother's news stunned me. I collapsed into the nearby kitchen chair. Ron rushed to me, knowing I needed his support. I tried to get my breath as I tried to process what I had just heard. The news took my breath away. "Ruth dead! This just can't be? How did this happen? Oh, Lord, you brought us together, healed us, and now you have taken her from me? What am I to do without her? Why, Lord! Why would you take away her away from me? How could you do this to me twice! If you had to take one of us, why didn't you take me? I don't have children who depend on me like she does. She was my lifeline, my encourager, and now she is gone! I know you have a plan, but it is hard to take. I need your help trusting your plan for her and me."

I had hoped the morning would bring a reversal of what I had heard. But that wasn't to be. Mother called with all the funeral arrangements.

Reverend Atkinson would officiate at the Honaker Funeral Home. This wasn't a nightmare; it was real. Ruth was gone.

After hearing about Ruth's death, Mother and Bill, Ruth's estranged husband and the girls' father, decided he should only bring Shelley, her oldest daughter, to the funeral, as Beth and Dawn were too young and impressionable to be there. In addition, she had decided I shouldn't come for the funeral either. Her rationale to me was Ron had just begun his job and the Lab wouldn't like him taking time off for the funeral. She didn't want us jeopardizing his job for this. Why didn't she want me there? As the conversation ended all I felt was utter despair.

She didn't want me to be a part of this tragedy. She had lost her pride and joy, and she certainly didn't want me there. I was her unwanted daughter. She wanted to be alone in her grief. I wasn't needed or welcome. Resentment reared its ugly head. With my anger at Mother at an all-time high, I made the worst decision of my young life. I would give her what she wanted.

She can have all the martyrdom she wants for her two dead children. If she doesn't want me there, I won't go. That decision I would regret all my life, as I needed to say good-bye to Ruth and have as much closure as Mother and Dad did. Even now, I still regret not being there for Ruth and myself. The anger that surrounded me covered the deep pain I felt with Ruth's death as well as Mother's rejection of me.

"God, how could she be so mean and vindictive? Ruth was my sister. I am not supposed to be there to grieve or say a final farewell to her? How could she do this to me? Help me understand what is going on here. Lord, help me grieve this loss. I miss my sister so much."

After the funeral, I called to see how she and Dad were. Answering, Mother said, "We're doing the best we can under the circumstances. If you had been here, she wouldn't have died." Again, she blamed me for Ruth's death. If neither Doc Coffee nor God could save her, how did she think I could? I didn't have that kind of saving power. I wasn't God!

"God, what am I to do? Since our wedding I have been the happiest person. Now Mother has broken me once again. Why does she hate me so much? What's so wrong with me she doesn't want anything to do with me? I wish I was the one dead. Maybe if Ruth was alive and I was dead then she would be happy or satisfied with me. With the pain and anguish I feel now, death would be freeing! Why can't she see and love me like you do? I know you care about me, but I have never felt she has. Help me believe you still love me, as she certainly doesn't."

During the next two weeks, I called daily to check on them. Usually someone other than Mother or Dad answered the phone. Because of my guilt I felt the person on the other end of the telephone wanted to ask but couldn't or wouldn't, "Why aren't you here?" This only made me feel guiltier than I already did. The coldness on the other end of the line cut through me. How could I have let my anger at her get the better of me so I made the most terrible decision of my life?

Day after day, I reeled from my decision. I knew I had been wrong and I couldn't get rid of my anger and guilt of it. I should have been there to say good-bye to Ruth, even if Mother didn't want me there. Ruth would have. She had been so wonderful to me, becoming everything I had wanted in a big sister. How could I let Mother ruin that for me?

Since I knew no one in town, I didn't have anyone to talk to about this. Poor Ron—I bombarded him with all my feelings. Church had always been my refuge, but now I didn't feel right there, even though I went weekly. I had failed God with my sin of anger, and I had failed myself as well. My anger turned me into a bitter and depressed woman. At times, the loneliness of not being home overwhelmed me, but I couldn't go back and undo what I had done.

"God, what do I do? God, help me! I need you."

As the days passed, my pain and anger didn't lessen. My relationship with my Lord became strained and almost non-existent. I had failed him, but I felt he had failed me by taking Ruth from me and leaving me alone. I cried out to him like a child looking for a warm place to hide and heal, but nothing came. At times in my lament, Ron didn't want to be there. He had heard enough. "Get on with it. You have your whole life and ours ahead of you," resonated from his lips more times than I wanted to count. Even he was closing off from me. Where was my faith? Where was God in my pain? "What am I to do with all these emotions, Lord? I am lost and I need you. Where are you?" He must have heard my cries, as a new path was about to become clear to me.

Joy Comes into My Life

"You have filled my heart with greater joy."
(Psalm 4:7)

As the weeks and months rolled by, I talked with Ron about doing something that would give Mother something wonderful to think about rather than Ruth's and Jim's deaths. I thought if I gave her something positive to latch on to, she would see me. Since the Laboratory had frozen new secretarial hires and driving daily to Santa Fe wasn't workable because we only had one car, I had to find a different avenue to fill my life other than clean our tiny apartment, cook, and watch the daily soap operas and game shows.

Ron and I started talking about starting a family but had made no decisions either way. This kept buzzing around in my head. The more I thought about it, the better the idea seemed. It definitely would serve two purposes: I would become the mom I always wanted to be, and it would give Mother something wonderful to look forward to.

That October, our housing rating with the Lab rose, so we moved into a one-bedroom upstairs apartment with a living/dining room, tiny kitchen, a real bedroom, bathroom, and two, yes, two closets. A bedroom all to ourselves! What luxury! Ron commandeered some of his work buddies to help us move. It didn't take but a couple of hours to move our furniture and things.

The following weekend we purchased our first bed, chest of drawers, and nightstand with a lamp. The salesman made us a deal we couldn't resist. Things would be a bit tight in the bedroom, but we would deal with it.

Ron and I watched the local newspaper and his "for sale" items bulletin board for a clothes washer. We had a small downstairs storage area where we could put the washer. All of a sudden I saw "For Sale—used washer in good condition $25." I called and we bought it that evening. One of Ron's colleagues took his truck to the home; he and Ron loaded it into the truck then placed it into the storage area. After they hooked up the electricity and water to it, I was in the washing business. No more waiting for the car to go to the Laundromat. I had my own washer. I loved hanging clothes and linens out in the fresh air and sunshine. They looked and smelled wonderful.

After the first couple of uses, we realized the washer's former owner had replaced its original motor for one much too powerful for it. It loved running all over the storage floor. I ended up sitting on top of it to stop its mobility. What a sight I must have been to passersby, but I did get some good exercise. Finally, Ron bolted it into the cement floor to keep it in place.

With November came our first Thanksgiving. Since Ron had both Thanksgiving Day and the following Friday off, we decided to drive to Denver for some Christmas shopping. What a treat! Big city life, all the shops we could venture into, and restaurants with various menus other than Mexican fare.

Once home, I wrapped the Christmas gifts and put them in the mail for our families. As Christmas drew near, Ron and I purchased our first Christmas tree, decorating it with a few strings of colored lights and my homemade ornaments and popcorn strings. With the star on the top of the tree, decorating was complete. I placed the traditional big white sheet around its base, and then I put our presents around it to make it look festive. Our first Christmas! Oh, how exciting!

About the same time, I felt as though I had come down with a virus from our Denver trip. We had walked in the cold and on the slushy snowy city streets and byways. I started wondering if I could possibly be pregnant.

I decided to check it out. I called the office of Dr. James Loucks, the obstetrician everyone raved about, for an appointment. He could see me the following Tuesday afternoon. Once I was in his examining room, the nurse weighed me, took my blood pressure and temperature, as well as collected a urine sample. My mind kept racing with thoughts of whether I was pregnant or not.

All of a sudden, this middle-aged, plump, cheery man came in. He said, "I am Dr. Loucks. So you think you are pregnant. What makes you think so?"

I said, "I haven't been feeling well for a week or so, and I don't think it is the flu."

He said, "Let's find out. Put your feet in these stirrups while I check out the possibility."

A few minutes later, after a thorough check, he said, "Mrs. Hurley, you are correct. You are pregnant. Congratulations! You look to be a month and a half to two months pregnant. From my calculations, I figure your due date is August twenty-ninth." His nurse came in and gave me some pink and blue pre-natal vitamins, a healthy diet, and the date and time of my next appointment with him.

I floated out of Dr. Louck's office. I was pregnant! I had something wonderful to look forward to. I stopped at our little grocery store and splurged on a steak, potatoes, green beans, rolls, and ice cream. I also bought a small bottle of wine; I had no idea what kind to buy but chose one with a good-sounding name. I purchased two wine glasses to create the right mood.

How I got home I will never know. My emotions were racing. Once in our apartment, I set the table with a tablecloth and real napkins from our wedding gifts. When Ron saw the table, he knew my news before I could open my mouth. His emotions ran every which way from excitement to shock. He was going to be a father, and he wasn't sure he was up to it. I couldn't wait. Seven months seemed like an eternity to wait for our little bundle of joy.

"Thank you, God, for this gift of life and love. Thank you for bringing hope and joy back into my life. Thank you, Lord, thank you."

We spent the evening talking about our new future. Ron would put our name on the housing list for a larger apartment. The Lab upgraded housing for pregnant spouses. We began thinking of names for both a boy and a girl. Ron insisted that we were having a girl, even though both his father and mother's families were 95 percent boys. With this data, I knew we would have a little boy.

After celebrating our new life, we called our parents the following evening. I thought Mother would be happy for us as well as for herself. Wrong again! First thing out of her mouth was, "How could you do this to me? I just lost your sister. You know you have had kidney infections and being pregnant you could die." I knew I had had a kidney infection when I was eight that summer with Gram and a bladder infection after our honeymoon trip. She was over the top, overreacting to my pregnancy; nothing to warrant this kind of comment or fear in me. "Lord, once again she is defining herself as concerned mother when it's all about her concern for herself that is in play. Help me to shake this fear and her unhappiness off me so I can be happy about our little gift from you. You are the one who has placed this life in me, and I want to be happy about him or her. I know you will protect both of us all through this pregnancy and deliver a beautiful little one to us in seven months. You are such a loving Father, and I love you and what you are doing in my/our life. Thank you, Lord. Amen."

Pregnancy wasn't a life-threatening situation. How dare she knock me down again when things were going so right for me! Once again, she had me reeling from her words. Not only had I not "saved" Ruth, but now I was going to die also. I couldn't believe what I was hearing. I went from extreme happiness to the bottom of the pit again. *Couldn't I ever please her? Why did I ever think I could have any kind of relationship with her?* All I wanted to do was scream at her

"God, be my strength in this and with her. Why does she do this to me? Can't you do something with her for me? What am I supposed to learn from all this? Teach me to surround myself with your breastplate so I can deal with what she dishes out. She doesn't care for or respect me at all. All she cares about is her and what she wants. I can't believe a mother can be so heartless. What did I ever do to deserve her or this? If you could, tell me what I can do to make it right with her, or help me deal with her. I just don't know what to do anymore. I lay this at the foot of your cross."

I don't know if it was depression, mourning my relationship with her and Ruth, or really morning sickness, but I stayed in bed much of the next month. Ron made wonderful-smelling dinners, but when I took one look at or smell of them, I ran straight for the bathroom. At the end of my third month, Dr. Loucks threatened to put me into the hospital, as I was so dehydrated and drawn. That frightened me! Ruth had died in a hospital, and I wasn't going there. He gave me a week and a new medicine. I began feeling a bit better.

Ron's mother suggested some brewer's yeast that could build me up. That didn't stay with me either. All of a sudden, I got a hankering for a sweet pickle, peanut butter, and banana sandwich. Ron looked and said, "What in heaven's sake are you making?" I told him that Gram had made these for her and me when I was a little girl. I loved these special, wonderful sandwiches. Believe it or not, it was the first thing I could eat and keep down. My days in bed were over. "Thank you, Lord."

By July, my little one and I had grown. I looked like I had a large watermelon for a stomach. One Friday evening Ron came home full of good news. Mr. Albertson had called to say he had a three-bedroom apartment available if we wanted it. All we had to do was have Dr. Loucks confirm I was at least seven months pregnant to get the larger place.

The following week I spent packing. By Friday, Ron had picked up our new keys, signed the rental agreement, and had his buddies ready for the Saturday move. Three moves in less than a year—I hoped this wasn't a signal of what our life was to be like.

Oh, what a thrill! Our new home was a two-story apartment containing a large kitchen with room for a washer and dryer, a living room, and a dining room on the first floor. Upstairs, we had three bedrooms and a bathroom. We even had our own enclosed chain-link fenced backyard. Good play area for our little boy or girl in a couple of years.

Since our old washer was bolted to the floor and we didn't want it, we decided to purchase a new one, possibly with a dryer, for our expanding family and diapers. After church on Sunday we drove to the Sears store in Santa Fe to purchase them. Now that we had a yard to mow, we also needed a lawn mower. Boy, did our budget take a hit that day. Sears would deliver the washer, the dryer, and the lawn mower the following Wednesday. What a luxury—a new home with a new washer and dryer set. We could live here for a long time, even if we had more children.

The following Saturday, we drove to Albuquerque to look for a crib, dresser, rocking chair, and curtains for the living room, the dining room, our bedroom, and the baby's room. Mother and Dad gave us money for the rocker.

In an attempt to get Mother excited about our first child and her fifth grandchild, I asked her to come out a week before my due date to be a part of this event. I hoped she would stay an additional week after the baby was born. All of a sudden, I realized this might not be the best idea. Her tendency to take over and dictate what should happen might lead to problems and tension for all of us. This made me nervous, to say the least. Since I was so huge, I thought our little one would come early. She told me she would come for two weeks. I began to think I should have had her come around the due date, not a week before. I thought, *I did it again. This isn't going to be easy with her, but I want her to be a part of this and be happy for us.*

" Oh, Lord, I need your help again. I am worried about having Mother here, as you know she takes over, and this is my baby, not hers. I am hoping her being here will help heal our relationship. I want to be able to talk things out and move on with her. Please show me the way to do this. You've always been my guide and supporter. Please help me with this important time. Thank you, Lord."

Suddenly, it was mid-August. My baby would be born soon. Excitement, as well as fear, traveled through my oversized, heavy body and stomach. The excitement was exhilarating, although fear of childbirth and delivery made me apprehensive. Could I deal with that as well as Mother?

The week before Mother came, our baby's godparents and some of my female friends threw us a baby shower. Oh, what fun! Opening all the gifts filled with cute sleepers, sheets, booties, and diapers made my impending motherhood even more real to me. After the party was over, the husbands joined us. I showed them all the goodies we had received before placing them into their appropriate drawers and closet. The baby's room looked ready. *"Oh, little one, I love you, and you haven't arrived yet. What are you going to be? Who will you look like? What will it be like when you come and I can hold and take care of you? Oh, come soon."*

The Saturday before my due date, Ron and I drove to Santa Fe to pick Mother up at the airport. She seemed perky and up ready for her forthcoming grandchild. She asked how I was feeling and what the doctor had said about the delivery date. I told her he was sticking to August twenty-ninth.

The Monday before my due date I saw Dr. Loucks, who told me the baby was in position but felt I still had a bit of time to go before things really started to go. By the following weekly visit, things hadn't changed much. Mother became more and more agitated that the baby wasn't coming so she could return home.

It became a drudgery to come down each morning, as her first question was, "Do you think today is the day?"

I would say, "I don't know."

Things became more and more tense as nothing was happening. At my last weekly visit, he told me Ron should borrow someone's jeep and take me on a bumpy mountain ride to get things going. Mother didn't care for his assessment of the situation.

That Saturday morning, September seventh, I knew things were beginning. Nine days overdue, I had had a show of color along with some simple contractions. After more than two weeks of her daily asking "Is this the day?" I could respond, "Yes, I do believe today is the day." Having her come out before the baby was born had been a stress on both of us. Why hadn't I thought this out before asking her?

She immediately instructed me to call Dr. Loucks and then go and see him. He told me he would be in the office in an hour and I should come in. After checking me, he said, "Go home, have a big lunch, and rest until the contractions become more pronounced." I was deflated, as I thought I was well on my way. I ate a little lunch, but things didn't move quickly. Mother questioned every twinge I experienced. At Mother's insistence, I called Dr. Loucks again at five o'clock. He told me to come in and let him see how I was progressing. Mother, Ron, and I got into the car, along with my overnight bag, and headed to the hospital. My pains were more severe. After checking me, he admitted me to the maternity floor, saying, "It looks like you're on your way."

By seven the pains had certainly intensified. I wanted this over soon. Dr. Loucks checked me again, telling Ron my progress was slow because it was my first baby. He told me just to relax and breathe deeply when my pains came. That would help. "Oh, Lord, get me through this soon." The pains only grew more intense.

He had planned to go to the Santa Fe Opera that night and felt it would be hours before my delivery. He told his nurse to give me something to slow my labor so he could go. The Lord had other plans for him. Just as he was ready to leave the floor, another of his patients arrived in full-blown labor. With one almost ready to deliver and me on the way, he realized that attending the opera was out of the question.

From time to time, Ron would update Mother of my progress. Hearing wailing from the labor area, she was embarrassed and surmised it was me, asking Ron, "Is that Nancy back there making such a noise?"

"No, Mom, it's the woman who just came in. She isn't tolerating her labor well," he reported.

As he wheeled the other woman into delivery, he checked me again. He told Ron it might be all night before our baby would be born. Well, that hit me like a ton of bricks! Fortunately, it caused me to give up and relax. A half hour later, after the other baby was born, the nurse checked on me. Immediately she yelled for Dr. Loucks. He checked me and then called for a gurney. I was on my way to delivery! Ron came tagging along behind. Mother became frightened that something was wrong with either me or the baby, as they were racing to the delivery room. Since dads couldn't be in the delivery room, Ron just stood outside, watching my progress through the delivery room door.

Within minutes, at 10:12 p.m., Ronald Gene Hurley II arrived kicking and screaming. I saw him for a moment before the nurses whisked him away to clean, weigh, and measure him. I would be able to hold him in the morning. Oh, how I wanted to hold him.

While Dr. Loucks finished his work on me, Ron ran breathless into the waiting room to tell Mother. He tried and tried to tell her what had happened. She panicked until Ron said, "It's a boy!" From the beginning of my pregnancy, he had told me he wanted a girl, but he truly wanted a son. He was afraid I would be upset if I had a girl and knew he wanted a boy. Having a boy just took the wind out of him.

Mother asked if all went well. He said I did well and Ronnie was fine—all eight pounds, one ounce and nineteen inches long. I would be out in a few minutes. She told him to call Dad and his parents. Dad took the thunder out of Ron's announcement by saying, "It's a boy, isn't it?"

Ron said yes. Dad immediately said he wanted to come and see his newest grandson. Ron's parents were thrilled, to say the least. Their first request was pictures as soon as possible.

Later that night, I panicked as woke up wondering why my nurse was massaging my stomach. She told me my uterus muscles weren't working as they should, and I had started hemorrhaging. A couple hours later she had the muscles functioning and all was fine. "Thank you, Lord. I don't want to die now that I have my little boy."

Since Dad planned to come and see Ronnie the following week, Mother decided to stay the additional week, which had its good and bad sides. I needed her to help with the daily household chores while I recouped my strength, but she was overseeing how I nursed, bathed, diapered, and did everything for him. Tension between Mother and me began to rise, and Ronnie felt it. Every time he cried, she was there. Nursing became difficult with her hovering over everything I did; he soon became colicky. This made my "motherhood" difficult. I felt like a complete failure as a mother.

Dad flew in. We had a wonderful two days with him. Sunday came, and I couldn't wait to get Mother on the plane home with Dad. Once the plane took off relief overwhelmed me. I couldn't stop crying. I hated Dad's leaving, as he was so gentle and excited about our little one. I would have loved to keep him around.

Finally I was alone with my son. What a joy! I didn't care if I was up nursing him every two to three hours; he was mine and I loved him. I loved the bonding and closeness that ensued. I felt sorry for Ron, as he could never experience that himself.

"Dear Lord, how can I ever thank you for this miracle of life you have bestowed on me? He is so precious! He is perfect: ten fingers, ten toes, blonde hair, and blue eyes. His eyes twinkle whenever he sees me. What joy you have given me! Help me bring him up in your love and knowledge. You are my Lord and Master. Help me pass you on to him so he can grow up in you also. All good things come from you. Ronnie is one true blessing for me. Thank you, Lord, for your gift of life and love to us. Amen."

"I will lead you in telling him about me so he will know me and come to me in prayer like you do. You will be a good mom. Trust and believe in me," I heard the Lord telling me.

Wonderful Visits

"Rejoice before God; may they be happy and joyful."
(Psalm 68:3b)

At nine months, our precocious little Ronnie began walking. What a terror on two feet he was! He investigated everything, opening and climbing onto anything he was curious about. He was a true all-American boy. What a wonder from God he was! Such a precious little boy! After Ron built Ronnie a sandbox, I spent hours watching him create sand castles and roads for his trucks and cars. During this time my thoughts rose to heaven. "Thank you, Lord, for this little one of yours and mine. Teach me how get him to know and love you as I do. I want to be the best mom in the world. I want this world to be the best for him. Please help me do that, Lord."

In no time it was the end of July and the Hurleys arrived. Ron met them at the front security gate, as they had no clearances to get in. What a shock to their systems! Seeing the guardhouse and armed guards, their thoughts and questions went in the direction of, "What kind of a place are you living in? You're living in an enclosed town with fences and guards everywhere." We assured them that since this was a top-secret government installation, it had to be guarded at every entry point so no one could get into the lab area or the residential areas. We were perfectly safe here and they shouldn't worry about us.

After four days on the road, they were ready to sit and enjoy Ronnie. Being Dad's first real vacation in a long time, we wanted him to enjoy every minute of it. Two days later, we drove them around Los Alamos, showing them our one grocery store, the drugstore, our five and dime, the beauty shop, the barber shop, the florist, our library, the bowling alley, our movie theater, the hardware store, and our luxury Baskin Robbins's 31 Flavors. That was the extent of our little town, other than the typical fire and police stations, a couple of gas stations, a few churches, and a couple of elementary schools, a middle school, and a high school.

Their first weekend, we took them on a tour of Old Albuquerque of Spanish times, the modern part of the city with its modern adobe buildings, then onto Santa Fe, which fascinated them. Santa Fe's town square was full of Saturday visitors as well as Native American Indians selling their homemade rugs, beautiful beaded and silver jewelry, and their sidewalk trinkets in front of the Palace of the Governors. We even witnessed a beautiful Spanish wedding in the center plaza. The shops and boutiques surrounding the square sold everything from cowboy boots, moccasins, squaw dresses, and western shirts, to pottery, art pieces, and rotas (sheaths of red hot peppers). Later that week, we drove them to the Via Grande, an enormous cattle farm high in the hills above Los Alamos. The rancher/owner lived in Texas, where he owned another large ranch with upward of ten thousand head of cattle. Each spring he flew them to Via Grande to graze for the summer and then flew them back to Texas in mid-October. The grazing here made for good cattle sales at the markets.

Another day, we toured Bandelier National Park, where we climbed up the steep, craggy mountainside then pole ladders to see inside their cave dwellings or homes. Years before, whole families lived together in these recessed hillside niches. In the center of the Indian living area were large pits, or kivas, where they cooked their food, held religious or tribal ceremonies, or whatever the community needed as a grouping.

As their time with us came to an end, Ron and I asked Mom and Dad if Judy could stay with us until it was time for her to return to school in the fall. We would drive her home as part of our vacation. We planned to be with the Hurleys for Ronnie's first birthday. They agreed, as long as we had her home for the beginning of school.

On the weekends, we drove around New Mexico showing Judy places nearby. The first was Espanola, a traditional little Mexican village off the hill from us, then to Taos, the artist's colony. As a high schooler, her eyes wandered from one painter to another as well as painting to painting. Another time, we toured the San Ildefanso Indian reservation, where she watched pottery workers mold pieces of clay then fire them into what would become Maria's black pottery. We ate tacos and enchiladas, as everything else was too costly for us. What wonderful times we had with her!

At the end of Judy's three weeks with us, time came to return her home for the start of her sophomore year. Knowing Ron, Ronnie, Judy, and I were all going to be in our little Beetle together for our drive to West Virginia, I attempted to pack as little as possible. That was so hard to do. We needed clothes but Ronnie needed clothes, toys, and diapers.

Our car was crammed to the hilt with an ice chest, Ronnie's necessities, and toys, along with food and snacks for the three-day journey. The roof luggage carrier held all our big suitcases, while the small ones we fitted behind the backseat and under the hood.

The Friday we left, Ron came home, had a bite of dinner, and then took a few hours' nap before we began our long trek to West Virginia. With us leaving around midnight, we hoped Ronnie would sleep through the night before we needed to take turns entertaining him during the day. Judy and Ronnie slept as best they could in the back, while Ron and I drove to Santa Fe and then caught the old Route 66 through Amarillo and points east. Morning came. We took time for a quick breakfast of sweet rolls, orange juice, and milk or coffee then took a five-minute walk to stretch out our cramped legs and bodies.

Back in the car, we drove and drove through flat, uninhabited land. Judy and I took turns reading to Ronnie and playing with some small new toys I had purchased just for this trip. We pushed hard, as Judy had to be home for school on Wednesday. After another stop for food and walking, we made Joplin, Missouri. After eighteen hours straight, we could hardly walk, much less stand up from the drive. We found a motel and rented a two double-bed room. After a quick dinner, we returned to our room. Those beds looked like a luxury to what we had had the night before. We each took a long shower to revive us before jumping into bed for some much-needed sleep. As exhausted as we were, we just fell into oblivion for the next eight hours. Even Ronnie slept soundly.

Morning came much too quickly for us, but we arose and climbed back into our spaces. Ronnie was more difficult, as he didn't want another day of being cooped up in the car. Just as we made Cincinnati late that afternoon, our car began acting funny. After two extended days of hard driving, it wouldn't turn off like it should. I kept hoping our little car would make it to Mother and Dad's in one piece, as we had a new Impala station wagon waiting for us when we arrived. It couldn't give out on us this close to home. It just couldn't!

"Lord, help us get home safely and that the car will be okay to trade in for the new one. We need the added room. Please help us, Lord."

The next morning, we set out. About an hour later, our car really started giving us problems. Being Sunday morning, we figured no gas stations or mechanics would be open and available for us. Fortunately, as we pulled into a little town, I spotted an open gas station advertising an on-duty mechanic that morning. "Thank you, Lord."

We pulled in. Again, the car wouldn't turn off; it just kept chugging on. To our terror, we realized the mechanic had never seen, much less worked on, a VW Beetle as he opened the hood looking for the motor. He said, "No wonder it won't stop; you don't have a motor. How did you get this far?" He asked where the motor was since he couldn't find it. The joke broke the tension building in us. Mom and Dad Hurley were waiting for us at my parents' apartment so they could take Judy home. We had to get the car home in working condition for the trade. The mechanic had no idea how to fix our car, much less what parts he would need or where to get them. "Lord, we are in a fix. What are we going to do?" I cried out in sheer desperation. What happened next amazed me. God had heard my cry.

Two of Ron's uncles drove tractor-trailers for Hormel Meats. Leaving their homes on Mondays, they used this road to get to Austin, Minnesota, on their weekly meat runs and then used it again on Sundays to get back home. Both uncles lived within five miles of the Hurleys.

While Ron continued to talk to the mechanic, I thought I heard heavy motors like those used in semis. "Lord, is this your answer to my prayer?" I ran outside, and what a beautiful sight I saw coming around the corner down our street. Chester and JE were heading toward us. I ran out into the middle of the deserted street and flagged them down.

After coming to a halting screech, they got out of their cabs. I couldn't stop crying for joy. Chester asked, "What are you doing here?" I explained our predicament. They strode inside to find Ron and the mechanic still discussing what could be done with the car. The mechanic was way out of his league with our Beetle.

Chester said, "You all get back in your car. Judy, come with me, as you'll have more room. Place your car between our rigs, and we will cradle you all to Huntington." That's exactly what they did. What a blanket of security we felt coming from our heavenly Father. What an answer to my prayer. "Thank you, Lord, once again for your help in our lives. You are always there for me. Oh, how special you make me feel. You are always there for me!"

We arrived at Mother and Dad's. What a relief, even if the car didn't want to stop again. My dad wasn't too happy that we had driven our Beetle as hard as we had, since we were turning it in for the Impala station wagon the following morning. "What if it doesn't work or has to be fixed before the sale can be made?" he said angrily. All we could say was we would deal with that in the morning. We were too tired to worry about it.

We unloaded our things. Mother had made a cold dinner buffet for all of us, as she didn't know when we would get in. After Judy and Ron's parents had some food, they left for home. I didn't really envy Judy another two-hour drive to their home, but she was so happy to see them she didn't care.

We spent a week with my parents and Gram before going to Ron's family, where we spent Ronnie's first birthday. They had planned a large family party for him so the family could see the newest Hurley. September 7, 1964, Ron's whole family (a total of twenty-nine) came bearing gifts. Excitement reigned. Ronnie ran from one gift or presenter to another. He just didn't know what to do with everyone and everything.

When the cake and candle came, he didn't know what to do. We told him to blow out his candle, but instead he put his hand in the center of the icing and took a big hunk of cake and icing. Within seconds, he had icing all over his mouth, face, and hair. Camera flashes flicked from every angle possible. Our precious was now a year old.

"Oh, Lord, how fast this year has flown by. Our little one has grown so and continues to be the center of our life. We are so proud of him and all he can do. He began walking three months ago. What a feat that was with all the pulling up and falling down he did along with his head being banged, knees scraped, and pants ripped in the process of learning. But that's how we learn anything by trial and error. We too are learning how to be better parents.

"Lord, help us to be the best we can, have the patience to teach him all he needs to know to succeed in your world, and not be frustrated by his failed attempts. Help us to not jump in too fast to do for him what he needs to learn to do for himself. Lord, lead him to be in touch with you through his prayers. Oh, Lord, this is a huge job and one I want to do well. Please guide us in each step so we can lead him in your way. Thank you, Lord, for this child—your gift of life and family I so love. Amen."

Another Gift from God

"Every good and perfect gift is from above..."
(James 1:17)

Christmas and Santa Claus had come and gone before I knew what had happened. By Easter, I began wondering if another little Hurley was on the way. When I checked it out with Dr. Loucks, he told me to expect my next little bundle of joy around the twenty-first of November. What exciting news! Telling Ron's parents about their impending new grandchild was uplifting, although they thought we should have waited a bit longer between babies. My parents were nonplused this time. Fortunately, this time Mother kept her views to herself.

Time moved slowly at first, but soon our little-one-to-be and I began to grow. Before I knew it, spring turned into summer; Ronnie and I walked daily and played in the sandbox. My thoughts turned to what a wonderful little boy he was and how I hoped our next little one would be as wonderful as Ronnie was.

That September, my parents came for a visit. Ron took time off, and we drove them through upper part of New Mexico into beautiful Colorado so they could see the ruins of the Mesa Verde cave dwellers in Colorado. The history of the cave dwellers—how they lived and the mystery of their disappearance—fascinated them I had to keep a tight leash on our little one so he wouldn't get too close to the cliff edges and fall. He certainly kept me busy.

From there, we continued on to Yellowstone National Park and the Grand Tetons for a holiday. What beautiful scenic roadways and landscapes! One morning while at Yellowstone, Ron and my dad took an exciting whitewater-rafting trip down the Snake River. While they were adventuring, Mother, Ronnie, and I stayed at the Lodge. Ronnie and I swam in the afternoon, as the sun had warmed the water so we didn't freeze.

The following evening, all of us took a hayride into an open mesa where the Lodge served a campfire dinner. Once the hayride began, I became concerned that all the jiggling and jostling wouldn't be good for the baby, but he or she took it all in stride. For the ride home, the manager strongly recommended I ride back with him in his truck. That was so much better.

After our holiday to the northwest states, we drove back home to Los Alamos. A couple of days later we took Mother and Dad to Santa Fe for their flight home. As good as it was to have them, they were exhausted from trying to keep up with our rambunctious almost two-year-old. My stomach grew larger with each passing day, making it more and more difficult to keep up with my little man. With the Lord's strength and love, I kept it all together.

November came, and the baby's due date was only three weeks away. Ron had gone for his weekly bowling night with his buddies. While I was sitting with my feet up watching Ronnie play with his blocks, a girlfriend called needing to talk. Before I knew it, my little one had climbed up the kitchen cabinets and was rummaging around in the medicine area. All at once, I noticed he was holding an open bottle of aspirin. I yelled for him to put the bottle down.

Fear struck as I wondered if he had taken any or how many. Immediately, I called Ron at the bowling alley. He and the guys thought I was in labor. When I explained what had happened, he said he would be home in a few minutes. He told me to alert the emergency room about the problem and we would be there shortly. While waiting for Ron to arrive, I kept asking Ronnie if he had eaten any of the pills. He just had this blank look on his face. Before Ron arrived, I put the aspirin bottle in my coat pocket then bundled Ronnie up.

On the way to the hospital all I could think was, *Did he take any of the aspirin? If so, what can the doctors do for him?* Oh, I hoped all would be all right. "Oh, Lord, be with Ron, Ronnie, and me as we work through this problem. Let the doctors know what to do for him. Let it not hurt. Please let him be okay. I am so scared of what lies ahead of us when we get him to the hospital. Please be with me as well as us as we go through another problem. Thank you for being with us."

As soon as we arrived, the doctor on duty gave him Ipecac to get whatever he had taken out of him. An hour later, after his stomach was empty from all his throwing up, he was as exhausted as we were. The doctor said he felt Ronnie would be just fine—"Keep him warm and watch him throughout the night." If there were any concerns, call his pediatrician in the morning. We thanked him and bundled him up again for the ride home. On the way home all I could say was, "Oh, Lord, thank you, thank you for bringing us through our first traumatic episode with Ronnie. I know you were there with us, as all went well and he is fine. Thank you; thank you so much."

About six weeks prior to our baby's due date, Dr. Loucks was shipped to the South Pacific. From my first visit with Dr. Wadstrom, my new obstetrician, I liked him from the moment I met him. He was gentle, thorough, and competent. I felt I was in good hands. My last checkup before delivery, Dr. Wadstrom couldn't believe I hadn't delivered, as I was so far along.

The day before my due date, I mentioned to our next-door neighbor that I had been in and out of labor for the past few hours and might soon need her to watch Ronnie. This time, I had decided to have mother come out *after* the baby was born.

The remainder of that day and throughout the night, my contractions came but weren't doing anything. Somehow, one of Ron's former college roommates found our address and then our telephone number and decided this was the night to reminisce about old college days. While I contracted mildly and grimaced, the two chatted about old times and their escapades. I wasn't interested in their talk; all I wanted was some rest before I would deliver this new little one of mine. An hour later, I dropped off to sleep.

At six in the morning, after a fairly decent night of sleep and a trot to the bathroom, I awakened Ron to tell him the baby was on his or her way. We alerted Dr. Wadstrom, who said he would be there as quickly as possible. After arriving at the hospital with my overnight bag in tow and checking in, Ron met Dr. Wadstrom coming off the elevator.

After checking me, he told me my baby was presenting head up instead of head down, so during the initial stage of delivery, he would attempt to turn him into the proper birth position. Again, I wished Ron could be with me during the delivery, but fathers still were not allowed in that inner sanctum. Within less than two hours, Dr. Wadstrom had manipulated our baby into the correct mode. At 9:23 a.m., John Christopher Hurley arrived—all eight pounds, ten and a half ounces, twenty-one inches, blonde hair, and blue eyes.

My prayer that beautiful Sunday morning was, "Dear Lord, thank you for your protection and care during my labor and delivery of this precious little boy. You are a gracious and loving God. I will never forget what you have done for me and us. Help me teach him your ways and keep him in your light and presence. Remind me not to be so immersed in my own life and family that I take my eyes off of you, Lord, for you are my strength, light, and guide. Amen." Once again the Lord said, "Nancy, I am here with you and your family. Just lean on me at all times."

While the nurses cleaned me up and readied John for the nursery, Ron went to call our parents. Both sets of parents were ecstatic with the news of their new grandson's arrival. "Send pictures as soon as possible," they cried. My mother retrieved her packed bag and boarded a plane to Santa Fe that afternoon. Ron picked up Ronnie from our neighbor, who was exhausted from our extremely active twenty-six-month little boy. Ron drove with Ronnie to Santa Fe to pick Mother up and bring her to our house. Arriving after visiting hours, she had to wait until morning to see John and me.

Within two days, my faith faltered. How quickly we can turn on him when something goes wrong. John had developed jaundice. I couldn't help wonder why this had happened and what would happen to him. Dr. Lee, our pediatrician, sounded ominous. Ron and I knew we had a blood inconsistency; he had A positive blood, while mine was O negative. All the blood work done prior to John's birth showed no problems. But when Dr. Wadstrom rechecked the lab work, he found that the lab had not done the most sensitive blood test because of its cost. This one would have alerted him, as well as Dr. Lee, to John's heightened sensitivity to my blood. He had taken on Ron's blood type, which put him at greater risk for change of blood transfusion.

As we watched the blood test results, Ron and I saw the billirubin numbers go up and up. I prayed, "Oh, Lord, make this problem go away and heal my little one. Why didn't you take care of this before it became a problem? Weren't you aware of this problem with my precious one? Don't you know how much my babies mean to me? Please, please put your healing hand on him and make the blood scores go down to normal levels. Please listen to my cries to you, Lord. I am like one alone in the wilderness crying for your help. Please, please help me as well as John. Amen."

On our fourth hospital day, Dr. Lee came in and said John's billirubin count was one point off his needing a complete blood change. This procedure was not easy and had life-threatening risks. Then he told us since John's blood was so sensitive to mine, any further children we might have would need an immediate blood transfusion. His strong suggestion was for us not to have any other children. Ron and I felt as though a Mack truck had hit us on both issues. The possibility of future children having to endure this procedure and maybe dying left us cold and in shock. I was devastated, as I had hoped to one day add a little girl to our family. That was not to be. But I soon realized we had two wonderful, beautiful boys and that's what God intended for us. No more.

Later that afternoon, after another blood test day, Dr. Lee came in and told us John's billirubin levels had started decreasing. If this continued, there would be no need for the transfusion. "Praise God." Dr. Lee told us John wasn't out of the woods just yet.

The next morning, Dr. Lee told me there had been further reductions in John's billirubin levels. If the levels continued into the normal level by afternoon, John and I could go home.

"Oh, Lord, thank you for the healing you are doing in John's body, and please continue it so he won't need the blood transfusion. Please forgive me for my distrust of you. I should have known you would bring him and us through this. Thank you, Lord. You are so wonderful to me and us. Amen."

The afternoon blood work proved John was in the normal range. While I bundled John up for his ride home, Ron pulled the car up to the hospital entrance. The nurse wheeled us out to the car and helped us in.

Arriving at our front door, Mother and Ronnie greeted us. Mother couldn't wait to get her hands on her newest grandson. I spent time reacquainting myself with Ronnie. His curiosity about his little brother got the better of him. He wanted John on the floor so he could play with him. I told him John wasn't a toy he could play with. He had to be careful around him until he grew some and could play with him. He didn't want to hear that. Seeing me nursing John upset him, as he wasn't the center of my world as before. He didn't like this little "upstart" invading his territory.

Mother's help with Ronnie, cooking, ironing, and cleaning was a Godsend for me. She still believed she was the expert on everything that went on within my house and family, just as her Mother had done to her. I wondered how she had totally potty-trained Ronnie in the five days I had spent in the hospital with John. She said she just told him his Mommy didn't need two babies in diapers. Since he was the big brother, he needed to use the potty properly, not his pants. This time I resisted getting angry, as I was truly grateful with the result and help she gave me, especially now that I had two demanding little ones.

Two weeks later, we packed everyone into the car to take Mother to the Santa Fe Holiday Inn, where she would spend the night before taking a taxi to the airport for her early morning flight back to Cleveland. What a blustery, cold November night we had. The winds were blowing, and the forecasters predicted snow before morning. After saying our good-byes, we started home.

Two weeks later, John became listless and had a 102 fever. Concerned it had something to do with his blood problem, I called Dr. Lee to find out if this was a possibility. Unfortunately, Dr. Lee wasn't in but Dr. Alexander, one of the pediatricians in his practice, was. The nurse said to bring him in and Dr. Alexander would look him over.

After a short examination, he said this condition wasn't normal for a two-week-old baby and ordered a spinal tap. I called Ron in shock, and he said, "Go ahead. We need to know what the problem is. I'll be there in a few minutes." Reluctantly, I signed the paperwork. Dr. Alexander, his nurse, John, and I went upstairs to the pediatric floor. After a few minutes they took him into a nurse's station for the procedure.

All I could do was call out to the Lord, "Oh, God, please watch over him. Please take care of him; hold him in your healing hands. Please, please, Lord, watch over him and don't let him be hurt."

Within moments, I heard a gut-wrenching scream coming out of that room, one I have and never will forget! With the procedure completed, they brought him out to me. All I could do was cuddle his shaking body until he relaxed and stopped crying.

Dr. Alexander said the fluid was clear, which meant it wasn't meningitis or any of the other possibilities. He would admit him, though, as his temperature had spiked to 103.5. John was put under an oxygen tent to make sure he breathed in pure oxygen. John hated being under the tent and cried out to be held and cuddled. The only times I was allowed to hold him were to nurse him and then put him back under the tent. Fortunately, after nursing, his little tummy was full and content, so he quickly fell asleep and then I could replace him under the oxygen tent until he was hungry or wet again.

The following morning, Dr. Wilson, the gruff senior partner in the practice, came in. After examining John and looking at his sleep-deprived mother, he turned and hurried out of the room. My first thought was, *Oh, no, what's wrong now?* I couldn't think of anything, as John had slept peacefully through the night except for needs and still was sleeping well. John felt cool to my hand and his cough had stopped. *What had upset Dr. Wilson?* I wondered.

Still holding John's chart, he walked straight to the nurses' station to talk to the nurses. All of a sudden, I noticed Dr. Alexander come into the pediatric wing. Dr. Wilson collared Dr. Alexander. Seeing Dr. Wilson heatedly talking to him, I knew something was wrong. He looked like a whipped puppy dog. After the discussion, Dr. Wilson came back into John's room and apologetically told me the spinal tap had been unnecessary. John wasn't suffering from a blood sensitivity relapse; all he had was a severe cold. At that moment I remembered the freezing night we took Mother to Santa Fe so she could fly home. He must have gotten chilled even in his heavy bunting. Oh, how upset and guilty I felt.

Dr. Wilson told me he would release John later that afternoon if his temperature broke and he didn't have any further breathing or coughing difficulties. Oh, what relief! "Thank you, thank you, Lord, for your protective and healing hand on John and your calming strength to get me through the procedure and last night."

Later that afternoon, Dr. Wilson visited us again. John's temperature was down to 100.5, and he hadn't encountered any further problems. He recommended we stay the night, as it was bitter cold outside and he didn't want John to get another chill, leading to further or new problems. I thanked him and said we would agree to that. Dr. Wilson removed the oxygen tent, saying he didn't feel John needed it anymore. If problems arose, he would be put back under it. He would check on him before heading home. I thanked him for all he had done.

The next morning, Dr. Lee checked his chart and John. He said, "If you bundle him up and Ron comes close to the hospital door, I will release him. Keep him warm and continue the penicillin. I want to see him in a week, unless there is a reoccurrence of the temperature or cough." After thanking him, I called Ron with the good news. He would come and pick us up as soon as possible.

"Oh, Lord, what a joyful day this is. The sun is shining in all its glory. I praise you for your watchfulness over my little one and me. What a wonderful, caring, and gracious God you are. My precious little one is healing, and I have you to thank for all these blessings. How can I ever thank you and repay you for your loving generosity to me and my son? Amen."

A New Beginning for Our Family

*"Whenever the Lord closes one door,
he opens another one."*
Helen Steiner Rice

As time passed, Ron and I discussed his future career aspirations in the scientific world; we realized he needed his master's and doctorate degrees to do that. Since going to the University of New Mexico part time would take years for him to finish his degrees, we decided he would leave Los Alamos and go to school full time.

After numerous applications, the University of Hawaii accepted him, offering him a teaching fellowship to help defray the prohibitive cost of living there. Penn State University offered him a full scholarship. We had to provide for our living expenses, though. What a change this would be! Dr. Gene White, his Penn State advisor and supervisor, worked out a small research stipend (two hundred dollars a month) from the US Office of Mining for him, so we had some money to live on. With the money from the sale of our home, we felt we could just eke out the next four years. We knew both degrees had to be completed within that time. Any longer and we would face real financial trouble. With two young sons, we had to make every penny count.

With his acceptance letter in hand, house sold, and our furniture on a moving van, we were ready to make the cross-country move. We would drive in tandem to our new life in State College, Pennsylvania, I in our station wagon and Ron in the secondhand Beetle we had purchased two years before. We left Los Alamos mid-December with the shining moon showing us the way from White Rock to our new life. Traveling at night always helped, as the boys slept.

Dr. White had sent us a few State College newspapers in order for us to find housing. Graduate school housing had been filled since September, so we needed housing outside the university. We rented sight-unseen a duplex containing two bedrooms, one bath, kitchen, living/dining room, downstairs laundry room, and a playroom for the boys. It would be quite a change from our home in New Mexico!

Being on our way to State College, we decided to spend Christmas with my parents. As we drove through St. Louis, we hit a frightening bump. In all our drives through that city, we never got through it without getting lost. This was no exception. As always, night driving made reading the interstate signs even more difficult for us.

Ron drove the lead car. All of a sudden, I noticed Ron had his right turn signal on to exit onto a wrong road. I beeped and beeped to alert him to his mistake while yelling through my windshield to get his attention, but to no avail. He had his radio on and was oblivious to the beeping or me. As soon as he exited, he realized his mistake. *Oops*. We ended up in a dangerous neighborhood. My body cringed and I began to panic—this was not the place where we should be. Adding to my frenzy of being in this unknown and dangerous-looking area, Ron pulled into a gas station, got out of his car, and then walked into the station to ask directions. I made sure my car doors were locked, leaving the car running. As he talked to the night mechanic, I noticed some unsavory young men eyeing the car. Now I was really scared!

My fervent prayer was, "Oh, God, please keep us safe and get us back on the interstate and on our way to Ohio." At that moment, glaring headlights beamed into my rearview mirror. My thoughts raced to, *What else can happen?* Now, boxed in, we could have all our worldly goods taken and be left for dead. My mind ran to panic mode.

But my Lord answered my prayer. The headlights came from a police cruiser with two beefy policemen inside. "Thank you, Lord, for your protection," was all I could get out. The policemen had noticed my out-of-state license plate, knowing I had mistakenly pulled off the interstate into this dangerous area. I explained to the first policeman that my husband had taken the wrong exit and we landed here. He had gone inside to ask directions. He stayed with me while the other policeman went inside to find Ron. The young men standing outside wanted no trouble with the police and moved on.

Ron and the policeman came out. Everyone got back into their respective cars. As Ron and I pulled out, the police car followed us until we got back on the interstate headed for Cleveland. What a harrowing experience, but with the Lord's protection through all of this, we were once again safe. "Oh, what an awesome God you are! Thank you once again for your protection to us. How special you are! You listen to our cries for help and protection and provide it. You are always watching over us. Thank you, thank you, Lord. Amen."

A day and a half later, we pulled into Mother and Dad's condominium complex. We had a wonderful Christmas with all the trimmings of the season: festive tree, Santa, turkey, and some much-needed relaxation time before moving on to our new home and life in Pennsylvania.

The night before we left Mother and Dad's, I prayed, "Oh, Lord, you have gotten us this far. Please keep us in your guiding and protective hands. Watch over us tomorrow as we finish our journey through Ohio and Pennsylvania to our new home. Help us to arrive safely, as the weather reports call for snow along our way, and you know how I hate driving in the snow. Remember that first winter I was driving when I took a left turn too fast, spinning two or three full circles in the road before stopping inches away from a telephone pole? You protected me by seeing to it no cars came either way on that road. Even though I came close to hitting the pole, you kept me safe from all harm. Thank you, Lord. .

"Oh please, dear Father, keep me safe and help me drive correctly and effectively, as I will have one or both boys in the car with me at all times. Keep us safe. Also, if I am not being too selfish, please give me the strength and courage to face all the trials of moving in and getting our new home ready for our new life there. We need you in our lives as we never have before. Thank you for listening to my requests once again. I seem to ask so much, and you don't ask anything in return. Thank you, Lord. Amen."

After saying our thank yous and good-byes, Mother asked us to call to let her know we had arrived safely. I said we would call from the State College Holiday Inn, as we wouldn't be able to move into our duplex for two days and I wasn't sure when we would have a telephone.

We stopped halfway on our route at a rest stop to have the turkey sandwiches, potato chips, pickles, and cokes that Mother had packed for us. Oh, how good that tasted; we even took time to stretch our legs and take care of nature's calls.

As we began our climb up Nittany Mountain leading to State College, the snow started. *Oh, this is not good*, I thought. I took it slow and made the incline without a problem. As we entered the town, all we could see were mountains of snow everywhere. The snowplows had cleared the main streets, leaving abutments of two feet on either side of the roads. What we didn't know, thank goodness, was that off and on snows had left State College with thirty-one inches of the pearly white stuff. I am so glad I didn't know that before leaving Cleveland, or I would have been a nervous wreck.

After uttering a prayer of thanksgiving for our safe trip and arrival, we drove through the snow to the Holiday Inn. After checking in, we called both sets of parents, letting them know we had arrived safely. With each call, we heard sighs of relief from the other end of the telephone line. Both sets of parents had become extremely worried after hearing television reports of the snowstorm in middle Pennsylvania. We told them we were fine and not to worry.

Next on our to-do list was a drive to see our yet unseen new home. As Ron drove us past our new home, it looked old but majestic on a small knoll near the university. Even though the driveway had been plowed, we were concerned with how the moving truck could climb the steep driveway to unload our furniture and things. Looking around the area, we delighted that there was a large park across the street where the boys could run and play. After viewing the brick duplex, we became excited to sign the final paperwork and move in the next day. We wondered what it would look like inside. On the way back to the hotel, we stopped at the boys' favorite dining place—you know the one—the one with the golden arches. We bought twenty-five-cent cheeseburgers and ten-cent fries all around. With our goodies in hand, we returned to the hotel to eat and watch a bit of television before crashing for the night. The drive and excitement of our new beginning had worn us out.

After signing the rental lease the following morning, we drove to our new home. He had cleaned and polished everything. The new blown-in tile in the kitchen and bathroom was beautiful. The boys had a playroom for all their GI Joe paraphernalia, games, books, and all manner of things. We would put Ron's desk in our bedroom so he could study out of the earshot of our boys playing. The duplex would be just right for us.

While he checked in with Dr. White, the boys and I waited for the phone company to connect our phones. We would call both sets of parents that night, giving them our telephone number and letting them know we were in and okay.

Since no one had lived in the duplex since mid-December and the landlord didn't pay for heating, the duplex was frigid. I turned the heat up gingerly as we had to pay for our heating. About a half hour later, things started moving quickly. I heard the roar of a large truck. Yes, it was the moving van. At that moment I turned the heat off, as I didn't want to pay for heating while the movers came in and out of our place with our things. Being frigid inside, the boys and I put on heavy jackets to keep us fairly warm until the movers left and I could turn the heat on again. To my surprise and concern, when I opened the door to the mover, I learned that he was the only one moving our furniture in. He needed all the money he could earn for his wife's mounting medical bills. Doing the job himself, he didn't have to pay a helper.

I couldn't believe this man carried our dining room hutch and base, along with its matching table and chairs, all our bedroom furniture, all the boxes of clothes, kitchen goods, etc. up the steep, slippery driveway incline then up the flight of steps into the main living areas. Lastly, he moved our heavy sofa bed, along with the washer and dryer into the basement area. I thought he would bust his back or heart lifting all those heavy things along with the boxes. When Ron came home and saw what the driver was doing, he helped him carry the remaining boxes upstairs. Within an hour and half, he had emptied his truck of our belongings and was on his way to another job.

I had the boys take their toys into the playroom and start organizing them into the built-in bookcases. While they did that, Ron and I began separating boxes and putting them into their respective rooms. We then moved our furniture into their proper places. What a help Ron was! After registering in with the university and Dr. White, he found he had two full days free before classes would begin. He had time to help me with the move-in.

At the end of our first day in our new home, we had our phones in, our beds up, clothes in their proper closets, knick knacks and books in their proper places, and my kitchen was complete and ready for my cooking. Anything not in place could wait for another day.

We ate macaroni and cheese for dinner, the boys' favorite meal other than MacDonald's and pizza. After doing the dishes, we called the parents, giving them our address and new phone number and telling them we were moved in for the most part. The last major thing on our agenda was the boys' baths, snuggling with them until they were asleep in the still-cool house. Afterward, Ron and I spent sofa time assessing our new life here.

"Life is good. Thank you, Lord, for helping us into our new adventure. You are wonderful watching over and caring for us. You are never far from us. You listen to our prayers and do what is in our best interest when answering them. Thank you again and again. Good night. Amen."

Summers in God's Garden

> "Then God said, 'Let the land produce vegetation:
> Seed-bearing plants and trees on the land that bear fruit
> with seed in it, according to their various kinds.'"
>
> (Genesis 1:11)

Winter produced freezing winds and snow. I kept the house temperature low so not to create huge oil heating bills. The energy crunch blossomed, and everyone was told to keep homes at sixty-five to sixty-seven degrees. When my parents came from Fort Lauderdale for Easter, they froze, saying we needed better housing. The windows let in cold air, and on top of that, the temperature in our place was insufficient for them. Our growing boys continuously had colds. "You must look for another place; this is unacceptable for living," Mother and Dad told us.

We explained our financial state and that Ron's stipend of two hundred dollars a month barely kept us above water. We couldn't afford to move. After some discussion, they said they would pay within reason additional rent money for us to move into a proper place to live. With our lease, we couldn't begin to do anything until May at the earliest, so we had to stay put. This additional money was an answer to our prayers. "Oh, Lord, once again you came to our rescue. Without this money I don't know how we would survive another winter in the cold. You heard our pleas for help and brought the needed answer so we can move to better housing. Now, Lord, another request: help us find the right house—warm, cozy, good neighbors. Thank you for all you do for us. You really do watch over and bless us daily. Amen."

As the year progressed, Ronnie's kindergarten learning grew. He was happy with his teacher, Mrs. Van Haven, a true blessing to him. His kindergarten teacher in New Mexico hated little boys and ridiculed those she couldn't get to do as she wanted. His first few weeks with her produced a belligerent child. She told me he just wasn't ready for school, take him out of school, and let him play a year before readmitting him the following fall. She made it sound like a benefit to him when in reality it only benefitted her. She only wanted compliant students; Ronnie was an overactive one. Unfortunately, she was his teacher the following year, as she was the only kindergarten teacher there.

The move to State College afforded us a new environment and kindergarten teacher. Mrs. Van Haven worked with him to bring him up to grade level. He liked her and did well with her. Since John was not school age, his days were spent with me. Both boys flourished in their new environment, as did Ron, who was finishing his first semester with his physics and metallurgy courses. Oh, how over-my-head his classes were! He was building some kind of x-ray spectrographic machine to do research on black lung disease for the Department of Mining. This research would lead right into his master's thesis work and later his doctorate. He spent hours designing, building, and producing results that led to scientific findings about the disease. My job was to keep the home fires and boys going.

By May we knew summer was coming. We had finally warmed up. After that cold winter with little heat, the thoughts of another winter in that duplex didn't intrigue us. We soon would begin our search for a warm place to live.

About this time, Ron learned that the university rented farming plots (forty by sixty feet) to graduate students for fifty dollars for the summer. We could raise our own vegetables, can and freeze them, and then have them available to us all winter, which would help with our grocery budget. "Thank you, Lord, once again."

Ron took our fifty dollars to the Agricultural College office and signed up for one of the plots. In late spring, the university plowed and partially cultivated the plot areas, but we had to bring the ground into planting mode, plant the seeds, and bring our own water to water the seeds and plants. I thought what a wonderful learning experience this would be for the boys. They would see nature at work. They could plant, water, and harvest their labors. Oh, what a blessing that would be for us.

The day after Ron rented our plot; the boys and I drove to a nearby farm store and looked at all the packets of vegetable seeds we might plant. We had to make some wise decisions, as we only had a small garden area. Ronnie wanted corn, green beans, and carrots. John wanted corn, lettuce (my salad boy), watermelon, and cantaloupes. I explained that melons needed a much longer growing season than we had, but we would try. I also picked up some zucchini, beets, onions, radishes, and tomato plants. Now we were ready to be "farmers."

That evening, we placed our hoe, rake, and a couple of shovels into the trunk of our car and took off like the forty-niners in the California gold rush days in search of the best piece of garden land. We picked out a back corner space, which would give us easy access to weed as well as water our garden. We staked out our perimeter and then strung rope with old shirt strips so other "farmers" wouldn't lay claim to our land. Now all we had to do was cultivate the soil, making it ready for planting. Ronnie and John expected us to plant seeds that night, but we explained that the ground had to be broken up, raked, and then crevice lines had to be created to receive the seeds. We would plant the following night. While Ron and I raked and hoed, the boys broke the big clods of soil for us. They were really getting into the idea of growing vegetables.

When we returned home, all of us sat around the kitchen table and planned out our garden. We drew three corn rows to the far left side, then two rows of green beans (Ron's mother had sent us pole bean seeds) then a dozen zucchini hills, followed by rows of lettuce, green onions, carrots, beets, radishes, a patch for our six beefsteak tomato plants, and finally a couple of mounds for the melons. Our garden was planned. Now all that was left was the planting and watering.

Late the following afternoon, when all my "men" were fed and ready, we filled the Beetle with our farming implements, seeds, and large jugs of water and then set off for our gold mine in the dirt. Oh, the anticipation of putting the seeds and plants in the ground filled the boys. Once there, Ron and I put in the rows for the seeds. The boys watched the garden map to make sure we were placing the rows in the correct spots. Once the rows were made, we put the seed packages in their rows to make sure all the seeds and plants were where they should be before planting began. It took all the strength and patience we had to keep the boys from planting the seeds until all was in readiness.

About a half hour later, we showed the boys how to take the individual corn seeds and place them securely and neatly in the rows and then pull the dirt over them. We felt that making them take their time with each seed would be the safest way for them to plant. Next came the beans. The radishes, lettuce, carrots, and other tiny seeds frustrated the boys, as they had to take incredible time to sow them into the ground. While they were planting the seeds, Ron and I created the mounds for the zucchini and melon seeds. When all was planted, we made the holes for the tomato plants then let the boys put them in the ground and cover over their roots. At last, we were almost done. With that done, the real work began. We had brought large water jugs; now we had to scoop out this precious commodity and pour it over the lines and mounds of plantings.

On the way home, the boys asked when the plants would come through the ground so they could eat them. We said it would take several weeks of sun and water to make them grow. They had to germinate then sprout before we would see them. I told them they just had to be patient. Oh, the sad faces, but I told them that every evening after dinner we would make a water trip to the garden so their plants would get the water they needed to grow. Before long, the vegetables would be ready for us to pick and eat. They seemed happier with that.

Simultaneously, we began another project—house hunting. After looking for a month, Ron and I found a wonderful home for us. The brick house had a living/dining room, kitchen, three bedrooms, so the boys would have their own rooms, and one bathroom on the first floor; the basement had a large playroom for the boys, a room we would make into Ron's study away from the daily goings on in the house, a laundry room, and a half bath. It was perfect for our needs. The elementary school was just up a little hill from our house. The first thing Mother and Dad wanted to know was would it keep us warm in the winter. We had checked that out and assured them the windows were well sealed. They told us to go ahead make the deal. Since they were helping with the cost difference, our finances wouldn't be strapped further than they already were.

"Oh, Lord, once again you came through for us. We have a home that is just perfect for our needs until Ron finishes his degrees. You even worked out the financing! How can we ever thank you for all the goodness and graciousness you have bestowed on us? Thank you for everything. Amen."

For the boys, the watering seemed like an endless task with nothing to show for it. We kept telling them just be patient. When the first green shoot made its appearance, you would have thought it was a monumental event. To them it was. We were farmers on our way to having food. Excitement reigned.

By midsummer we were feasting on harvested tomatoes, lettuce, radishes, carrots, beets, zucchini, and the corn began tussling. Oh, the excitement. Sadly for the boys, the melons grew no bigger than baseballs. I tried to explain that melons didn't grow well in this environment; hopefully by the end of the growing season we might get one or two we could eat.

As the season progressed, I canned tomatoes, froze some beets, and began using the mounds of zucchini in breads, sauces, and salads. Oh, did we have zucchini! I even rented a three-cubic-feet freezer space for our overflow of zucchini and other vegetables. Guess what took up more than half that space? You're correct if you said zucchini. When our neighbors or the people walking down the sidewalk saw me coming with those beautiful green sticks, they wanted to turn and run. They had been as overrun as we with my zucchini. I knew I had way, way too much and next year we would only sow two or three hills of this "delicacy." Oh my, did we eat well that summer. Our food pantry and freezer were stocked full for our winter meals. What abundance for us and a savings to our dwindling funds. This had been a wonderful learning experience for the boys about being out in God's creation and finding their own abilities.

"Oh, Lord, what a glorious God you are. You let me see how you provide for me through your creation of food and bounteous goodness to all of us. As we watched your seeds grow into ripeness, you taught us of your love and concern for our daily needs. Through this, we came to a fuller love of each other as we toiled and worked together in your soil. You brought us to a home where we could be warm and healthy. You provided us with a loving environment of peace and joy, which helps us grow in you and each other through these tight years. Your love is so evident in all you do for us. You are such an awesome God! All praises and glory go to you always. Thank you, Father, Creator, Protector, and Sustainer. Amen."

All I could hear was the Lord saying, "Nancy, you are special to me, as is your family. I will be there for you in the good times as well as the bad ones. I will supply you with your needs, not all your wants, to keep you with me always on the path I want you to walk with me. Remember I love you."

Our three and a half years at Penn State were some of the best years of our lives. The boys flourished not only in school but in body and soul. Weekdays, Ron researched and studied, the boys learned reading, writing, and arithmetic, and for extra money, I worked as a cafeteria aide at the boys' school, which helped us financially. Another bonus was that the boys' and my schedules were the same. Our last year there, I was offered and accepted an educational aide position at another elementary school, which increased my hours from three to six and even my pay by a dollar and a half more an hour. What a luxury that was. I felt "rich," even though we weren't. We could do things with and for the boys we couldn't before. What a joy that was!

Fall Saturday afternoons found the boys, Ron, and I eating hoagies and chips while drinking wonderful apple cider in the student section of Beaver Stadium, watching our Nittany Lions run and dodge opponents to make touchdown points or tackle opponents to keep them from advancing their touchdowns points against us. We all enjoyed those exciting, crisp, sunshiny afternoons and being part of this tradition of college life. Oh, how glorious it was to watch Franco Harris, Steve Smear, John Cappeletti, Lydell Mitchell, and others do their jobs to make us winners.

All too soon, our time at Penn State came to a close. Ron received his master's degree in Solid State Science (a combination of chemistry, physics, and metallurgy) mid-December 1971, a year after he started classes. On June 16, 1973, surrounded by our parents, we all watched as Ron received his PhD in Solid State Science. *What a brilliant husband I have!*

We hoped for a warm sunshiny day, but we ended up with rain. Washed out was the important part of the ceremony—the PhD candidates being hooded as they received their diplomas. I felt so bad for him; he had so looked forward to that moment. He hadn't gone through his master's ceremony, as he wanted to be hooded during his PhD ceremony. His commencement speaker was Joe Paterno, who gave an inspiring talk about going out into the world and making it a better place for everyone.

After the ceremony, we returned to our home to celebrate our years there, his graduation, and the beginning of our new life in Michigan. "Oh Lord, how gracious you are to us. Ron has finished his master's and doctorate degrees. I feel your presence and love all around us. You have created all this for our good. Thank you, Lord, for loving us so much. Thank you for always being there for us. You are truly awesome. Amen."

Our New Life in Michigan Begins

"Many, O Lord my God are the wonders you have done, the things you planned for us no one can recount to you."

(Psalm 40:5)

A month before graduation, Ron interviewed with Ford Motor Company for a position in its new emissions program. A few days later, he received and accepted a job offer from them. That weekend, we all drove to Michigan. Ron's new boss, John Bomback, recommended we look for housing in Plymouth, as its school system was the best in the area. He loved the area, especially the town's New England town square reminiscent of Boston, where he and his family had come from.

We quickly found out that the housing market catered to buyers. As soon as we saw something and returned to the real estate office to put in an offer, we found it had already been sold to another buyer. We returned to State College without a house. Although discouraged, we had hope. We asked Ron's parents to come and watch the boys so we could return for an intensive, long weekend of house hunting. They loved to do it.

Two weeks later, we returned to scour the market with hopes of purchasing a home. On our third day there, we found a lovely, older, two-story. After putting in a bid, we waited an hour and then drove past it again just to look at it. To our shock, a sold sign had been placed in the center of the front yard. We hurriedly returned to our agent and told her of the sold sign. She said it had been sold. We almost collapsed with the news, until she said, "You bought it." What joy! We had a home.

Returning home, I began boxing up everything for our move and new life in Michigan. Two weeks after graduation, Ron drove off in his decrepit, little Beetle for Michigan and his new job there. The boys and I couldn't go with him, as the present owners hadn't moved out and would be there for another two weeks. Dr. Bomback knew Ron was coming alone and generously suggested Ron stay with them until we could join him.

His first day on the job, July 16, 1973, Ron spent signing all the usual W-2 forms, health and dental plans, etc. That evening, knowing Ron played handball, John took him to the Livonia YMCA for a couple games. During the match, as Ron went to the wall to hit the ball away, he accidentally hit his right fourth finger into the wall. John told him to just shake it off. A bit later as he returned another shot, Ron banged the same finger into the wall. This time Ron moved his finger, which felt like broken glass inside. John took him to emergency at St. Mary's Hospital, where they spent the next six hours while a hand surgeon removed bone fragments and placed pins in Ron's knuckle to save the finger. Ron's second day at Ford was taken as a sick day. What a way to start a new job! John would never let Ron live it down.

Ron didn't want me worrying, but he let the cat out of the bag a week later when he mentioned his doctor's appointment the next day. I asked, "Why? Do you have another physical for Ford?" With my questioning, he told me about his injury and surgery. Oh, the guilt I felt not being there to take care of him. He told me Tanya, John's five-year-old daughter, was taking good care of him and bringing him whatever he needed, whether a glass of water or something to read. So the Lord had placed an angel in his midst to take care of him when I couldn't. "Thank you, Lord, for yet another blessing!"

My nightly prayer included, "Once again, Lord, thank you for coming to our aid in time of trouble and aloneness. You are always there for us. Lord, I can't thank you enough for being with Ron at the hospital, having the best hand surgeon on call that night, and protecting him during his surgery and recovery. Watch over his knuckle and heal the bones, muscles, and tendons, bringing them back to full use. Thank you for keeping him from further hurt. You have blessed us so many times and continue to do so. You show us daily you are with us in all things. Thank you, Lord. I will praise and glorify you and your name always. Amen."

The following week, the Mayflower van drove up to our house. Four men picked up our furniture, washer and dryer, boxes of clothes, household things, the boys' toys, and bicycles, finishing off a three load truck almost to the brim. Before driving on to Michigan, we turned in our keys and then began our trek to Michigan. I praised God for his bounteous gift of life and the happiness that he bestowed on us as we began our new life.

The next afternoon, Ron met us at the Holiday Inn. What a joyous time to be together as a family again! Later that afternoon, we went to our Realtor's office to pick up the keys to our "new" home. The boys wanted to see their new home and stake out their territories. I needed to size up where the furniture would go. With that accomplished, Ron, the boys, and I returned to the motel, where my guys spent time playing in the pool together. After more than two weeks apart, and me having full responsibility for the boys and the move, I spent the afternoon relaxing by the pool. It was wonderful not having anything pressing on me or my time. It was good to be a family again.

The next morning, Friday before a nice weekend, we drove our cars to 10123 Wolfriver Drive. Our new home impatiently awaited us, as did the Mayflower truck. I directed the positioning of all furniture so there would not be any mistakes. When Ron realized I had everything under control, he told me he wanted to get into the office early so he could leave early to help me with the unpacking.

By the time he returned later that afternoon, our furniture had been placed, the beds made, and some of the kitchen put together. Not wanting the house to be a total mess of opened boxes and wrapping paper, I worked feverously to put everything in place so it looked like a home and not a house.

At about five o'clock, three of our new neighbors knocked on our front door, introduced themselves, and brought dinner in. Oh, what a blessing they were! The Lord never ceases to amaze me with his gifts of love. As exhausted as I was, I hadn't even thought about dinner. The women even brought paper products and a large jug of iced tea, as they figured I hadn't been able to unpack the kitchen things in order to fix something for dinner. In fact, I hadn't had time to get any groceries for the refrigerator or cabinets yet. Nothing could have been more welcome! They asked if there was anything they could do for us. I told them no, bringing dinner was such a blessing. I asked them to stay for dinner, as there was enough to fill us and their families. They said, "Another time; you must be exhausted." That began a wonderful seventeen-year friendship with these three families. In the years to follow, we became extended families for each other; our lives intertwined.

"Lord, you provided for us. You brought us to this new home, surrounded us with friends, and brought us to this new life where our sons can grow and mature into the wonderful young men they will become. How can I ever repay you for the joys you give me, the protection you provide, and the care you give us? In all things, I thank you and will devote myself to you and the work you have planned for me. In all things I pray in Jesus's name. Amen."

Reconciliation with Mother

"Again I ask, 'Did they stumble so
as to fall beyond recovery?'"
(Romans 11:11)

I always felt I had an ongoing love-hate relationship with Mother. Looking back now, I realize that my part in this relationship was my jealousy of her putting Ruth first. Anytime Ruth wanted anything, Mother was there to finance it for her. Mother routinely compared Ruth to me. Ruth was eighteen years older than me. Mother's seemingly endless comparisons of the two of us made me feel incapable of doing anything right and feeling unloved, and so inferior to both her and Ruth. Ruth was her perfect one, while I was the inept daughter. Never could I live up to her expectations of me. The more she saw wrong in me, the angrier I became. The anger turned into a wall of resentment that neither of us could penetrate.

After Ruth's death and her telling me not to come home for the funeral, my wall got thicker, higher, and stronger. The following years did nothing for our relationship, as Mother couldn't or wouldn't deal with Ruth's death. She reminded me of how much Jim and Ruth's deaths had taken out of her. I knew she hurt deeply, but I couldn't seem to do anything to help her. We were two ships sailing on the same turbulent sea with no landing site to engage each other.

But even in my anger, I loved her and wanted to be close to her. I attempted many times to talk to her about how I felt about her comparisons of Ruth and me and how I felt being nothing to her. Since she refused to talk about this, her response was to turn and walk away. Every so often I thought I saw the beginning of a tear or a possible breakthrough with her. In our family, feelings were never talked about, so she steadfastly refused to share herself and her feelings with me, whether they were joy, sadness, anger, or depression. She kept them all bottled up inside her.

Mother and Dad used alcohol to defuse any semblance of feelings. Its numbing effects worked wonders, so they didn't have to deal with whatever was bothering them, whether it was Dad's insecurity in dealing with the corporate world, Mother's anger with her mother living with her, their disappointments with their life/lives in general, or us children, or just plain stress. For them, the bottle helped them deal with whatever without openly dealing with it. I learned years before, the night with Dad's anger, to let him have a couple of drinks before trying to discuss something he didn't want to talk about. The only way I could talk to him or be close to him was through his on the rocks glass.

Mother, on the other hand, was full of anger at having her mother living with us. Gram daily imposed her opinion on Mother's incompetence at household duties, child raising, husband needs, or anything that came down the pike. Wanting Dad to be a success, both Dad and Mother threw themselves into making Dad a business giant. Both needed subconsciously to show themselves and their parents he was capable, influential, and important in the business world. For Mother, she needed to prove her worth to her mother as a perfect wife, mother, housekeeper, and daughter. With their plan in mind for Dad, they kept to themselves, drinking and planning further business successes for Dad. In doing this they eliminated once again their need of enjoyment with family, friends, good times, and most importantly, life. Their refuge was alcohol. With it they could relax and forget.

Without the permission to show or talk about feelings, they had no outlet for their bottled-up feelings. Their only refuge to eliminate or numb their feelings was their alcohol. With this family rule, nothing could be reconciled between Mother and me. What might have been if we could have really talked?

My Lord had a plan; a plan for reconciliation. On Thanksgiving afternoon 1976, I called to wish her and Dad a happy Thanksgiving. They had invited some people in for drinks and appetizers before going to the club for dinner. Maybe it was the drinks or the sentimentality of the day, but she seemed different. She even seemed pleased that I had called. I wondered what had brought about this change in her. *Could there have been a breakthrough in her feelings toward me? What had caused it?* We talked for fifteen minutes about Thanksgiving and what she might like for her seventy-third birthday two weeks away. When we finished, I felt as if the world had been lifted off of me—a new beginning. "What a Thanksgiving gift! Thank you, Lord."

A week later, we talked again, and things seemed fine but not as jovial. *Oh well, I had my moment of joy.* "Dear Lord, whatever you did to create that wonderful conversation, please let it come again. I felt for the first time that we had a chance of having a real mother-daughter relationship. At Thanksgiving, you gave me a glimpse of what could be. If it is in your plan, please cultivate this in both of us. Thank you, Lord, for whatever you do in this situation. Amen."

About ten days later, while I was eating my lunch at school, I felt this incredible need to write Mother. The urge only got stronger as I taught my afternoon classes. Whatever was happening inside me, I knew from its intensity God was pushing me hard to do this. Why, I didn't know, but I knew I had to do this and it had to be in that evening's five-o'clock mail. No later! The intensity only got stronger and stronger. It wouldn't leave me. I couldn't wait for school to be over. "Lord, why does this have to be done today and be in the evening mail? Why is this so crucial? Why do you want me to do this?

I will do it, as I know you want it done. You don't ask much of me, so there is some reason for it. I will obey you."

Arriving home that afternoon, I sat down and wrote Mother a letter telling her only the things I loved about her. Once our relationship truly began, I felt I could broach the things needing to be dealt with. After making sure I had said all I needed to say, I ran it up to the post office so that it would go out in the five o'clock mail. Relief hit me. I couldn't help but wonder the meaning of it all.

On December seventeenth, the day after Mother's birthday, Ron and I attended a Christmas party given by three different parts suppliers for some Ford, Chrysler, and General Motor engineers at the Dearborn Country Club. What a wonderful time we had socializing and celebrating the season. When the valet brought us our car, we noticed a thick new layer of snow on it and the roads. Everything looked so magical, almost like a winter wonderland. The long ride home from Dearborn through Hines Park in the new fallen snow filled us with the awe of God's creation in full splendor.

When we arrived home about midnight, the boys were in bed, as the next day was their last school day before the Christmas holiday. Ron and John, now thirteen and eleven respectively, attended middle school together. As I passed through the kitchen to get my nightly glass of water, I noticed young Ron's note telling me to call Grandpa as soon as we got home. I woke him and asked when and why Grandpa had called. He told me he had called earlier in the evening and hadn't said why I needed to call. He had tried to stay awake for us, but it was a losing battle, so he went to bed after leaving his note. He told me, "Grandpa wants you to call whenever you get in. He will be up."

I knew something was seriously wrong, as he wouldn't leave a cryptic message like that otherwise. Once I heard Dad's broken voice, I knew something was drastically wrong. He told me Mother was in the hospital. After fixing breakfast, they opened the mail. As she read my letter, she began to sob. Dad asked her what I had said to upset her so. If she told him, he didn't tell me. He read it but didn't say anything about it to me. After breakfast, they played their usual gin rummy games. After complaining of a severe headache, Dad suggested she take some aspirin for it.

About eleven, they got dressed to go to the airport to pick up an old business acquaintance and his wife. The couple planned to stay the night with Mother and Dad before going on to Miami the following day.

Once in the condominium elevator, she complained that the headache had become excruciating. He thought it was just a lot of tension from getting ready for their company. En route to the airport, she spied Holy Cross Hospital as they made the left-hand turn heading toward the airport. She pointed to the hospital. He pulled into the emergency entrance. By this time, she was heaving and becoming more and more disoriented. He went in to get someone to help him with her. The orderlies placed her on a stretcher and took her to an examining room.

A half hour later, the hospital called in a nearby neurosurgeon, Dr. Blakely, to come and examine her. After all kinds of scans and X-rays, Dr. Blakely came to talk to Dad. He explained that Mother had suffered a massive cerebral hemorrhage. He wished it had been only a clot, as he could surgically remove it, but the hemorrhage had flooded her brain. Little could be done for her, as the damage was so extensive. She would be in intensive care until she was stable enough to be moved to critical or acute care unit. I was amazed at how calm he was, but with his stoic, Scottish upbringing, that's all he could be. Denying his feelings was instinctive with him, whether he felt devastated, confused, or angry.

I told him I would fly down as quickly as I could. I remembered Delta had a daily nine-thirty flight to Fort Lauderdale that we had used before. I just prayed that with the holiday travel I could get a seat. I would rent a car so he didn't have to leave Mother to pick me up. Oh, how relieved he sounded when I told him I was coming. I felt he needed me in this crisis.

Ron immediately called Delta. Fortunately, there was one seat remaining on the early flight; he booked it with an open-ended return, and then he booked a Hertz compact car for me. With all the details done, I packed a small bag with only the things I felt I would need for a week or so. I left a message on the school voicemail apprising them of the situation. Ron said he and the boys would fly down on the next day, as Ford shut down over the holidays and the boys would be out of school until two days after New Year's. I asked Ron, "What do we would do with the boys' Christmas gifts?" He said he would wait for the boys to be in school, box them up, and ship them to Dad's. We could do some last-minute shopping after he got there.

Before the boys left for their school bus, we told them Grandma was in the hospital and Grandpa needed me there. They would fly down as soon as Dad could get the flight booked. I gave them big hugs, telling them I would see them soon. Ron and I had another cup of coffee before he drove me to the airport. The flight seemed to take forever. After arriving in Fort Lauderdale, I went to Hertz and picked up my little Escort. I couldn't believe I remembered how to get to Holy Cross Hospital.

After asking reception how to get to the intensive care unit, the woman asked Mother's name. She told me Mother had been moved into acute care and then she gave me directions to it. Once on the sixth floor, I walked toward the unit. Dad saw me coming down the hall, and I ran into his arms. I controlled my emotions, as I knew that would upset him to no end. He didn't need me falling apart when he needed me to be strong.

"Oh, Lord, hold me together so I can be a strength to him. Falling apart would only make this situation harder for him; he has enough on his plate right now. I don't need to add to it. Give me your strength to help him deal with Mother's problem. Help him, Lord, give him strength, and hold him close to you so he knows you are with him as well as Mother. Keep her close to you, as I know she will soon be in your loving arms. Make her journey to you as smooth, swift, and pain free as possible. Amen."

After my prayer, I asked Dad how she was. He said, "No change." He told me the doctors had her hooked up to so many different monitors that I wouldn't be able to really see her. I took a deep breath before walking into her room. Completely hooked up to every kind of contraption, including a ventilator, she looked so vulnerable and frail. This woman had given birth to me, been a thorn in my side growing up, as well as my adulthood, and now she was just lying there. This was also the woman I had hoped to have a closer relationship with. As she lay there motionless, I knew I could do nothing to help her but be there for her.

"Oh, Lord, how can this be happening to me again? I can't save her for Dad or us. Oh, Lord, help me with this. Help me with Dad. Help me help her in these last days left to her and us. Guide me in what I am to do. Tell me. Be with me during this time and afterward. I need your strength and presence to get through this! I pray you hear me and help me now as you always have. Amen." I knew I needed him more than I ever did. He was my rock. To be all I could be to Dad and Mother, I needed his strength and courage. I knew he would sustain me to be the person I needed to be.

Later that day, Dr. Blakely checked on Mother. As he was leaving, I followed him into the hall. I asked him what her prognosis was. I told him to be straight with me; no sugar coating. I needed to know in order to help both Mother and Dad. He told me her brain had been flooded during the hemorrhage. Nothing could be done for her. She would remain this way for as long as she lived, and that timing he couldn't predict.

As I returned to Mother's room, Dad asked me what I was doing. I said I wanted a little chat with the doctor. He seemed upset I had talked to him personally without him. Dad didn't agree with Dr. Blakely's diagnosis and then said when she got better he would take her home. He would take care of her himself. I stopped the talk by saying, "Let's see how things progress." He seemed adamant that he was going to do this no matter what I or the doctors said. He expected her to recover, and that was that.

The following afternoon, I picked up Ron and the boys at the airport and then drove to Dad's apartment. After telling them to stay in the apartment and watch television, Ron and I left for the hospital. The boys wanted to come with us, but we explained the hospital rules stated they had to be eighteen before they could visit someone in acute care. They reluctantly agreed. I was relieved, as I really didn't want them to see her like she was anyway. Even though the doctors and nurses said she couldn't feel them suctioning out her tubes, I knew she felt it, as she had a pained look on her face after each procedure. I agonized with her every time the nurses came to suction her. I just pitied her, but I knew when she passed she wouldn't have to endure any more pain.

"Oh, Lord, as I look at this woman I want to love so much in such pain, I ask you not to let her suffer like she is. Let her feel your presence during this time. I realize her body must catch up with the devastation her brain has gone through. I know this process is getting her body ready to come home to you. Again, I ask that her journey be as smooth and pain free as possible. Let her be joyful in her return to you and being reunited with Ruth and Jim, as well as her other family members already with you. Lord, be there for her. Be ready to help Dad when Mother leaves. Sustain him in the days to come with funeral preparations and learning to live without her. Help me to know how to help him. Help me with the loss I am about to experience as well. Give me the strength to fill my life with joy so I don't pass this grief onto my family. Lord, I know you are listening. Please answer my prayer. In all things, I ask this in Jesus Christ's name. Amen."

Dad and I kept vigil with her until Christmas morning, when we returned to give the boys some semblance of Christmas. Mother had decorated the apartment and trimmed the Christmas tree, so the apartment looked festive. Santa did visit, making the boys quite happy, as they didn't think he would find them. I made our traditional Christmas breakfast of orange juice, scrambled eggs, bacon, sour cream coffee cake, and coffee. Afterward, Dad returned to Mother. I remained with Ron and the boys to help them celebrate Christmas. Later that afternoon, I drove to the hospital to be with Dad. No change in Mother, much to Dad's disappointment.

As the New Year approached, Mother's condition remained the same. I suggested to Ron that he and the boys return home a day or two after New Year's, as the boys had to be in school on January fourth. He agreed, unless Mother's condition worsened.

The afternoon of January second, things began to go downhill for Mother. After each of her aspirations, the red color of blood became more pronounced, her skin was graying, and her coma was deepening; all of which signaled Mother's death was nearing. I attempted to help Dad realize that, but he refused to listen to anything I had to say on the subject. She would come home with him, and that was that.

When Dr. Blakely did his afternoon rounds, Dad was curt with him, downplaying all the doctor was telling him about her. By the evening, her vital signs made the immediacy of her death all the more clear. Trying not to think about her and her condition, Dad paced furiously. At that moment, I realized Dad knew the end was coming and there wasn't anything he could do about it. Mother was in God's hands now.

While Dad went to the nurses' station for some coffee, I said my good-byes to her. A psychiatrist friend of mine had told me that before a death you need to tell the person all the things good and bad you feel about them so you both have closure. I told her how I felt about being neglected and rejected, her criticalness with my imperfections, her total control of my life decisions, and how I ached, as she and I would never have the relationship I so craved. I wanted to leave her with love and good feelings. Then I finished with all the things I loved about her: her elegance, her courage in facing the deaths of two of her children, her stamina to put up with her controlling, critical mother living in her home, as well as my impertinence. I ended with, "I love you, Mom. I know you need to go home to be with our heavenly Father, and I am giving you permission to do so. I will miss you and what we could have had together." I kissed her tenderly. About ten o'clock, I left her with Dad in tow. All the signs were telling me she wouldn't make it through the night. I knew I would be grieving her loss very soon.

When Dad and I arrived home, the boys were asleep. Being the wonderful, caring husband he was, Ron had made dinner and kept it warm for us. He, Dad, and I sat around the dinette table eating leftover chicken; our moods were somber and talk was nonexistent. After a few bites, Dad excused himself and went to bed. I knew he was thinking the same thing I was. Her monitors and gauges told her fate: Mother would soon be leaving us, possibly in the next few hours.

After getting into bed, I cried out to Mother and God. "Oh, how I need you. After telling you tonight I loved you, I truly missed out on you telling me before you died that you really loved me. I needed to hear that. I realized I would never have had the mother-daughter relationship I so wanted, but I just kept hoping, especially after you read my letter. How could you die without letting me know what you felt about what I said? I hoped to make peace with you, and now I can't. That dream is gone forever. Lord, you have brought me the realization this will never happen now. I need a parent more than ever who will love me no matter what. I want you to be that parent or friend I can lean on. I know you have always been with me and in my life. What I need now is a deeper relationship and love with you and from you. Can you do this for me? Only you can create in me the person you want me to be so help me be that person. In all things I thank you for all you have done for me in the past and look forward to more in the future. Amen."

The Lord's voice spoke to me. "You needed to go through this with your mother to tell her how she hurt you as well as tell her of your unspoken love for her. This is my gift to you. I know it was hard but healing for all the pain and anger you have held onto for so many years. I will be with you to lead and love you through all of this and your life."

A little after midnight, the telephone rang only once. I knew Dad had picked it up immediately. Within minutes, a rap came on our bedroom door, and Dad said, "Mother is gone. We need to make funeral arrangements." For the next several hours, Dad and I sat around the dinette table sharing memories of her. It was at that time he talked about my letter to her. As she read it the morning she entered the hospital, tears streamed down her face and she cried softly. He was concerned about what I had said to upset her again. He told me how moved she had been by my words to her. Now I knew why the Lord had urged me to write and post that letter that particular afternoon. If I hadn't, she would never have received it knowing what I had told her. The letter was my and God's gift of love to her. What I told her were things she needed to hear from me to feel good about herself and her life, things my grandmother had never told her. My letter was the last thing she read before she entered the hospital that day.

"Oh, Lord, you are the ruler of all things and men. You made sure Mother received my letter with all the things you wanted her to hear before her hemorrhage. You are so wonderful, your plan so perfect. Without you, none of this would ever have happened and she would have died without the words she needed to hear from me. How can I ever thank you for your wisdom and generosity to her and me. You are a most loving God. I thank you for your great love for us. I know you took her home to be with you. Thank you, as she is not suffering any more. Please watch over Dad and my family as we begin and go through this time of grieving and remembering her. Help Dad with his grief and let him feel your presence and love for him. In all this, I ask these things in Christ Jesus's name. Amen."

By morning, Dad and I had shared many memories of her and begun the process of preparing her for her final resting place. He and I had selected her burial outfit, the baby blue two-piece dress and jacket she loved. Years before, she told me she didn't want to be buried with her engagement and wedding rings, as she wanted them saved for young Jim, my nephew. She wanted him to give them to his bride when he selected one.

We went to Fannin Funeral Home to pick out her casket and make the arrangements for her Florida viewing and transportation to West Virginia, where she, and later Dad, would be interred alongside my brother and sister. We chose a beautiful rose-colored metallic casket with ivory inside coverings. Her viewing would take place the following evening.

The following evening, Mother and Dad's Florida friends paid their respects before we took her north. A day later, we boarded the plane for West Virginia. Two days later, their Huntington friends, some of our relatives, along with some of Dad's former business associates and Ron's family, drove through blinding snow on slippery, snow-covered mountain roads for the viewing and the funeral. What a beautiful service Reverend Thomas conducted for her! During the service, I upset Dad with my soft weeping. That wasn't ladylike.

After the interment, we went to the Frederick Hotel for a buffet luncheon. Many memories of her were shared with us by those attending. Some people left right after the funeral, as the roads had become worse.

After saying our good-byes to everyone, Ron, Dad, the boys, and I returned to our hotel for a bit of rest. I talked to Ron about my returning with Dad for a week or so to get him acclimated to life without Mother. When Dad came to our room later, I approached him on this. He said, "Definitely not. You can come down in six weeks or so, but I need time to adjust alone." I tried to persuade him, but nothing I said would change his mind.

The following morning he said good-bye to us and boarded his plane home while we waited for our departure. I prayed, "Oh, Lord, be with him during his flight home, his return to the apartment where he and Mother lived. Help him through the loneliness and grief he will encounter now that Mother is gone and we are not there to help him. See that friends surround him with love and support. Let him know you are with him and will remain with him all his life. Love and care for him just as you do for us. Lead him in the path you want him to follow. In all these wishes I call on your name and that of your Son, my Savior, Jesus Christ. Amen."

Six weeks later, during my school winter break, I spent a long weekend with him. Although deeply grieving, he was managing better than I expected. He continued having their cleaning lady come in to clean, do his laundry, and fix some of his evening meals. He ate his other meals out with friends or alone. He promised to come up in the summer and spend time with us. He planned to drive up, visiting the places where he and Mother had lived. He planned to see family and friends as well as us along his way back to his home.

"Oh, Lord, continue to be with him as he goes through this process of loss and grieving. Love him through it. Keep him close to you and us. And in all things, I ask this in your name. Amen."

My Life Changes

"Praise the Lord, O my soul; all my inmost being, praise
His holy name. Praise the Lord,
O my soul and forget not all His benefits."

(Psalm 103:1–2)

The winter term for school had started before our family returned from Mother's funeral. We had only missed a couple of days, but our schools understood. I threw myself into my family and my teaching. The teachers I worked for—I was a special educational aide for two teachers—had expected me to take a week off, but I needed to keep my mind and hands busy, so I returned quickly. Life resumed quickly for me with the boys' activities. Ronnie's daily swim practices and weekend swim meets, kept both the Rons, John, and me hopping and on the road. I enjoyed the fastness of my life, as I didn't have time to think.

I loved teaching and being with my students in the resource room (special education). Working one-on-one with these special students, whether learning disabled or emotionally impaired, kept me on my toes. I saw their problem areas, either with reading or math, and then I created games that made learning fun for them. I loved my work.

This time became a proving ground for me. The teaching techniques I learned from these teachers would be invaluable in years to come. After two years working in the resource room, I moved to a special reading program working with students two or more years below their classroom reading levels. The reading specialist in this room was a caring, effective, and special woman. She helped me gain confidence in myself and my teaching abilities. She demonstrated how I could get the most learning out of each of our students: demanding their best and not letting them slack off their tasks. I learned so much from her about myself, life, and teaching. I will always be indebted to her.

Unfortunately, in April 1980, a disk in my lower back herniated. I attempted to work through the pain for more than a month. After seeing Dr. Stanley Haney, a recommended orthopedic surgeon, his recommendation was total bed rest for a month to six weeks to let the disk heal. Now how was I going to do that with three men in our house? My teaching was over for that year. Oh, how I hated the thought of not being with the kids and doing what I loved to do.

After six weeks, I returned to him. Although everyone said surgery was his last resort, it was the first thing out of his mouth. "You need surgery to repair your spine. I will fuse some of the disks together and then you will need additional bed rest to finalize your recovery." Stunned, I called my doctor cousin, Dr. Jim Tisdel, in Port Huron to ask his advice. Jim had an orthopedic doctor friend who had had similar back problem fixed, and Jim would approach him for his recommendation.

Two days later, Jim called to say his friend highly recommended my seeing Dr. Sayad Farhat, a neurosurgeon at St. Joseph Hospital in Ypsilanti. Dr. Farhat had performed his friend's back surgery, and he was up and walking within days. He went so far as to say that if he ever needed additional surgery done, he would definitely go back to Dr. Farhat. With his earnest recommendation, I called and made an appointment with Dr. Farhat. He couldn't fit me in for two weeks, so I just laid there letting overwhelming concerns overtake my thoughts. I hoped Dr. Farhat would find an alternative method of dealing with my back problem. After his examination, he ordered a myelogram to show him exactly what the problem entailed, and then he would make his recommendation.

"Oh, Lord, what am I to do? You have always been with me to tell me what I need to do. Please calm my fears. If it is possible, please heal this disk of mine and keep me from any surgical procedure. You know how afraid I am of surgery since Ruth's death. I will trust you in whatever you say, as you are always with me. If surgery is needed, I know you will be with me in it. I put my life in your hands. Amen."

Two weeks later, at noon, I entered St. Joseph Hospital for my myelogram. Two hours later, I was prepped and being wheeled into the surgical room. Fear hit me when I realized Dr. Farhat's resident was performing the procedure, not him. Again, I cried out to God. "Please protect me in this and let nothing happen to paralyze me. Keep his hands steady, the needles to go exactly where they need to be, and help me to be calm and at peace during this process and recovery. Amen."

The nurses turned me on my stomach, placed sheets over me, and then told Dr. Craine, Dr. Farhat's chief resident, that I was ready. He was a young man of thirty or so with a strong build and a calming presence. He explained the procedure and told me he would walk me through each step of the procedure so I knew what to expect and would not be afraid. First, he told me he would deaden the area where the procedure would take place. Then he would insert the needle in the correct disk area, release the inky, radioactive fluid into my spine, and take the necessary x-rays. Then he would remove the needle and all would be over. The x-rays would reveal for Dr. Farhat the information he needed for my care. Dr. Craine was so gentle and reassuring that I was calm throughout the procedure. It went quickly and smoothly.

After the procedure, I was placed back onto the gurney and wheeled into my room for the night. For the next twelve to eighteen hours, I had to remain perfectly still on my back so the fluid would flow properly out of me and I wouldn't get a headache from the dye. The nurses monitored me through this process. If all went as planned, Dr. Farhat would release me in the morning.

With a sleeping pill and pillows holding me in place, I slept through the night. Eight o'clock the next morning, Dr. Farhat made his appearance. I could tell from his stiff face the news wasn't what I wanted to hear. I did indeed have a herniated disk that needed to be repaired. He planned to have his surgical scheduler get me the first possible surgical day he had, but it might be a couple of weeks before a bed would become available. I needed to rest and not worry; he would take care of me and my problem.

A few days later, his office called, saying there was a cancellation and could she schedule my surgery for the following Wednesday morning. I said yes. The nurse instructed me to be at the hospital by two o'clock Tuesday afternoon for the prep and pre-op workup. Dr. Farhat would see me during his evening rounds. Surgery was scheduled for eight o'clock Wednesday morning. I would remain for a day or two, depending on my recovery.

Once again, prayers went up. "Oh, Lord, you were with me during the myelogram and the diagnosis. Please be with me during this time, keeping me in your loving arms so I do not become frightened. I know you are with me and want only the best for me. I know this surgery will cure the problem, making me whole again. Please calm my fears and strengthen me in all that is to come. I ask this is Jesus's name. Amen."

I was so fortunate that Ron's mother was visiting us. Ron's dad had died almost two years before. She spent the fall with us until Ron's sister, Judy, and her boyfriend, Mitchell, came to pick her up at Thanksgiving to take her back to Philadelphia for the winter. She would care for Julie, Judy's daughter, and Mitchell's son, David, while they worked.

I loved her spending the fall with us. God's creation and care showed through the vibrant leaf colors of yellow, orange, and red; the days turned crisp, and the pumpkins readied themselves to be made into Halloween jack-o-lanterns. Mom, Ron, the boys, and I went out to Foreman's Apple Orchard in neighboring Northville to pick out wonderful bushels of Paula apples to make her luscious apple pies and applesauce, which we froze for wonderful winter treats. After all the apple buying, we usually splurged on a dozen cinnamon doughnuts coming right out of the fryers, along with a gallon, sometimes two gallons, of their fantastic apple cider. Oh, how I loved this time of the year with Mom.

She and I spent hours talking about life, the boys, and anything that cropped up. Mom had always been the mother I wished I had, as she was loving, supportive, and my encourager in all things. She treated me as a daughter and not as a daughter-in-law, making our relationship so special. I loved her dearly.

"Oh, Lord, thank you for this wonderful woman you placed in my life to give me the love I so lacked in my growing-up days. You have handed me a bounteous gift. She is so special, and I know you sent her to me. Thank you Lord. Amen."

With my bag packed for my hospital stay, my courage holding up, and good-byes to the boys, knowing they would be well cared for with Mom there, I felt relaxed as I got into Ron's car for the drive to the hospital. After checking in and signing all the admission papers, I rode the elevator to the third floor and walked to room 324. I waited and tried to relax until Dr. Craine came in. He began the pre-op questioning about allergies, family histories, and any questions I had about the procedure. While he talked with me, my phone rang. Surprised, I answered it, thinking it was a wrong number. The call was for Dr. Craine. Overhearing his side of the conversation, I learned that whoever was on the other end of the line, possibly another surgical resident, wanted to know if he had performed the surgery on the chief of surgery at the University of Michigan Hospital. Dr. Craine said, "No, the old man did it himself." I could tell he wished he had done it, but knowing the importance of the patient, he knew he wouldn't be allowed.

Relief overwhelmed me. I knew I had the best. God had answered my prayer. Dr. Farhat had been chosen for me, and I would be all right. "Thank you, Lord, for once again providing for my care and blessing me with a special surgeon to make my back right again and the pain to go away. Thank you, thank you. Amen."

That night, Ron and I talked about everything and nothing just to keep me from thinking about what would transpire in the morning. Ron would be with me before surgery, which made me feel secure. As he left, he gave me a hug and kiss. I told him to give hugs and kisses to all, saying good night to them for me as well.

Before I knew it, the morning nurse came in and told me to shower, brush my teeth and hair, go to the bathroom, and then rest in bed until the gurney came for me. When I came out of my bathroom, Ron was sitting in a chair waiting for me. We just held hands and talked about the boys and their day. Before long, the orderlies came for me. Within seconds, I had scooted onto the stretcher. Ron came with me as far as he could go. I kissed him, and then off we went into pre-op.

Once in pre-op, the nurses hooked me up to monitors and began the IV drip to relax me. All of a sudden, I noticed Ron coming in, which puzzled me. He told me Dr. Farhat had an emergency; he would do my surgery once the emergency one was completed. I was groggy but relaxed, and we talked some more. Ron prayed, "Oh Lord, watch over Nancy as she undergoes this surgery. Hold the surgeon's hands steady, and give him the wisdom to do what is necessary to fix her disk problem. Relieve her pain and bring her back to full life and energy. In all things, I ask this in Jesus's name. Amen."

The more I waited, the sleepier I became. Before I knew it, Ron kissed me and wished me God's blessings. In my twilight sleep, I remember being placed onto the surgical table then being asked to help the nurses turn me onto my stomach. The anesthesiologist told me he was beginning the anesthetic; I was to start counting back from one hundred. I think I got to ninety-five or ninety-four. I never knew when Dr. Farhat came in. The next thing I remember was being gently taken off the table and placed on the stretcher. As soon as I returned to my room, the nurses carefully positioned me on my bed and then placed pillows all around me so I couldn't move even a smidge. I dozed off again.

When I woke, Ron was sitting next to me. He had been there since I went into surgery. He bent over and kissed me, telling me the surgery was over and I was back in my room. I nodded and fell back asleep. Two hours later, I was awake and feeling some surgical pain. The nurse gave me a shot of painkiller and told me to call her when the pain started again. The sooner she could give the shot the faster the pain would leave.

About two o'clock, Dr. Farhat made his surgical rounds. From the smile on his face I could tell things had gone well. He told us, "Your ballooning disk surprised me, as it was larger than I had expected. It was the size of a large pea. I cut it out and didn't have to do anything else. In an hour or so, I want you to let the nurses help you sit up on the side of the bed for a bit. Later, again with the nurses, get up and go to the bathroom. Then this evening, I want you to walk a bit down the hall. I will see you in the morning. Have a good evening." He left as softly as he came in. He was a gentle, caring man, and I felt fortunate to have him as my surgeon.

In an hour, the nurses came in to see if I felt up to sitting up. I said, "I'd like to." With one on either side of me, they balanced me, keeping my back straight while they maneuvered me into a sitting position. Oh, how good that felt! I realized my pain was nonexistent. Oh, what a relief. After months of back and sciatica pain, I was pain free. I sat there for about ten minutes, and then they helped me back into my lying-down position. Another hour later, the nurses had me sitting and then standing. Oh, how good that felt. I even took a few steps to the bathroom and back. Wanting to be home when the boys got home from school, Ron left to tell everyone I came through the surgery well. That evening, the boys wanted to come, but Ron told them I was still too groggy. By the time he returned, I was fully awake and happy to see him. After another shot of painkiller, the nurses came in and started me down the hall for a short walk to their station and back. They couldn't believe how well I was doing. Once back into bed, I felt exhilarated but exhausted. Ron and I talked and watched some television.

Before Ron left, I took another walk down the hall with him on one side and a nurse on the other. We walked past the nurses' station this time. How gratifying that was! I felt like I had run a marathon and won! My, did I feel good!

"Thank you, Lord. You kept me safe and gave Dr. Farhat the wisdom and hands to do the work needed to take care of my problem. You are such a good and gracious God. I am so glad you are my loving Father who cares about me. Without you I wouldn't have found the right surgeon and care I needed. Your surrounding presence 'through the valley of the shadow of death' calmed me, so I didn't fear what lay ahead, as I knew you were with me. Thank you for all you do for me. I love you. As always I say this, in the name of Jesus Christ, my Lord, Savior, and your Son. Amen."

Early the next morning, after a decent night's sleep, Dr. Farhat came in to see me. After noting my progress on his chart, he told me he was pleased with my progress. If I continued to do well the rest of the day, he would release me in the morning. I couldn't believe it. I called Ron to tell him I could possibly be coming home the next day. "Astounding! You just had back surgery a little more than a day ago, and Dr. Farhat says you may be able to come home tomorrow. Amazing!" The words flowed out of his mouth.

The rest of the day I spent walking more and more. Toward late afternoon, the nurses let me walk alone as long as they could see me. I only required one pain shot in the morning and none afterward. That evening, Ron brought Ron, John, and Mom to see me. Oh, how wonderful to be surrounded with their love. The boys feared to hug me, but I said, "Just do it gently. I won't break. I love your hugs." The boys and Mom stayed for a bit and then went to the waiting room for cokes so Ron and I could have a little time alone. He and I walked the hall again. He couldn't believe how well I was doing and was eager to get me home.

"Oh, Lord, what a gift of your love you have given me to be surrounded by such love, caring, and support. Ron is your gift to me, and I thank you from the bottom of my heart. My sons are precious to me as well. Mom being here is another of your gifts to me. Thank you, and continue in your care and love for us. Thank you for the complete surgical healing and my speedy recovery. You are a great and wondrous God and my heavenly Father! All glory and honor to you. Amen."

The following morning, Dr. Farhat remained pleased with my continued walking and pain-free condition and signed my release papers. He told me to live on one floor for the next two weeks until he would see me, reassess my recovery, and remove my back staples. He instructed me to walk every day, beginning with a short walk down the street and then add at least one step each day to it. I thanked him for all he had done then said good-bye.

Ron and I packed up my nightgown, robe, slippers, and toiletries. I dressed in my loose-fitting exercise suit that I had worn to the hospital. The nurse brought in the usual going-away conveyance: the wheelchair. She told Ron to get the car and bring it to the entrance doors. She would have me there. Within minutes, I moved from the wheelchair to the front passenger seat of our white and wood-sided Pinto station wagon—my chariot to the awaiting world. I was homeward bound. Home! Oh, how good that sounded. I could get back to life without pain. "Oh, Lord, what an awesome God you are. Once again, thank you for your tender loving care of me. Amen." "You are back to living your life without that pain and can now go on with your life," I felt the Lord relay to me.

Dad called that evening to check on me. He hadn't called earlier, as he had been on a tour of India and had just returned. He had wanted me to go and be his companion, but my back problem prohibited that. The poverty and unhealthy living conditions he had seen along the trip had overwhelmed him. Both he and I agreed this was not a place for me to see. He didn't talk long, as his exhaustion had overtaken him. He would call in a couple days after he was rested and could talk longer. I told him the surgery was a success and my pain was gone. Oh, how thrilled he was.

Every day, Mom and I walked farther and farther down the street. The walk was good for both of us; to be out in the fresh air and sunshine just accentuated the season and my recovery. When Dad called a couple days later, we talked for an hour about my surgery, recovery, and his trip. How relieved I was to know he was home safe, although he still sounded so exhausted.

"Thank you, Lord, for Dad's safe return. Restore his stamina and physical health. Thank you also for all you are doing in my recovery. You are an awesome God, and I praise you daily for all you do for me and my family. I love you. Amen."

After two weeks, I returned to see Dr. Farhat for my staple removal and a checkup. He had me bend over, walk for him, and asked how I felt. I told him I walked daily with Mom, adding a step and sometimes more each walk we took, even stopping if either of us needed a rest. She had a heart condition, so we had to take it easy for both of us. He continued to be pleased with my progress, telling me to continue with my daily walk, no heavy lifting, and now I could go upstairs once a day. He wanted me in for a final checkup in a month. He warned me that with the staples out I would feel free but not to overdo it, as I was still recovering.

In the following days and weeks, I began to wonder what to do with my life. The school year had already begun, and my job had been given to someone else. The teachers I had worked with told me to go back to college and finish my education degree. I needed to be teaching in my own classroom. I thought long and hard about that idea, especially since college fees were escalating. When I mentioned my interest in returning to school to finish my degree, Dad offered to help with the financing. Oh, what a relief and gift! Now came the next big hurdle. Could I get into a college since my grades from the University of Cincinnati stunk?

In November 1980 my search began: University of Michigan, Eastern Michigan University, and Wayne State University. A month after sending them my transcripts, résumés, and enrollment forms, I had two rejections, one from the University of Michigan and the other from Wayne State University. I did get an acceptance from Eastern Michigan University. Oh, the undeniable joy, but at the same time, fear struck! How could I ever compete with students fifteen and twenty years younger than I was? I needed to get the okay from Dr. Farhat as well.

It just so happened I was to see him for my six-week checkup. He told me college would be fine as long as I didn't carry too many or heavy books around with me. I told him I planned to take only one class to check out the waters before I truly began in earnest. He thought that was an excellent idea, especially for my back. He told me I could resume driving and most everything I had done before the surgery. I needed to remember to take it easy and let my back tell me when I needed to stop doing something. I should continue my daily walking with Mom. She and I really enjoyed that time together out in the fresh, crisp, sunshine-filled mornings. He discharged me and said if I had any problems or concerns to call him. His success rate with this surgery was 96 percent with only 4 percent needing further surgery. Oh, how happy I felt! "Life is good," I told him. He agreed.

The next day, I drove to Eastern Michigan and enrolled in the History 121 course for the winter 1981 term. That should be easy enough. Again, the excitement and fear hit me, but I planned to persevere and see how it and I turned out. I hoped I wouldn't completely embarrass myself. It had been twenty-five years since I had sat in a college classroom as a student. Oh, what a change this would be. The teacher was now the student. I realized I had to learn how to take notes again and find the precious time needed for study if I was to make a go of this new adventure in learning.

On the first day of class, I realized from the syllabus that a lot was expected of me: lots of reading and study time. I loved history, so that shouldn't be too much of a problem. After my first exam, I talked to Professor Schmitt about my not-so-good B grade and how I could improve it. He spent an hour with me, reminding me of how to take notes and exams. His time and wisdom paid off with good test grades for the remainder of the semester. It also paid off for me in my future classes. "Thank you, Dr. Schmitt!"

After three and a half years of toil, sweat, tears, papers, and exams, I graduated with a 3.24 grade point average. What a change from beginning with a 1.20 average from the University of Cincinnati. I had worked my buns off, and it had paid off big time. I graduated the end of April 1985 with a Bachelor of Science degree in English and American Literature and Composition with a minor in Business Education.

Ron and the boys had a wonderful celebration for me with all our neighbors and friends. I wished Dad could have seen me graduate and be a part of the celebration afterward; but unfortunately, as I worked through my college classes, his health had slipped, making it hard for him to travel. He had encouraged and supported me through those years since Mother's death. Not having him with me left a sadness that wouldn't leave. What was to happen with him soon would leave an even greater sadness inside me and the family. During my last two college years, I juggled Dad's Alzheimer's disease, our family and home, the boys' various activities, along with their and my school work. A weighty problem, but with the Lord, Ron, and the boys' help, I managed it. "Thank you, Lord. Amen."

DEALING WITH DAD'S SAD SITUATION

"To you I call, O Lord my Rock; do not turn a
deaf ear to me. For if you remain silent,
I will be like those who have gone down to the pit."

(Psalm 28:1a)

On June 16, 1982, our son Ron graduated from Canton High School. Dad had driven up to be a part of his graduation and the celebration afterward. Our time with Dad was wonderful. We took him out to the Huron River, where Ron and the boys sailed our little Sunfish boat and had picnics afterward.

The following year, June 19, 1983, John graduated from Canton High School with the same bells and whistles as Ron had the year before. Dad drove up, as he wanted to visit family and friends along the way.

Sensing he hadn't been functioning as well as he should, and feeling his own internist hadn't found out even with all his testing what was wrong with him, Dad wanted another opinion. He called his nephew Dr. Jim in Port Huron. Dr. Jim told him to come over and he would set him up with Dr. Rowans, his internist, who would put him through a complete workup of blood tests and exams.

After all the results were in, Dr. Rowans pronounced him in perfect health except for a small abdominal aneurysm. Since Mother's death, Dad's faith in their internist had dwindled. Now that he hadn't found his aneurysm, he decided he would seek a new internist on his return to Florida. Dr. Rowans told Dad to let him know the name of his new internist and he would send him all his test results and recommendations. Dr. Rowans said the aneurysm was small, so all his internist needed to do was keep a watchful eye on it. Growth might require surgery. Relieved, he returned home feeling good and resumed all his golf and social activities.

Christmas that year came, and he flew up to spend it with us. What a great time we had together. Our whole family, including Dad, went to our usual Christmas tree farm to cut our tree, and then we decorated it and placed our presents under it. While I played the piano, our family sang the traditional Christmas carols, making the season all the more wonderful. We all attended our usual midnight Christmas Eve service. Coming out of the church, we were greeted with beautiful, fluffy snowflakes.

Christmas morning traditions remained with breakfast and then gift opening.

Antsy to get home, Dad left two days later. I hated to see him leave, as we saw so little of him, but he was adamant that he needed to get home to pay bills, etc. After our good-byes at the airport, he said he would call to let us know he was home safe and sound.

The day after New Year's, he called, telling me he had received the bill from Archer's Florist for Ruth, Jim, and Mother's mausoleum Christmas flowers. I told him I was glad they remembered the annual standing order. He asked me what he was to do with it. I said, "Write a check for it." His asking that question concerned me, as he knew what to do with it.

He asked where his checks were, and I told him in the bottom right drawer of his desk. Again, I couldn't believe the questions he was asking me.

He said, "What do I do with the check?"

I replied, "Put it in an envelope and mail it." Now the red flags really began to rise.

Then the ultimate question came, "What is an envelope?"

At that moment I knew something was amiss with him. There were some things he had said and did that I should have been aware of, but with Christmas I shrugged them off. I told him I would fly down in a couple of days after I cancelled my winter classes, which fortunately hadn't started, and help him sort out the problem. His relief became evident. "I am glad you can take care of this for me. I look forward to having you here."

The following morning, I drove to Eastern Michigan University and cancelled my winter semester courses, bought an open-ended plane ticket, rented a compact car for a week in Florida, and then packed. The following day, Ron took me to the airport for what would become a three-month stay with Dad.

When he opened his door to me, his relief and joy radiated through him. We spent the afternoon writing the Archer check, taking him to the grocery to stock up his refrigerator and pantry, and getting him organized. I knew this problem wouldn't go away anytime soon, if ever. I realized a major change had occurred in his thinking pattern. I just couldn't understand what had happened. His whole being was so different; I was shocked by what I was seeing and hearing.

I remembered when he came for John's graduation he had complained about something being wrong with him, and then I realized the problem hadn't been physical but mental. I totally missed the signs of his mental decline. He had faked his abilities so we wouldn't notice them. Oblivious or through denial of this problem, I now knew this would change not only his life, but ours as well. Being so busy with family and school, I hadn't really taken notice of the small but subtle changes in his thinking. I never saw this coming.

The change in him from Christmas to that day had been unbelievable. Now the once capable, intelligent, businessman was incapable of dealing with most daily functions dealing with finances or, for the most part, caring for himself. He had no idea what to do with a kitchen. He never did, as Mother always took care of all the cooking, cleaning, and washing. He had no idea how to do any of those activities. Fortunately, he retained their cleaning lady, who continued to do his cleaning, washing, and some meal preparation. He was totally lost.

I wanted his new internist, Dr. Guida, to check him out and tell me what the problem was. Dad resisted this idea, insisting he had just had a total physical six months before. I persuaded him to do this for me.

The following Friday afternoon, I drove him to Dr. Guida's office. After his examination, Dr. Guida called me in for a consultation while his nurse kept Dad busy. He told me he had never seen a patient go downhill so fast mentally. His abdominal aneurysm had also grown a bit but was nothing to be alarmed about, which was a blessing. I asked what he would recommend. He suggested his moving in with us or into some kind of retirement situation that had facilities for later assisted living and nursing care.

Shock reeled through my body. How was I going to talk to the dad I loved, although still feared, into this life-changing decision? This would be a major change for him, but Dad needed help.

After driving Dad home, I just sat there in a daze while he watched the afternoon stock market show. I decided to fix us both a drink before dinner. He always had a couple before dinner. That night, I needed one just to calm my nerves and help me adjust to what I had heard and what lay ahead for me and the family. I needed to talk to Ron and find out what his thinking about this new turn of events meant to us and what we should do about it. I needed serious advice.

After dinner, Dad asked me what the matter was. I said I was just mulling over his doctor's visit; no big deal. I knew he didn't want to hear what I thought about it. On top of that, I hadn't talked with Ron yet. When Dad finished his television shows, he stalked off to bed. I knew the appointment had unnerved him. Going into the den, I put a call in to Ron and told him what I had learned. He said,

"Sure, bring Dad home with you. We can deal with this here better than there." I was relieved to have his support.

The following evening, after he had had a couple drinks and his dinner, I broached Dr. Guida's idea of his moving to Michigan.

"What do you mean? He didn't say anything to me about that," he rebutted.

I said, "He mentioned to you about moving up to our home or to a place where you would make new friends, you could fix your breakfast and lunch, and then have someone cook your dinner for you. You could even drive wherever you wanted or go places with other people to the theater, shopping, and the like."

Agitated now, he said, "Oh, I don't need anything like that; I am just fine right here. I don't plan to move anywhere. I am happy here."

With that, I hit a brick wall. I suggested his coming up and spending more time with us. He immediately told me, "No, that wouldn't do, as you have your own life and family with all their activities. I would just be in the way, and your house isn't big enough for me to stay for any longer than I already do. This is my home, and here is where I am going to stay."

I knew I had a battle coming, and it was one I couldn't win without help. I tried to get him to see things my way, but nothing was going to change his mind. He wouldn't discuss it any further and immediately went to bed.

After Dad turned in for the night, I phoned Ron. He knew the instant he heard my voice that something was wrong. I explained our conversation and his refusal to listen to any of my ideas. While I cried it out, he offered his support. He was just as much in the dark about how to deal with this situation as I was.

With Ron's help, I developed a plan. I would enlist the help of a lady friend of his, Mary Lou Ruelle. I put a call into her and explained Dr. Guida's concerns about Dad and his recommendations for his care. She had noticed his diminishing mental capacity. She and I combined forces to get Dad to consider living in a retirement village, explaining all the positives of it.

For short periods, I would leave Dad, giving him a sense of freedom from me and my ideas for his future. During this time, I searched for suitable communities that fit Dad's needs. Dr. Guida stated that Dad needed a facility that had advanced nursing care as his mental capacities dwindled further and further. Somehow, Mary Lou and I had to convince him into this new life, especially since he was adamant about not moving in with us. He refused to listen to any talk about this change in his living status.

One day while Dad and I were out for a drive, I drove past Abbey North Community. Open house signs adorned its entrance, and I suggested we just take a look and see what it had to offer. Being in a congenial mood, or maybe out of curiosity—so he could tell me this wasn't the way of life for him—he agreed to look at it. After a full tour of the retirement facility, he seemed to like the staff and their programs. He learned he could bring his furniture as well as his car and drive anywhere he wanted. His whole idea of these places was that they were prisons for aging parents and adults. After all of his questions were answered, he decided to think it over. That was a step in the right direction, but we still had no champagne ending.

As we continued to discuss this, I brought my sister-in-law, Eileen, and my nephew, Jim, into the discussion. Eileen disagreed completely with my assessment of Dad's situation. I explained that he had refused to move in with us and he needed some supervision. Even after I related what Dr. Guida had told me, she proposed overseeing him, as they only lived thirty minutes away. I shuddered as I thought how she intended to supervise him, as they only saw him once a month or every six weeks. That wasn't the kind of supervision he needed.

At that moment, I knew I needed additional help from Mary Lou if this was going to work. We continued our discussions with Dad about the advantages of this move for him. He said he would give it more thought. As the days went on, I realized his "thinking" was a delaying tactic so he could stay in his apartment and I would stay and take care of him. In his mind, I was Mother and it was my duty was to take care of him like she did. I had to find a way to break this deadlock.

Again, I took him to see Abbey North Community and had Mary Lou meet us there. With both of us going on another tour of the facility and going over all its positives for him, he finally broke down and signed the papers. Now, the work began.

After I privately talked with Dad's trust officer at the bank about Dad's diminishing mental capacity, Dad and I went to see him. Pat told us he would put Dad's place on the market and then find a good mortgage deal for Abbey North. The furniture and anything else Dad couldn't take with him, Pat would sell. After receiving three different moving company bids, I took the best and cheapest one and made the move arrangements. Draperies and valances for his living room, bedroom, and the guest bedroom were the next step. Dad couldn't decide on what he wanted, so I took a cushion from the living room sofa, a sham from his bedspread, and one from his guest room in order to match fabrics for the window dressings with the drapery coordinator. I wanted to make things look as much like his apartment so the transition to his new one would be as easy as possible. My prayer in all this was to make the move as simple and smooth as possible. Dad wouldn't be able to adjust to his new surroundings if there were problems. "Oh, Lord, I am hoping you can help me with making this move as easy as possible for Dad. You always are with me, giving me your strength, wisdom, and support. Once again, I am looking to you to help me be the tower of strength and poise to make this move as easy on Dad as possible. He can't take a lot of agitation along with this move. Help me; be there for me. Be with me throughout this process, showing me how to best help him adjust to his new home and environment. With you at my side, I know things will go well. Thank you for all you do to help me in all I do. I love you. Amen."

Moving day came. The movers finished our packing and off we all went to Abbey North. The next couple of days, Dad and I worked feverishly getting everything in place. During that week and the next, I drove him around his new area, getting him acquainted with the places he would frequent: the grocery store, drug store, bank, gas station, and any other places he might want to go. I quizzed him on how to get to these places so I knew he knew how to get to them alone. I wanted him to have it down pat before I left for home. Home! I had been with him almost two months getting all this done.

As I began getting ready to leave, I made sure his pantry was filled with the necessities. In his freezer, I put some frozen dinners and two half-gallons of his favorite chocolate ice cream. "My, you have a lot of food here just for me," he said, sizing up the situation.

I reassured him, "Just in case you get the munchies, you'll have something at hand." He seemed all right with everything.

I remained an additional few days to make sure all was in place. Toward the end of the week, I called Delta to open up my return ticket to Detroit for Sunday. Totally exhausted mentally and physically, I was ready to go home. I needed some down time. Mary Lou promised to keep an eye on him for me and let me know how he was doing. I hated to leave him; again, he made it abundantly clear he would visit us but not live with us. Now, parting time had come. I needed my family, and he needed to show himself and me he could be independent. "Lord, be with him through this transition time. Help him make the needed adjustments. Help him find peace and happiness here. Also, help me say good-bye to him without a waterfall of tears. Give me the strength to leave him and return to my family. Keep me in your care as well. Amen."

After getting into my taxi for the airport, I sobbed, as he looked so lost. He looked like I had the night Mother and Grandma left me at St. Anne's. I just wanted to rush back to him, put my arms around him, and make things better for him. I knew he desperately wanted me to remain with him, but I had a family I loved and needed to take care of as well.

After my two stressful months with Dad, then my two-and-a-half-hour flight home, I was fighting total exhaustion. Walking off the plane in a total daze, I walked right past Ron without realizing it was him until he said, "Nancy." I looked at this man, realized who he was, and then flew into his open arms in total acceptance of the love he was offering me. "Home at last," was all we could say to each other.

Ron and I had a few hours alone before the boys arrived home from school. They seemed taller and more mature than when I left. They told me not to go away like that again, as they couldn't stand any more of Dad's microwave potatoes. I said I would be home for a while. Little did I know this statement wouldn't last.

Knowing how exhausted I was, my family let me sleep in. What a blessing that was. I hadn't realized how tired I was. I slept twelve hours solid. I finally understood the total emotional exhaustion I had endured over the past months.

Around two o'clock that afternoon, I received a call from Abbey North reporting Dad was missing. "Missing! What do you mean missing!" I replied indignantly.

The resident manager said, "Did he have access to a car, or could he have gone with someone? We don't know where he is. He didn't sign out. If he had a car, we didn't know about it." I was stunned to say the least.

I returned, "I told you when he signed the contracts that he had a car. We registered his car with you, and then you issued him a parking sticker and parking place."

He continued, "Well, he isn't here, and we don't know where he is."

I asked, "How long has he been missing?"

The reply was, "We don't know."

I called Ron at work and explained the situation. I asked him to call the Florida State Police, as it would sound better from a man rather than from a hysterical daughter. After talking to them, he told me the Florida Highway Patrol couldn't do anything, not even look for his car, as he hadn't done anything.

At that moment, I let out a cry of desperation. "Oh, Father God, watch over my dad, wherever he is. Keep him safe until he returns home. Don't let anyone hurt him. Protect him. Amen."

All I could do for the rest of the afternoon and evening was call his apartment and pace the floor like an expectant father waiting for the birth of his child. I always paced when one of the boys was late; now I did it for my dad. The more I paced, the more frantic I became. Ron talked me into lying down for a bit. "You should try to get some rest;

someone will call you with information about him, and you need to be rested to deal with that information," Ron pleaded.

About two o'clock that morning, the phone rang. I knew it had to be about Dad. The man on the other end of the phone line introduced himself as Sergeant Clark Johnson of the Florida State Police at Delray Beach.

He asked me, "Are you Nancy Hamilton Hurley?"

I knew he or someone had opened Dad's wallet and taken out the simple sheet of paper bearing my name and address on it. I had placed that information there after Mother's death just in case he needed me or something happened to him.

The next thing out of my mouth was, "Yes. Is he all right?"

The burly sounding sergeant said, "Your father is shaken up and very confused about what happened to him or where he lives." I explained that he had recently moved to Abbey North Community.

My next question was what had happened. He explained, "Your father became quite disoriented, believing someone was pursuing him for his money. As he became more confused and frantic about his whereabouts, he forgot how to stop his car. He reasoned the only way to stop his car was to run it into another, which he did, plowing into three unoccupied cars along the beach. The sound of the collisions brought the police, who found him slumped back in his seat. The police then brought him to the Delray Police Station."

Sergeant Johnson told me one of their on-call doctors had checked Dad and physically he was all right. The doctor had prescribed a tranquillizer to lessen his agitated state. He needed someone to come and take him home. The only one I could think of was Mary Lou. I hated to call in the middle of the night, but she was the only one I could think of. Knowing Eileen's opposition to Dad's move and living about a half hour or so away from her, she wouldn't make herself available for this. Mary Lou graciously said she would pick him up at the police station, take him back to Abbey North, and stay with him until I could get there in the morning. *Now, what was ahead for him?* What I had thought would be the best solution had turned into a disaster.

2 Sunday, December 26, 2010

inside

New party clothes make the new year festive.
$34.95

veries on page 2

-and-sho

oliday,

At nine o'clock that morning, I boarded the Delta flight to return to Dad and face this new crisis with him. As I picked up my rental car and proceeded up A1A to Abbey North, I thought of what lay ahead for us. *How could I leave him to fend for himself? What was the next step for him and us as a family?*

As soon as I arrived at Abbey North, Mr. Cudahy, Abbey North's director, whisked me off into his office. He explained that Dad could no longer remain here, as he was a risk to himself and his other clients. How could he be assured Dad wouldn't leave the stove on, causing a fire in his apartment that might spread to adjoining ones? He demanded he move out at once. He didn't care where I took him; he couldn't remain here.

I immediately called Pat Burkett and explained the events of the last twenty-four hours, as well as Mr. Cudahy's order to remove Dad. As our tense conversation continued, I asked Pat if Dad's apartment had been sold. When he said it hadn't, the solution became evident. I would move Dad back into his old apartment, where things were familiar, thereby settling him. Now I had to organize another move back to his old place. Then the next problem appeared: Dad's apartment association wouldn't agree to his return without around-the-clock care for him. The association's concern about Dad's mental state was the same as Abbey North's. Pat would organize nursing care, while I made the move arrangements.

Leaving Mr. Cudahy's office, I went to Dad's apartment. He was asleep from the sedative he had been given. Mary Lou told me he was resting. I explained what I knew about his situation. I called Ron, assessing him of the situation. Ron reassured and calmed me. He asked if I needed him to come down.

I said, "Right now, with things in such an uproar, it would be better if I dealt with Dad and the situation alone."

"Okay, call me when you need me or if you just need to talk," he replied. I knew I could rely on him for anything.

"Thank you, Lord, for such a wonderful man and husband!"

A few hours later, Dad woke and came into the living room. As soon as he saw me, he lit up like a Christmas tree. He didn't want to talk about what had happened. Pat called later, saying one of his trust clients had used Kimberly Nursing Group and was quite pleased with them. While I made the moving arrangements, Pat would sign the around-the-clock nursing service contract.

After I made dinner, I told Dad that because of his episode last night, Abbey North wouldn't allow him to remain there. He could move back into his old apartment, but the Homeowners Association required someone to be with him at all times. Explaining this set Dad off with unbelievable anger. He didn't need anyone to care for him. He didn't want to hear of any of this. I told him the women would be there just to do the cleaning, laundry, and cooking. They would take him anywhere he wanted to go: to the store, meals out, whatever. He wouldn't be a prisoner. Oh, what a ruckus he gave me. He was perfectly capable of taking care of himself. I explained that his accident had made that impossible. That only angered him more. I attempted to talk him into moving in with us, which he indignantly refused to even listen to.

"No, you have your own family, and I can take care of myself. Don't you understand that? I am capable of that. Now, don't talk to me any more about that," he roared. Anymore talk of this would only make things worse.

As his tirade continued like a child having a temper tantrum, I prayed. "Oh, Lord, I now realize that the move to Abbey North wasn't the best choice for him. He now needs help, as he cannot live alone anymore. How can I broach his living with us again? I need discernment here. I need your guidance in this new situation. Help me find the right place for him. Help him accept this new wrinkle in his life; help me to know how to deal with him; and get him to accept what will become his new way of life. Lord, help me deal with his anger, as you know how afraid of it I am. You have always helped me in the past; please do so again. I ask all this in Jesus's name. Amen."

Relief came slowly as I let go and let God take the lead. Oh, how difficult this was for me, as I had always thought I could do this all myself. What a humbling experience for me, but one I needed to confess and ask forgiveness for. "Oh, Lord, forgive me for my thinking I could do all this myself. I can't do this alone; I need you to take the lead in this. I am powerless in this. Help me work through this new crisis in both Dad's and my life. I confess to you my prideful actions and ask for your forgiveness. Return to me with your love and guidance. I place all of this in your power and hands. Amen."

Later that day, I contacted the moving company, who could move us back into his apartment in two days. After cancelling all the utilities, I made ready for the move. I called Pat and told him of Dad's return move to his apartment and his insistence he didn't need anyone to take care of him. I had to work on that problem.

After the movers had finished moving us in, I made the beds and then took Dad grocery shopping. While I fixed his favorite meal—steak, baked potato, tossed salad, and an apple pie with ice cream—he had a couple of drinks to unwind. After watching some of his nightly television shows, we prepared for a good night's sleep. My only concern was would he get up and attempt to leave the apartment alone. I half slept, as I needed to hear if he was moving about.

The next day, I took him to see Pat to go over the finances of selling Abbey North and the provisions for the nursing staff that would start the following week. Dad again became hostile, but Pat made it clear that the apartment building required it and there was no getting around it. After a heated discussion, Dad finally sulked out, knowing he couldn't fight what was about to happen. Anger encircled his whole being; he knew he was losing this fight.

The first of the following week, I began talking about the nurses and their duties. He again began with, "I don't need them and I don't want them."

I had to continue with, "This is the only way you can stay here." On Friday, the nursing administrator, Shelley Abram, and one of her psychiatric nurses came to talk to us about beginning their duties and routine. Anger abounded again, but Shelley calmed him by saying, "Mr. Hamilton, you are to tell them what they are to do."

Again he angrily said, "I don't need them to do anything; I can do it all myself."

She overlooked his remark, saying, "You need to tell them how you like your laundry done, what and when you like to eat, where you like to go shopping, etc. You are in charge."

He retorted, "If I was in charge, you wouldn't be coming, as I can do this for myself!"

Shelley came with the first nurse, Sophia, the following evening. Shelley told me then that I could stay for a couple of days, but after that, my being there would make his transition into this new situation difficult not only for him but for them as well. The following morning I called Ron, telling him I had made my flight reservation home for the next afternoon.

The Battle Lines Are Drawn

"This is what the Lord says to you: Do not be
afraid or discouraged because of this vast army.
For the battle is not yours, but God's."

(2 Chronicles 20:15)

Things progressed well for a few months, until my sister-in-law, Eileen, and her boyfriend, Jerry, decided to get involved. Dad had bitterly complained to them about the nurses and his not needing or wanting them there. After one of their visits, Jerry said he would talk to Pat and see what could be done. Jerry told Pat he would take over Dad's care if Pat would pay for his expenses. From the way Jerry presented himself, Pat realized this offer wasn't to take care of Dad properly but to get to his money. When Dad told me a couple of nights later Jerry was going to take care of him and not the nurses, a huge red flag signaled trouble ahead. This was not good.

By this time, Dad's capacity for understanding money and Jerry's manipulation of him alarmed me considerably. The following morning, I called Pat to discuss this new ripple in Dad's life and Jerry's plan. I was shocked to learn Jerry had already contacted Pat about this very thing. Both Pat and I were troubled by Jerry's intervention in this situation. Something had to be done and quickly.

Later, I called Shelley and asked her how many times in the past couple of months Jerry, Eileen, and Jim had come. Shelley checked her records and said they came every other Sunday and spent about an hour with him, leaving him distraught after each visit. I couldn't prohibit their visits, as I didn't have that right, but their visits and conversations with Dad concerned me greatly. Jerry just seemed to be stirring up the anger pot so he could get control of the situation. Dad believed Jerry could get rid of the nurses and he would be free of them without seeing Jerry's true intent.

After talking to Pat again, he suggested I visit and make my own assessment of the situation. Once again, I flew down to visit. When I knocked on his door, he opened it and didn't recognize me. What a shock to my system! Once he heard my voice, he knew who I was. He now only knew me through my telephone voice. He was overjoyed at my visit. He expected I was there to send the nurses away and then to stay and take care of him myself. I knew I had another struggle ahead, but I needed to see what was going on before hitting the situation head-on.

First, I called Dr. Guida's office, making an appointment for the next day. Telling Dad that Dr. Guida wanted to see him for a checkup, he agreed to go. After doing a basic mental evaluation and some basic physical checks, he told me he was distressed with Dad's deepening senility. He would not put a diagnosis of Alzheimer's disease on his chart, as Blue Cross would refuse to pay anything toward his care. Senility was a diagnosis the insurance company would accept without a problem. He told me that Dad's abdominal aneurysm had grown a bit, but it was nothing concerning yet. If it grew larger, we would have to discuss the options open to him.

I discussed Dad's accident, moves, and nursing situation since I had had Dad in for his last physical with him. I suggested taking Dad home to live with us. He said, "Definitely not. To change his surroundings again would just accelerate his dementia and make him even more belligerent. Nancy, you need to understand that your dad may look like your dad, but he now has a different brain. His brain doesn't function as it used to. He's not the fearless leader of industry he was but a man who can't deal with daily functions of life." Now I knew steps had to be taken to protect Dad and his money so he'd have enough to take care of his medical needs for the rest of his life.

Upon returning to Dad's apartment, I called Pat, telling him of Dr. Guida's medical assessment of Dad and asked for his recommendations on how to protect Dad, especially from Jerry or anyone else. Pat said he would call Steve Lauer, Dad's attorney, and discuss the matter with him. The following day, I had Sophia, the on-duty nurse, take Dad out to lunch and then grocery shopping so I could have a strategy meeting with Pat and Steve on this Jerry situation. Steve said the only way to totally protect Dad was to become his legal guardian. That meant I would be responsible for all his physical and mental needs while Pat and he watched over his financial and legal needs. Then I asked how this was done. This was a huge step!

Steve said, "You have to contact the probate court and legally go through the procedure to become his guardian. You need a Florida lawyer to take you through the process. I can't do it since I am your father's lawyer. I can recommend a good lawyer with experience in this field. His name is Larry Smith, and his office is down the street from me. I suggest you keep a daily journal of all your conversations, interventions, and anything you do concerning your care of your father." I left Pat's office in shock. I needed to go to court to legally protect Dad. Steve said the evidence of his automobile accident and Dr. Guida's assessment would be all needed to do this. The more I thought about the road ahead of me, the more I just shook and trembled.

"Oh, Lord. What am I to do? I am so scared about this new wrinkle in my life as well as Dad's life. Help me get through this so it is in his best interest. I want to protect and help him live the best life he can without any pain or hardship. Lord, show me the way. You have always helped me do the right things, although the decision I made about Abbey North wasn't for his good. You know how to do it; let me see what has to be done. Give me the courage to do what is necessary. Be my guide and be with me every minute as I go through this process. Please, help me, lead me, and keep me calm and safe as well. I ask this in Jesus's name. Amen."

I know God heard my cry. He kept me calm and helped me through this traumatic time. When I saw Larry, I explained Dad's past months and present situations. He drew up the papers and told me to take them to the probate court. He would represent me legally during the court hearing. Oh, how unnerving and scary this was becoming.

At this same time, we received a call from Aunt Winifred, Dad's sister, saying she was taking Dad up on his invitation for a week's visit. She was pleased I was there and asked if we could pick her up at the airport.

I said, "Certainly. Just let us know when."

The following morning, she called, saying she would be on the afternoon flight from Kennedy. What a blessing this would be. With her staying with us for a week, it would afford me to talk to her candidly about Dad and give me time to do the legal work that needed to be done.

After talking to him, she was in disbelief about his mental deterioration. She understood why I had instituted the nurses, as he couldn't live alone anymore. This helped eliminate part of my guilt about this situation. I explained that he didn't like the nurses being there; he wanted them gone, as he could take care of himself.

During cocktail hour, he began talking to her about her staying on and taking care of him. Now it was obvious what his plan was by inviting her down: to take care of him. She said she had her own family and friends in New Jersey and didn't want to leave them. She would stay for the week, but her son Bob was to pick her up at the airport the following Saturday. Bob had purchased her non-refundable ticket and expected her home then. That really didn't sit well with Dad. I knew this would not be the last time either Aunt Winifred or I would hear him talk of this.

Two days later, I made an appointment with the probate court to start the paperwork toward Dad's guardianship. Oh, how I trembled as I talked to the probate registrar! I shook so much I thought I was going to be sick standing there in front of her. I gave her a list of all his relatives so she could contact them about this action. Then she really shocked me by stating an officer of the probate court would have to serve Dad with the papers of this pending action.

At that moment, she realized how shaken I had become and asked if I was all right. I said, "Just give me a couple of seconds so I can take a couple of deep breaths and go on." I told her not to process the papers until Friday of the following week. I needed to talk to my lawyer before the papers were served. I didn't tell her what a coward I was. I needed to get both Aunt Winifred and myself out of town before he was served. He would be over the moon with this, and I didn't want either of us to be there. I had to apprise Shelley about this forthcoming situation as well. As I left, the shakes and nausea hit me like a ton of bricks again.

I needed to talk to someone.

"Oh, Lord, help me. I am so scared and need to feel you are with me to help me through this situation. Be with me; let me feel your presence; keep me on the path I need to be on; protect me from harm. Just stay with me and help me through this. I ask this in your name. Amen."

I drove directly to Larry's office to discuss the next steps. Once Dad was served, a court date would be set. Pat and Steve would also attend in their capacities. He would represent me in court; I didn't need to be there. He felt the accident and his doctor's report would be all the judge would need to rule in this case.

We discussed the great responsibility I was taking on for Dad's physical, emotional, and environmental needs. Was I sure I wanted to continue with this? I explained Jerry's involvement and how I feared what he would do to Dad financially and emotionally if Dad wasn't protected.

He reminded me of what Pat and Steve had told me: keep a record journal of every talk I had with Dad, the nursing staff, doctors, any legal and financial discussions with Pat and Steve, and anyone who had anything to do with Dad. This way I had ready access to any information the judge or the court might ask of me. I would also need it for my annual report to the court.

At that point, I made calls to Pat and Steve, telling them the paperwork had commenced and would be processed the following Friday. I also alerted Shelley at Kimberly Nursing Group to the coming situation. She would have a psychiatric nurse on duty that entire day to help deal with the situation.

Still shaking as I left Larry's office, I returned home. Dad questioned me about my whereabouts, and I said I had had a meeting with Pat. I realized I should have told him I had gone shopping or anything else.

He was livid and said, "Why did you go without me? What did you two discuss behind my back?" he bellowed. I lied, saying Pat had concerns about some questionable bills that had come in to him.

"Well, he could have asked me about them!" Dad angrily said. I said that was true, but we just needed to talk. Any talk with him at this point was pointless. I attempted to change the subject to get his mind off what I had done. I fixed Dad a drink to calm his nerves and relax him while I fixed dinner. By the end of dinner, he had forgotten about my trip without him.

The next morning, Maria, one of the nurses, told me Shelley wanted to talk to me. That phone call would shake me to the core! After our discussion about the pending suit the day before and discussing it with her staff, Sophia and Maria had told her Dad had threatened them with bodily harm or he would jump off his balcony. He told them he had a gun and would use it on them if they didn't leave. Fortunately, they had been able to get his mind off that and onto other things, settling him down. She asked if he had any guns in the apartment. I had to tell her he did and I would dispose of it that afternoon. I felt sure he didn't remember the combination to his hall closet safe, but I couldn't take the chance. Some of his long-term memory was intact and accurate, so I needed to make sure he didn't harm the nurses. What I didn't divulge to her was he had three hunting rifles that he kept in his clothes closet. He hadn't mentioned them since moving, so I didn't think he remembered them, but I didn't know. They had to be taken out of the apartment.

After lunch, I asked Aunt Winifred to take Dad for a long walk around the pool area. I told her I had to do something and Dad couldn't be here when I did it. She looked deeply concerned. I said, "I will explain it to you later. It will be okay, but I need about fifteen to twenty minutes without Dad around." She said she could do that for me.

She found Dad in his study and asked if he would like to go for a walk with her. He was delighted, like he was getting out of prison. Sitting on the living room sofa pretending to be reading, I told them to have a good time. Off they went. I asked the Lord to help me with this task. I didn't know how to handle guns, and I didn't know if any of the four guns were loaded. I just had to trust the Lord, praying he would protect me in this. First, I went to the safe and retrieved his handgun and bullets. I wrapped the gun in a towel, then the boxes of shells, placing them in a small overnight case. Thinking about it now, how did I ever think the towel or the overnight case would stop a bullet if the gun went off? Once they were secure, I found his three hunting rifles tucked in the back of his bedroom closet and retrieved them.

Now I had another dilemma. How could I conceal them so I could get all the rifles and the small suitcase past the security cameras in the hallway and onto the elevator and then into Dad's basement storage unit? I couldn't let the security people know what I was doing. All of a sudden, I noticed Dad's traveling golf bag cover. It was just the right height and size. Again, with all the courage I could muster, I put the three weapons in the golf bag and zipped it up. From there, I went into the kitchen and rummaged in his junk drawer until I found the storage unit keys.

Armed with the key, suitcase, and golf bag, I left the apartment and rode the elevator down the twelve floors to the basement. As I entered the basement, I became aware of the security cameras, but I walked calmly to his unit. Putting the key into the lock, I hoped it opened the cage. Fortunately, it did without a hitch. I quickly placed the guns behind some storage boxes where he would never find them if he ever realized the guns were gone. With a quick step,

I exited the cage and relocked the unit. Unless he remembered this basement storage unit, he would never find his guns. What relief I felt leaving the storage area! The Lord had provided protection for me so none of the guns fired, hurting me or someone else.

"Thank you, Lord. You are awesome in your help and protection to and for me. Your being in my life has matured me into who I am today. Thank you, Lord, from the bottom of my heart and being. Without you I would be nothing. Amen."

By the time Aunt Winifred and Dad returned from their walk, I was back on the sofa reading a book. He never knew I was gone. I would have loved a cold glass of chardonnay to calm my nerves, but he would have asked why I was drinking in the early afternoon.

After his walk, Dad was tired, wanting a short nap before dinner. This gave me time to explain to Aunt Winifred what had been going on in the last few months. I told her of his dementia problem, his doctor's advice, the car accident and its ramifications, Abbey North refusing to let him live there, and the apartment complex stipulating he had to have twenty-four-hour care for him if he came back. She hadn't known any of this. I thanked her for taking Dad on a walk, as I needed to get his guns out of the apartment. She couldn't believe he would threaten the nurses but understood my need to get them out of his way. Finally, I told her of the legal action I was taking to protect Dad from Jerry. The action incorporated becoming Dad's legal guardian. She agreed this would be in his best interest. Oh, how relieved I was that she understood.

The rest of the week flew by, giving us a lovely time together. Thinking I could spare Dad the legal proceedings by having him come live with us, I talked to Dr. Guida once again. He reiterated that changing his environment would only worsen his limited mental capacity. He strongly urged me to reconsider taking him with me. I just sat there shaking and softly crying, thinking how helpless Dad seemed and concerned about what was going to happen to him on Friday when he was served with the guardianship hearing papers.

Thursday morning, Dad pleaded with Aunt Winifred to stay and take care of him, but she firmly told him she couldn't do that. After a tearful good-bye, I drove both Aunt Winifred and myself to the airport for our flights home. Oh, the guilt and sadness that surrounded me. I wished I could take him home with me.

I called that night, knowing he would be upset. I tried to soothe him as best I could. He asked when I was coming back, and I said in a few weeks to make it sound better and more encouraging. He told me Eileen, Jerry, and Jim had stopped by and spent some time with him. Since Aunt Winifred and I were gone, they proceeded to discuss the possibility of their taking care of him, giving him false hopes.

Friday morning, I alerted Pat to their visit. Pat told me Eileen and Jim had just left his office, telling him of their plans to take care of Dad. Dad could be there by himself during the day, and then one of them would stay with him during the night in case he needed something. They expected to be paid for their time. Pat sensed from Jerry's previous discussion with him he was the mastermind behind this venture, even though he hadn't come with them. Pat sidestepped the issue, as he knew the guardianship hearing papers would be issued today. He didn't mention any of this to them, as he didn't want another problem with the hearing looming in the background.

All day I paced the house like a "Cat on Hot Tin Roof." Nothing could rid me of my worst fears and guilt. I knew I was doing the right thing, but that didn't alleviate my foreboding feelings. That evening, I called him. Mad wasn't the word. A volcanic eruption would have created less sound than the anger in his voice and words. This, by far, was worse than the night I wanted to go to the movie with Grandmother Hamilton.

"How dare you say that I can't take care of myself? I can take care of myself. You certainly don't have that right. Why did you and Winifred conspire against me? How could you do this to me? You're not my daughter anymore. I don't ever want to see you again."

I knew he was hurt, scared, and angry, but hurt was the worst of it. I knew I deserved every bit of his wrath, but I felt I had done it for his own good. I would wait it out.

For days when I called he refused to talk to me. This was not good. How could I attend to his needs as I legally would need to if he wouldn't even talk to me? I called Pat and explained the situation, which he agreed was not good. Dad had been in a couple of times, ranting and raving about what I had done to him. Pat and I had hoped things would change, but as of now they hadn't, leaving me with deep concerns.

A couple of days later, the Lord intervened in this situation. Dad had been in his office that morning to get his weekly allowance. During his visit, Dad had waved around the guardianship hearing papers, telling him what a hideous, selfish, ungrateful daughter I was. While Dad was there, Pat asked him if he could look at the papers to see what could be done. When Pat had the guardianship papers, Pat turned the discussion to some financial issue to get his mind off me. Without Dad noticing, Pat swiftly put the papers in his desk drawer. After finishing their discussion, Dad left, not remembering the papers he'd given Pat.

That afternoon, Pat called and told me what had transpired in his office with Dad. I couldn't believe he got them away from Dad. Pat suggested I wait a day or two and then call to say hello. I needed to know if he remembered the guardianship papers. Two days later I called when I knew he had had his dinner. What a turnaround! He was loving and thoughtful. He asked how the boys were, how Ron's work was, and how my schoolwork was going. I explained I had completed my bachelor's degree and graduated two weeks before. He seemed sad that he hadn't been there for it. I couldn't believe the change. The Lord had changed his mind and heart toward me.

"Thank you, Lord. You have been with me through all of this, and led me out of this valley of darkness. Thank you, thank you. Amen "

A week later, the guardianship hearing was held. Judge Robert O'Hare listened to the police report from Dad's car accident and Dr. Guida's report about Dad's mental capacity. At that point the judge asked him some basic questions: "What day is it? How old are you? What did you eat for breakfast? When and where were you born?" He couldn't answer any of his questions. Pat, Steve, Larry, Shelley, and Sophia, his morning nurse, were in attendance. Eileen and

Jerry attended the hearing but said nothing, just wanting to hear the judge's ruling.

Things went smoothly until one morning late in May. Tom, one of the apartment front-door security guards, called to tell me Dad had come down alone and had talked to him. On top of it, he seemed confused by his surroundings.

I said, "Tom, did he say why he was alone?"

Tom said he didn't seem to know why. "Now that I think about it, he seemed drugged," Tom said, quite concerned about Dad.

I asked, "How can that be? A nurse was to be with him at all times."

Tom said, "Yes, I know. I hate to tell you, but Maria, the night nurse, signed in at eight last night, left at eleven, then signed back in at six this morning. I have a record of it, Mrs. Hurley. She didn't want Sophia to know she hadn't been there all night."

I answered, "Both you and I know he has to have twenty-four-hour care."

Tom said, "Yes, but he was alone for seven hours while she went on a date or something. She must have given him something strong to make him sleep until she returned."

I was fit to be tied. I thanked him for calling me and told him I would fly down immediately and take care of this. "Don't say anything to anyone, especially the nurses. I want them and the service caught unaware. This won't do," I replied. He agreed and said he hated to call but was really concerned about Dad. I told Tom I was so grateful he did. He could have saved Dad from a real catastrophe.

I called Delta immediately and booked the one-o'clock flight to Florida. Upon landing I called Kimberly Nursing Group, telling Shelley I needed to see her immediately. She said she would stay until I came in. I didn't discuss the reason for my visit, but she knew something was wrong. Within fifteen minutes I was on my way to see her.

When I arrived at her office, she ushered me in. I explained Tom's call and asked for an explanation. She denied that could have happened. I explained that everyone who entered and left the building—including the nurses—must sign in and out; the security guard then placed the times in and out next to the person's name. He had the log for the previous night's signing out and this morning's return documented in black-and-white. She would look into it. I said, "If this is the way your nurses take care of patients, then I need to find a new service, one that I can trust to take care of my father." She said she would get back to me.

From there, I drove straight to Dad's apartment. Again, he didn't recognize me. Once he heard my voice, he was overjoyed to have me there. He did seem a little out of it but not as bad as Tom had told me. The following day, Shelley called to tell me she had talked to security and learned Maria had left Dad alone for seven hours. Maria finally admitted she had given him some sleeping pills so she could go out on a date. I told her how furious I was, as he could have gone out his balcony and fallen over or he could have taken the elevator to the basement become disoriented and unable to find his way back to his apartment. He could have been lost and frightened for hours. This would only increase his agitated state, thereby making him more belligerent and difficult to work with. Shelley told me she had suspended her without pay for two weeks. I told her I didn't want Maria on his case again. She said she would work it out, but Dad knew her and worked well with her, which was a plus. I acquiesced but said this could never happen again. She agreed and would keep better tabs on the situation.

I spent a long weekend with him, as graduation was over and all I was doing was sending out applications for fall teaching positions. Since most non-returning teachers didn't resign until the summer vacation was over in order to keep their benefits, schools couldn't make new staff decisions until early August. I had time to send out my résumé and transcripts to various districts.

Dad and I enjoyed each other's company. I took him shopping. We ate out a couple of times or just sat and watched television, walked the malls or beach, or whatever. What a great four days.

In July, Ron surprised me with a Caribbean cruise for my graduation. We had a fabulous time. When we returned to Miami, we decided that rather than flying directly home we would spend a couple of days with Dad for his eighty-second birthday. He couldn't believe we were there and welcomed us in with open arms. "What are you doing here?" he asked. I told him Ron had surprised me with a graduation cruise and then we decided to stop in and spend his birthday with him. He was thrilled. After dinner, the three of us just talked the night away.

The following day, we took Dad to pick out his birthday gift. He loved watching television and sometimes took a nap in his uncomfortable loveseat. Ron and I had decided to get him a recliner so he could watch his television shows and take a nap if he wanted. After driving him to a nearby furniture store, he looked quizzically at us when we took him inside. We explained we wanted to get him a recliner so he could relax while he watched television or even took a nap.

He said jokingly, "I don't nap while watching TV."

I returned, "Well, if you ever wanted to, we want something nice and comfortable for you to do it in." We checked out all possible choices. He fell in love with a soft, chocolate corduroy recliner. We bought it. The store would deliver it the following morning.

We had a wonderful, long weekend with him. We took him out to his favorite restaurant, Seawatch, for his birthday. After dinner, we sang "Happy Birthday" while we served him his favorite: chocolate cake and vanilla ice cream. He looked like a little boy enjoying the limelight of a special party.

Unfortunately, both Ron and I noticed how he had aged due to the toil of his dementia. The light once in his eyes had dimmed, and he looked so frail. He no longer was the dynamo he had been before Mother's death. It was so sad to see what was happening to him. Not only as Dr. Guida had told me he had a different mind; now his body was frail also. He sadly remembered the good times and birthdays he had had with Mother, and I just wanted to cry seeing him missing her so. I wanted to take him in my arms and make everything all right for him, but that could never be. Against my will, a tear fell from my cheek; fortunately, he never noticed it. The doctors and court had said this was his life now.

On our way back to the airport, I stopped in to see Pat to check on how Dad's finances were holding out with his medical care. Pat stated, "The money is holding. Nothing to worry about unless something catastrophic happens, which neither of us believe will happen. Just know all is being done for your dad. If there is something to do, I will call you." Nothing had to be done with the court or Judge O'Hare, as all my reports had been filed and recorded.

Little did I know when we left for home that that would be the last time we'd see him in his apartment. Things were moving that were completely beyond my control. The winds of change had begun. Within a month, the change would be evident to all around Dad

Life Changes Come Swiftly

"I lift up my eyes to the hills—where does my
help come from? My help comes from the Lord,
the Maker of heaven and earth."

(Psalm 121:1–2)

I called Dad on my birthday; our birthdays were only nine days apart. Dad told me how comfortable his chair was; he even wanted to sleep in it at night. I said, "Napping there is okay, but for a good, restful sleep, you need to be in your own bed." He assured me he would do that, since the "girls" wouldn't let him do it anyway.

The following Wednesday afternoon, I received a call from Dr. Guida's office telling me Dad was there. I asked why. Maria had brought Dad into his office, as he was complaining of stomach pains. By the time they arrived, he was doubled over in pain. Dr. Guida checked him and realized the abdominal aneurysm had burst. He called an ambulance and sent Dad and Maria on their way to the Holy Cross Hospital. Dr. Guida's nurse explained the hospital would be calling for authority to perform the necessary surgery to close the aneurysm. Within minutes, Holy Cross Hospital called for that authorization. I told them to do everything they needed to do to save him.

"Oh, Lord, be with Dad during this time and surgery. Give the surgeons the wisdom and skill to know what to do for him. Heal him if that is your plan for him. Keep him as pain free as possible, and let the recovery time be swift. Watch over Ron and me as we fly to him. Oh, Lord, be with all of us. Help us to be calm and reassured that all that is being done for him will be within your doing. I ask this in Jesus Christ's name. Amen."

I called Ron immediately and explained the situation to him. He called my friendly airline, Delta, making reservations for us on the first plane going to Ft. Lauderdale. After calling both the boys at their jobs and apprising them of their grandfather's pending emergency surgery, I told them we were flying there as soon as possible. They both told us to take it easy and let them know we had arrived safely and how Grandpa was doing.

I quickly packed a few things for us and then drove to pick Ron up before heading to the Detroit Metro Airport for our afternoon flight. The only flight we could get had an hour layover in Atlanta, Delta's hub, before flying on to Ft. Lauderdale. While we waited for our second flight, I called the nurses' station for information about Dad. All they could tell me was he was still in surgery and it could take another hour or so. I told them we would be there about midnight. She told me she would let security know so that we could be admitted not only to the hospital but to intensive care.

About eleven thirty, our Delta wheels touched the ground with a thud, and then the pilot reversed the plane's engines, slowing us down so he could taxi us to the passenger walkway. As quickly as possible, we raced to our rental car. After throwing our small overnight bag into the backseat, we sped to Holy Cross Hospital. God must have been with us, as we arrived quickly without any police involvement. We told the security guard who we were, and he let us in and then gave us directions to intensive care.

Just as we arrived there, the head nurse reported that Dad was coming up from recovery. He had had a rough time and was heavily sedated. He wouldn't be awake, but we could see him for a minute. She told us to go to the waiting room so they could get him into bed, cleaned up, and hooked up to their monitors. She said after we saw him we should go home and get some rest before returning in the morning. She would keep us posted, especially if there were any changes. I thanked her.

About a half hour later, she returned and took us to see him. Oh, how pale he was. He looked like he had been hit by a huge Mac truck. I wanted to hold him and surround him with my love. As I began talking to him, his blood pressure skyrocketed so much they had to administer more sedatives to him. His surgical nurse explained that he had heard my voice and wanted to wake up to see me. She told me, "You better not talk to him anymore, as a raised blood pressure would do more harm than good, especially this soon after surgery."

She again told us to go home and get some rest. She would be on all night and let us know of any changes, good or bad. I once again thanked her. I gave Dad a kiss on the forehead and cheek, took Ron's hand, and tearfully left.

I prayed as we walked to the elevator, "Lord, this is a monumental evening for both Dad and me. I am filled with all kinds of fears and concerns. Dad is my last family member, and I love him. I don't want him to die if at all possible. I know his quality of life isn't what I want for him, but it is the way it has to be for him to be safe and taken care of. I want to hear his voice and tell him I love him. I want more time with him. Please keep him as pain free as possible and help him recover from this surgery. Keep him cradled in your loving arms throughout the long night that lay ahead. Lord, do all that's possible to help him and bring him back to us. I know you have a plan for him as well as me, and that will always override my prayers. I hand him and his care over to you. Please take care of him through this long night and the rest of his life, whatever that may be. In all things I ask this in Jesus's name. Amen."

About nine o'clock the next morning, Ron and I entered the intensive care unit where a nurse stopped us, asking who we were. I explained that I was James Hamilton's daughter and wanted to see him. She said his doctors were examining him and it would take a few minutes before they would finish, so we needed to wait in the visitors' room.

Shortly after, Dr. Ross, the surgeon, came out to talk to us. Dad had come through the surgery remarkably well, but he still had a long way to recovery. He would keep him heavily sedated to hold the pain threshold as low as possible. I could talk to him, but he probably wouldn't respond. Dr. Ross would be watching for blood clots, blood circulation in the stomach and extremities, and any signs of infection or pneumonia, as these could bring fatal results. Dad would remain in ICU until he was stable and out of danger. Oh, how pale and frail he looked. I could tell the surgery had taken a lot out of him physically as well as emotionally. He was hooked up to so many monitors and machines that I could only brush the hair off his forehead and then give him a kiss. As I began to talk to him, his blood pressure began to rise, and nurses came in to check the monitors for inconsistent numbers. Since Dr. Ross hadn't left the hospital, they paged him to see what he wanted done with Dad. He checked Dad, saying he again was responding to my voice, hoping to regain consciousness to be with me. This couldn't happen. They needed to keep him in a controlled state of unconsciousness in order to keep his pain level as low as possible. Dr. Ross immediately ordered more sedation to be added to his IV bag with additional doses given as needed. Dad settled down almost immediately.

"Oh, how long will he have to remain this way?" Dr. Ross didn't give me a definite answer, except that when his pain level diminished he would let him come out. My inner cry was, "I need you, Dad. Just get well quickly." Ron and I sat the rest of the morning with him in silence.

All of a sudden it dawned on me that I hadn't contacted Pat with the news about Dad. Concern filled our conversation. He wanted to come, but I told him that wouldn't be possible, as only family could visit. I would keep him abreast about his progress. I didn't know how long he would be in intensive care or the hospital, and I would be here until Dad came home. Pat asked if there was anything he could do. All of a sudden, I thought he needed to call Shelley and tell her not to send any of the nurses for the foreseeable future. We would call them when we could reinstate them. I also called Eileen to tell her of Dad's condition. She was shocked.

That afternoon, one of the nurses, a big, burly one, came in to see me while I sat with Dad. She told me from her experience Dad wouldn't survive this ordeal, and I should consider taking him off life support and let him go. Horror filled me that she could be so brazen and unfeeling. I internally called her "Mrs. Nasty." I told her I wouldn't do that. He was my father, and I wanted him to get better. She told me I was just prolonging his suffering.

I said, "Excuse me, but I think you have said enough. I want you to leave now. This is not your decision, and I don't appreciate your 'words of wisdom.'"

Shaken by Mrs. Nasty's words, I needed to get away. Ron suggested we eat something since we hadn't eaten anything since our morning toast and tea. Driving down the street, he spied his favorite place, McDonald's. We went inside for a Quarter Pounder, fries, and coke. It felt good to get away for a moment, although I felt uneasy leaving Dad in that woman's care.

When we returned, the evening nursing staff was coming on and getting their instructions. Relieved that Mrs. Nasty was leaving, I went in to see Dad. Nothing had changed. As Ron and I sat there, Mrs. Cummings, Dad's new nurse, came in and introduced herself to us. I felt her warmth and care surround all of us. I just felt encouraged by her presence and knew she would take good care of Dad.

"Thank you, Lord. You are an awesome God. You heard my prayers and concerns and sent Mrs. Cummings to us. Thank you, thank you. Amen."

About eleven o'clock that evening, Ron and I left Dad in her good hands. On the way back to Dad's apartment, we picked up some chicken and a salad for our supper. We sat holding each other for a long time before getting into bed for some much-needed rest. We didn't know it then, but we would need to be rested for the morning's news.

As Ron and I came into the intensive care unit the following morning, the nurse on Dad's duty said Dr. Ross had just seen Dad and needed to talk to me. I asked if he was still in the hospital or if I needed to call him. She said she would page him and see if he was still in the hospital. Within minutes, he came to see me. He explained the circulation in Dad's legs had slowed considerably during the night, especially in the right one, which had almost no blood circulation. He needed to go in and clean out the blockage(s), or he Dad could lose one or both legs.

This news threw me into a spiraling tailspin. I asked what other alternatives he could recommend so Dad didn't have to undergo additional surgery. He had just gone through major abdominal surgery fewer than thirty-six hours before. He told us it was necessary to do this not only to save Dad's leg(s), but possibly his life. The circulation problem had to be rectified, or he would die. I looked at Ron, and we both agreed that if this was the only way to save Dad, it had to be done. I gave Dr. Ross the authorization to proceed. I couldn't believe what was happening. This frightened me, as I could lose my Dad with or without the proposed surgery. What else could I do? Things for Dad were going downhill fast, and there was nothing I could do about it but pray.

"Oh, Lord, here I come to you again with another hurdle to overcome. Please be with Dad as he undergoes this surgical procedure. Keep him in your loving and caring hands. Keep him as pain-free as possible. Help him as he struggles back to health if at all possible. Help me to cope with whatever happens to him. Help me accept your outcome and will for him. In all things, I ask this in Christ's name. Amen."

About four hours later, I learned he was in recovery. Another hour passed, and finally, Dr. Ross came to tell us things had gone as well as could be expected. He had been able to open up the leg arteries, giving him the blood circulation he needed. He might need additional surgery if the circulation slowed again. "Oh, I certainly hope this does the trick," I said to Dr. Ross. He didn't look as hopeful as I wanted him to be. I thanked him as he left to check on another patient. I didn't realize how emotionally drained I was since Dr. Guida's call to alert me of Dad's problem. I collapsed into the chair behind me and just started crying and wishing all this would go away but knowing that was impossible.

I hadn't noticed while we were waiting for Dad's return that Mrs. Nasty had come on duty. Approaching us, she told us that this was an additional sign Dad wouldn't survive and it was time to let him go. We both asked her to leave and not mention this again to either of us. I planned to talk to her supervisor if she didn't stop this talk.

Coming into Dad's room, we noticed how much paler and pained he looked since he left for surgery. All I could do was run out of his room so he wouldn't hear me sobbing at what I saw. Once I got control of myself, I returned to his cubical and kissed his forehead. He felt warm and sweaty. Oh, how my heart went out to him. I kept thinking *How could I have put him through another surgery? He is so fragile and is suffering so. Oh, God, help me deal with what I have put him through.*

We stayed with him the remainder of the afternoon and evening. I wouldn't leave his side even to eat. My thoughts of Dad consumed me.

About ten o'clock, the nurses shooed us out, saying there was nothing we could do for him. They said, "Go, get some rest, and eat something so you don't get sick yourselves. That won't do your dad any good. You need to be healthy to care for him." I agreed that I didn't want that, as I needed to be there for Dad; we took their advice and left for home. They would take good care of him and advise us of any changes.

Returning to the apartment, I found some eggs, tomatoes, and bacon in his fridge, along with some sliced bread in the pantry, and proceeded to make us sandwiches for dinner. It was good to be doing something positive, as there was nothing I could do at the hospital other than watch Dad, his monitors, and pray. We watched the late-evening news and then turned in for what would become another restless, sleepless night. It was good to stretch out, though, and just relax a bit.

When we arrived the next morning in the intensive care unit, we found additional bad news from Dad's monitors. His heart rate, pressure, temperature, and other bodily indicators were slowly but diligently decreasing. At eleven, I saw Dr. Guida, who broke additional bad news to me. Things were not good and wouldn't get better. He didn't expect him to survive the week. Stunned, I fell backward into Ron as he caught me. I figured he—of all the doctors—would give me some positive news, but that wasn't the case. He told me to brace myself for what was to come and call him anytime I needed to talk. I said I would.

Again, Mrs. Nasty voiced her opinion about Dad. I told her I had had enough of her opinions and if she didn't stop bothering me, I would report her to her supervisor and to the hospital administration. I wondered how many other patients' relatives had had the same treatment from her as we had. I hoped that would put an end to her. With that, she stayed out of my sight for a while.

"Oh, Lord, help me deal with this nurse who continually is saying I need to let Dad go. She is a real thorn in my side. If Dad is to go, please don't let her be on duty. Please have Mrs. Cummings to be with him and us at that time. She is so caring. Please grant this request, dear heavenly Father. In all things I will accept your will, even if it is hard. Amen."

As the morning progressed and the monitors revealed more dire numbers, I called Eileen and explained Dad's situation, the monitor readings, and his bodily functions decreasing steadily. If she and Jim wanted to see him before he passed, they needed to come as soon as possible, as I didn't think he would make it through the day or night. She said she would see. I thought it strange, especially since she and Jerry had proposed taking care of him with Pat. I hoped she and Jim would come, as they hadn't been to see him for several weeks prior to his entering the hospital.

By two o'clock, the monitors became more and more ominous. I asked Ron to go to the apartment, get Dad's navy blue suit, and take it to the cleaners, as he would need it soon. Ron was puzzled by my request. I explained that the numbers on Dad's monitors told me. Dad's time with us was very limited. He would need his favorite suit cleaned for his burial. Ron had difficulty realizing what I was telling him. He got up then and asked me if I wanted him to bring me anything back; a sandwich, coffee, or anything to eat. I said, "No, I couldn't eat anything. You have something if you want, I am not hungry." After I kissed him good-bye, Ron left on his errand.

Hovering but staying away from me, Mrs. Nasty had no intention of coming near me after our talk. Again, I prayed Dad wouldn't die with her around. We both needed someone gentle and comforting. Watching the monitors, his respiration, and blood pressure numbers continue to slide more quickly now, I prayed that Mrs. Cummings would be here with us when he died.

About three o'clock, still in prayer and paying total attention to Dad, I was unaware of the changing of the nursing staffs. A little later, Mrs. Cummings came in to check Dad. After taking one look at the monitors closing in on single digits, she gently and softly said to me, "I know you know his time is close. Go into the waiting room and let me clean him up. Once I have taken care of him, I will come and get you so you can spend what limited time he has with you." She asked where Ron was, and I explained he was taking Dad's suit to the cleaner, and she nodded.

About the same time, a terrific thunderstorm began. The sky had begun to darken as well, but I really hadn't taken much note of it. I kept watching for Ron so he could say his last good-bye as well. By now, I figured Eileen and Jim weren't coming. That upset me, but I couldn't do anything about that, as my focus had to be on Dad and the little time we had remaining.

Mrs. Cummings came for me, and we walked back to his room. Silently, she left. Sitting close to him, I grasped his hand, wanting him to know I was there for him as he took his final journey. As the numbers dropped ever lower, I put my head to his and told him it was okay for him to go and be with Mother, Ruth, and Jim. He had fought the good fight, and now it was time for him to be with them without pain. I told him how much I loved him and that I would miss him dearly. A sob or two came out, which I knew he wouldn't like, as he hated any show of emotion. Oh, how he detested it; but he was my Dad, I loved him, and now he was leaving me forever. This hurt to the base of my heart and soul.

As his numbers finally got to ten, I said good-bye and talked him through his last journey across the beautiful bridge to Mother, Ruth, and Jim, who were waiting to welcome him home. Lastly, I told him I would miss him, but I knew he needed to go and be out of his pain. Someday we would see each other and give each other big hugs. "Good-bye, Dad."

With that, the monitors above and around him signaled his demise. Mrs. Cummings came in and turned them off. She said, "I'll give you a few minutes alone with him before we need to move him out. You will need to tell us the funeral home that will be taking care of his arrangements." All I could do was sob. My dad was gone!

At that moment, I looked out his window; the storm had subsided, and in its place I saw the most beautiful rainbow in the sky. I knew God was telling me Dad had made it safely home. I thanked him for taking him easily. He just stopped breathing. He had no pain at all at the end.

"Thank you, God. You are awesome."

After I had said my good-bye, Mrs. Cummings came in and steadied me so I could walk to the waiting room.

"Would you like some coffee?" she asked.

"Thank you, but no thank you," I softly said.

About fifteen minutes later, Ron returned and saw me in the waiting room.

He asked, "Why aren't you with Dad?"

I said, "Dad is gone. He left us about fifteen minutes ago." The shocked look on his face rocked me, as I saw the tears in his eyes. He hadn't been able to say his good-bye. It wasn't until much later that I told him I really believed the Lord had sent the thunderstorm so that Dad and I would be alone for those special last moments so I could walk him home. Again, I saw God's work in Dad's and my life.

"Thank you, Lord. You are so wonderful and caring."

The hospital staff asked what funeral home Dad would be sent to. I told them Fannin Funeral Home, where Mother had been laid out, and Dad wanted the same as Mother. They would call Fannin and have his body transferred to them within the next couple of hours. We called them to make an appointment to see Mr. Fannin at ten the following morning.

As we were leaving the intensive care unit, I thanked Mrs. Cummings for all she had done for Dad and for helping me with Dad's last moments of life. She was a true treasure of care, support, and love; a real gift from God. I don't think I could have gotten through the afternoon without her.

Ron drove me to a nearby Denny's restaurant since I hadn't eaten anything other than coffee since the previous night's egg, bacon, and tomato sandwich. Ron ordered sandwiches and cokes for both of us. He ate his, and I just shuffled mine around the plate. I did drink my coke, which gave me some energy and calmed my stomach. Ron kept talking to me, but my mind was in another world. He could have been talking about dog meat and it wouldn't have registered with me.

After we arrived at Dad's, Ron and I placed the sad calls to Ron and John telling them of their grandfather's passing. You could hear and feel the sadness they felt through that telephone wire. They dearly cared about their grandfather. We told them not to come to Florida, as they were both working, but to drive down to Huntington for the funeral. They told us how sorry they were and hoped we were okay. We said we were doing all right. It had been a rough day, but he died peacefully, which was a blessing. They asked about Eileen and Jim, and we said we had not seen them.

After talking to the boys, we called Ron's sister Judy to tell her about Dad's passing. She said she couldn't come to the funeral, as she couldn't get time off from work. Then I called Eileen, who was shocked by the news. I told her we were making his funeral arrangements at ten o'clock in the morning if she wanted to be a part of it. She said to just let her know of the arrangements.

After regaining some composure, I called Pat to tell him of Dad's death. The news crushed him, as he and Dad had great respect for each other. They had known each other for over ten years. I felt sorry for him. I told him to relay the message to Steve. I told him we would be taking Dad to Huntington for his funeral and interment next to Mother. The Florida visitation would be the following night. He asked if Eileen and Jim had visited him, and I said no.

The next day, we met with Fred Fannin and picked out a casket identical to Mother's. He would see to all the arrangements for Dad's death certificates, death notice in the *Fort Lauderdale Herald* with the visitation times, Dad's plane ticket and shipping papers, and billing receipts. He told me he would contact Honaker's Funeral Home in Huntington and arrange for them to pick Dad up, take him to the funeral home, put his death announcement in the *Huntington Herald Dispatch*, and any other items that needed to be done. I would arrange for Reverend Robert Thomas of Trinity Episcopal Church in Huntington to perform the funeral service and burial rights. I told Mr. Fannin I would bring Dad's clothes and suit in later that afternoon, after we picked them up from the cleaner. He said that would be fine.

Arriving home, I called Eileen and told her the arrangements. She said she and Jim would come to the Florida viewing, but they wouldn't fly to Huntington for his funeral or interment. The following evening, Ron, Eileen, Jim, and I visited with Dad's friends we had called or who had seen the death notice. We talked about the times they spent with him and how admired he was. We laughed and cried together. The bittersweet evening flowed smoothly and was over before we knew it. Ron and I said good-bye to Eileen and Jim and returned to Dad's.

We packed our suitcase. Again, we waited for sleep to overcome us and give us some much-needed rest.

The morning came swiftly, and we headed for the airport for our ten-o'clock flight to Cincinnati and then shuttle to Huntington. Dad had to go in a cargo plane through Baltimore, just as Mother had. We took the cheaper flight through Cincinnati.

After registering at the Radisson Downtown Huntington, I called the funeral home. All was in readiness for his nine-o'clock arrival.

The minister presented a problem. Reverend Thomas was vacationing, but the church would contact St. John's Episcopal Church to see if Reverend Collingsworth would perform the burial and interment services. None of us had ever met him.

About four that afternoon, Ron and John arrived and registered into our adjoining room. Oh, how good it was to see them. Lots of hugs, kisses, and tears ensued. The funeral home called in the morning, saying all was ready for the visitation that evening. They wondered if we had been able to contact a minister for the services. I told them Reverend Collingsworth would officiate and gave them his phone number if they needed to contact him.

The rest of the day, we drove around showing the boys Marshall University, where Ron received his bachelor's degree and where we met. Young Ron had also attended Marshall. We drove past the house where I lived on Enslow Boulevard as a teenager. We lunched at the old Stewart's Hot Dog and Root Beer Stand, where Ron and I always went when we were dating. Stewart's had been and still was a hallmark of the community and university life for almost fifty years. Later that afternoon, we all went to Honaker's to check on Dad and the arrangements. The visitation would begin at six and finish at nine. Dad looked good, but I still had trouble seeing him in his coffin. The boys were weepy and overcome at one point but were able to shake it off, as they thought it wasn't the manly thing to do. I said it was okay for them to show their feelings for their grandfather.

Six o'clock came quickly. We met with some of Dad's friends and business associates before the visitation time had finished.

The next morning Reverend Collingsworth conducted a lovely funeral service, and then we drove to the Abbey of Remembrance for the graveside service. Afterward, the mausoleum men told us they would be placing Dad in his cubicle and resetting the stone. We could go outside while they did that and then come back in to say our final good-byes. I said I would remain, as I wanted to make sure he was taken care of until his and Mother's name plate was back in place.

"If that is what you want, that's okay with us. Most people don't want to do that, as it is too emotional for them," the men said.

After all was in place and the men had left, I spent a few moments alone with Mother, Dad, Ruth, and Jim before Ron and the boys came in to say their final good-byes. Tearfully, we left arm in arm.

Later that afternoon, the boys left for home, as they had to be at work in the morning. Ron and I planned to spend the night in Huntington and then fly home to Michigan the following morning.

It felt good to be home and surrounded by all that was familiar and meaningful to me. I was home. Ron and I were both parentless now. We had lost all four parents in a period of eight years. We were the matriarch and patriarch of our families. How alone we were, but yet we were together. What a wonderful thought.

"Oh, Lord, you helped me through this painful time. Without you sustaining and comforting me, I would never have known I could be the woman you wanted me to be—caring, intelligent, and able to deal with problems with you at my side. You have given all of us your guidance, peace, comfort, and the togetherness we needed to get through these past days. Without you being with us, we would never have realized the extent of your love for us, Dad, and our family. How can we ever thank you for all your presence and the love you so generously bestow on us. Thank you for your rainbow of reassurance to let me know Dad is home with you and our family. That gives me much comfort and peace. Let Dad and the others know I am all right. I miss them, but I know one day I will see them all and then we can work out whatever differences we had. Again, thank you, heavenly Father for your love and being there for us and me. Thank you. Amen."

The Lord's voice spoke to me so gently, almost as a whisper. "Nancy, your dad is home with me, along with your mother, Ruth, Jim, and his parents. Know you did all you could do to help him through these last years of frustration, pain, and life. You had many hurdles and arrows thrown at you, but you weathered them with my help. I have always told you I am with you, love you, and you are special to me. You don't need to grieve, as he is home safe with me and family and pain free." I fully felt the Lord's presence in me. He truly loved me and wanted only the best for me. "Thank you, Lord."

Beginning Again

> "Therefore, if anyone is in Christ, he is a new creation;
> the old has gone, the new has come."
> (2 Corinthians 5:17)

Fall and school came much too quickly for me. I needed time to adjust to Dad's death, but the hope of a teaching position in our oversaturated market left me without a full-time position. Since the school districts had no teaching positions open for a first-year teacher, I began my teaching career as a substitute. I quickly learned from the timing of those early morning calls which school district and grade level I was being called to work in. Plymouth called at 5:15 in the morning for high school and 5:45 for middle school. Northville called at 5:30 for high school and 6:00 for middle school.

My nerves frayed from not knowing if I would teach or not, what I would be teaching, and how the students would accept or not accept me into their routine and classroom. After two months into this early morning drill, Sister Mary Alexander, principal of Ladywood High School, an all girls' Catholic high school in Livonia, called with an offer of a six-week substitute teaching position in English. Oh, how wonderful! My own classroom, of sorts, until the teacher returned from her medical leave. No more early calls, different daily classrooms, and students. No more students testing my limits. What a joy that was!

I had five classes: one freshman general English, a multi-grade Creative Writing, and four senior English Literature classes. The senior classes were in the midst of making Victorian hats to go with their study of Victorian prose and poetry. Some girls were clever with their designs, while others needed help designing and producing their hats. The freshman class consisted of grammar, short stories, poetry, and essays. The creative writing class kept me on my toes, trying to find innovative ways of writing. I hated to pray that Bettianne King, their teacher, wouldn't be able to return in January. I loved my job there. When Bettianne returned, I went back to the substitute pools, which became a great proving ground for practical classroom management and teaching.

I continued that winter and summer investigating other teaching opportunities. Finally, in August, I received a call from Sister Mary Alexander offering me Bettianne's position. Oh, what a blessing in more than one way! I didn't have to be in the substitute pools anymore; I had a full-time teaching position in a school where I loved working. I immediately said yes, even before I knew what classes I would be teaching. She told me I would be teaching two American literature classes, along with three junior religion classes. I thought it strange, as I wasn't a Catholic. I had taken religious training from Madonna College when I planned to go into religious education.

The Thursday before classes started, I spent a full day at a faculty get-together meeting. During the afternoon break, I talked with the chair of the religion department, mentioning I was an Episcopalian and would be teaching the junior morals class. I explained I had the training, but I still thought it strange.

Friday, bright and early, Sister Mary Alexander called me into her office. She told me she thought I was a Catholic, as I had that certain glow about me. What did that mean? Episcopalians can't glow in their love of the Lord? I reminded her I had specifically identified myself as an Episcopalian on my application. To that, she replied, since I wasn't Catholic I couldn't teach the religion classes. She would change my teaching schedule. That afternoon, she informed me I would be teaching the two junior American literature classes, along with three typing classes (my minor had been Business Education). I understood it was a Catholic school, but I was definitely not happy. There was nothing I could do; my hands were tied, as I didn't fit the criteria.

After school one day, Sister Mary Alexander caught me in the hall and asked me if I would consider being English department head. I said I was new at the school; other teachers in my department should be given first choice of this position. She told me no one else wanted the job. I thought to myself, *I have only been out of college a year, and she wants me to be department head!* She explained there was a twenty-five-dollar stipend with it. I considered it; the money wasn't important to me, but the title would look great on my résumé if I ever changed schools. I told her I would do it. That became the hardest job—no one wanted to come to department meetings or work with one another. Now I knew why no one wanted the position. Boy, was I naïve! "Oh well," I said to myself. "This is just another learning experience."

"Oh Lord, help me with this new adventure. I am going to need it."

The next five years were the best! After my first year, I taught four American literature classes as well as the prestigious advanced placement senior English. My fifth year there, Sister Mary Alexander added a basic freshman reading class. Needing more students to pay for her increasing finances, she had lowered the freshman standards to let in students with below-the-needed reading level. Some were more than a year or two behind in their reading and needed study skill training to manage the work expected of them. She knew I worked well with all learning levels and had the patience to help them along. She almost pleaded with me to take on the task.

She explained that the Livonia public school district would send a reading professional to assist me with testing materials, reading machines, and reading materials to get my program started. After the first month, Mrs. Barkley, the teacher provided to me, became less and less visible. She felt her time would be better spent helping public school students rather than parochial ones. She left me high and dry. I didn't have the training to really help these students and felt at a complete loss in this endeavor. At that moment, I knew I needed further training in how to teach reading classes if that was to be part of my teaching schedule.

At the end of the school year, I told Sister Mary Alexander of my intention to return to Eastern Michigan University to study for my master's degree in reading. At my age, I needed to go full time and finish as quickly as possible. She deeply regretted my decision and stated she couldn't hold my position for me. I told her I understood but hoped when I finished there might be a place for me at Lacywood. I asked her not to tell my students, as I wanted to do that on the last school day. She said she wouldn't.

The final school assembly came, and the seniors were eager for graduation. At announcement time, Sister Alexander had information she couldn't resist telling. Sister Rose Mary had been singled out for a journalistic position at the Vatican and would be leaving in a couple of weeks for Rome. For whatever reason, she decided to break her promise to me and announced that Mrs. Hurley would not be returning as well. After telling them, a gasp resounded through the room and then silence; you could have heard a pin drop. I had not even told my peers of my plans to return to school for my master's degree. I truly was upset with Sister for breaking her promise to me, but she wanted to blow her trumpet about Sister Rose Mary's appointment.

When the assembly was over, everyone returned to class. The atmosphere throughout my classes could be cut with a knife.

"Mrs. Hurley, please say it isn't so. Why are you doing this? Is it because you are too close and honest with us about everything that they fired you? Why? You can't leave us! You're the only one we can turn to when we need help. You're deserting us."

I even had sophomores wanting me for their American literature classes asking me to reconsider my decision and stay. I told them I couldn't. I had been accepted for the fall term, and I needed to do this. I hoped in time they would understand and forgive me.

As I readied for my leaving, I remembered the years with my students—helping them through their good times as well as their crisis times, as they had become the hallmark of who I was. I had never realized what a lifeline one of my writing assignments had become for them, as well as for me to really get to know each of my students. I required them to journal twice a week and once on the weekend in a spiral notebook about what was going on in their lives. My contract with them was what they wrote in their journals was confidential between them and me. They could write about anything, even the tough stuff. If they discussed their journal contents with anyone outside of me, that was their right, but I wouldn't divulge their contents to anyone else. They had to bring their journals daily to class, as I could and would pull them in at any time. If a student didn't turn hers in, she had no grade for that time. My practice was to pull individual classes in without notice, scan their notebooks, make comments to each girl in the margins, and then return them when I was finished. I did this usually twice during a marking period. The first year I instituted the journal, their initial entries were generic, as they didn't know if they could trust me with their inner thoughts.

After I pulled their journals in for the first time and made comments in their journal margins, they relaxed a bit. They liked reading my comments of "how did you feel about this," or "what do you plan to do about this," or "I think this is a great idea," when I returned them. As they came to trust me and my confidentiality, they wrote more deeply about themselves without realizing it. I really got to know each of my students: their hopes, dreams, joys, fears, happy and sad times, and even asking for answers to questions they felt they couldn't ask elsewhere. They even shared what they didn't feel comfortable sharing with each other. This sharing unburdened and enlightened them, as I tried to support them in whatever.

During my first year teaching at Ladywood, I had a sophomore typing student, Lisa, who seemed very insecure and at times hostile if I suggested an easier way to do an assignment that she didn't want to attempt. When she resisted, I asked if something was wrong. Her scripted answer was, "There isn't anything wrong, Mrs. Hurley." I felt something was bothering her, but she wouldn't divulge to me. Her wall thickened during the semester. Nothing could penetrate it.

The following year, I had her in one of my American literature classes. At the beginning of the semester, her journal spelled out nothing significant to me. I kept an eye on her. When her grades dropped or she seemed down, I generally pulled that class's journals in to see if anything in her journal would give me a clue to her or her problem. I did that twice before Thanksgiving. Nothing, other than generic information, did she include there. As time progressed, my concern increased. She definitely wasn't going to talk about anything.

One afternoon after Thanksgiving break, she popped into my room and revealed that her best friend had a drug problem and had been hospitalized for the second time. She almost died. Lisa's parents were giving her heat about this relationship. She planned to go with her friend to a drug twelve-step class. Her parents didn't want her doing this. This information was a major breakthrough. I suggested she talk to Mrs. McClane, the school counselor, to get some help dealing with her and her friend's situation. She refused, saying Mrs. McClane was an open pipeline to Sister Mary Alexander, who would discuss this with her parents. She didn't want that. She had enough going on in her life with her parents without adding another lecture. She thanked me for my concern and left.

For the next week or so, her burden seemed lighter, and then her grades took another nosedive. I figured more trouble. Hoping she had written about the problem, I pulled her class's journals in. I never took in only one student's journal, as the other students would wonder why I had singled out one student's journal and not all of theirs as well. To my regret, she didn't reveal anything wrong with her friend or at home, only her usual generic talk.

Just before Christmas vacation, she seemed even more distraught. After class, I quickly mentioned her friend to her; all she said was she was okay. They had begun the support classes even with her parents' displeasure. I attributed her mood to her parents.

One afternoon after the Christmas break, she came in after classes and asked if she could talk to me. I replied, "Certainly." She closed the door, meaning something major was coming. Our classroom doors were not to be closed at any time, especially with only one or two students inside with a teacher. I realized Lisa was quite upset.

She began with, "Mrs. Hurley, I lied to you."

"What do you mean you lied to me?" quickly came out of my mouth.

Her next words rocked me. "I told you before Christmas my friend was okay. I lied; she died."

Sobs wracked her body. I put my arm around her and let her weep for her friend. Her parents had made it clear that her friend wasn't the girl she should be hanging around with, and her death proved that. I could see Lisa was struggling with her parents' comments, as well as her friend's overdose and death. Her parents were right to be concerned about their friendship. They were concerned Lisa's friend Susan* (name has been changed to protect identity) would lead her down into the same drug path. Lisa, on the other side, wanted to help and even protect her friend. This turmoil was overwhelming for her. She was torn in two inside. Two loyalties of diametric opposites! As we sat together, I listened to her litany about her friend's problem and Lisa's attempt to support and bring her to rehabilitation. Unfortunately, it all ended in tragedy.

The pain of losing her best friend encompassed her. Her weeping over this grief was the beginning of her own recovery. She and I talked a number of times during the remaining months of her junior year. I told her about my dealing with the death of my sister and how it had affected me. I told her she could talk about her sadness in a safe place with me. She couldn't do this with her parents or the few friends she had at school. I was the only safe haven she had. I do believe her journal became her lifeline, as she began pouring out her various feelings.

Another junior I had another year had parent and boyfriend problems. She loved him, and her parents didn't want her to be so serious. Through her journal, she unloaded her struggle with them about her boyfriend and their dating. I tried to explain how parents only want the best for their children. Since I had been through a similar situation in high school, I helped her see she was too young to cleave to just one young man as the end all to her dreams. She needed to take a realistic look into what she wanted for her future: college or a family. Did she need him to complete her? What need was he fulfilling for her? Could she find a way of filling this need without him? I wanted her to see she had options she didn't want to face. Unfortunately for her, later that year, she found out he was dating and professing love to her as well as another girl. The devastation and the broken trust overwhelmed her. She didn't need me as well as her parents saying, "I told you so!" That, she wouldn't hear from me. I just let her talk it out so she could get on with her life. She did, but her trust level with boys was jaded now.

Sally was a boisterous, self-centered, argumentative junior. Through the year, she and I had our tussles, as I kept a strict code of manners with all my students. By the end of the year, she had settled in with other classmates and teachers, becoming an excellent student. It took patience and leading to help her unwind her behavior and move into another way of relating to and with others around her. Unfortunately, a few years later, I learned from a peer that my leaving had sent her back to her old ways, as she couldn't relate to other teachers as she had me. Sadness filled me, but there was nothing I could do.

My problem areas didn't always involve my juniors. The year before I left Ladywood, I had two students in my advanced placement senior English class. Michelle, a creative, vivacious student, and Jackie, a self-absorbed, non-imaginative student, presented me with a problem that could have wide ramifications. As with all my longer, more intricate projects, I routinely paired the students with different partners. The grade for project could incorporate up to 15 percent of their quarter grade. This particular assignment was to include a biography of a known English poet, plus a poem using his or her technique. As usual, the partners worked together, but their finished products had to be their own creations. The timeframe for this project was three weeks. We spent time in the library researching their various poets and writings; afterward, we spent time discussing the poets, their lives, and their modes of writing.

After their projects had been turned in, I spent the weekend reading and digesting their contents. I was so pleased by their insights and expanding knowledge they had gained from their studies. As my policy, I gave each girl a new number to be placed on the top of her paper in place of her name to make my grading more objective. All of a sudden, as I read one of the papers, I stopped, finding it suspiciously familiar. "Oh, it couldn't be!" I said to myself. The further I read, the more sure I was. After I finished the paper, I rifled through the others to find the one I sought. Looking at the numbers and checking them against student names, I realized Michelle and Jackie had not only worked together but had turned in the same paper. Their papers were identical, even to the crossed t's and dotted i's.

Since both girls belonged to the merit scholarship program, it was mandatory for me to consult their advisor following the weekend grading. One girl had turned her partner's work in as her own, which created a plagiarism problem. As a result, I gave both a failing grade, which would jeopardize their overall grade point averages.

Bright and early Monday morning, I went to Leah Holland, the merit scholarship advisor, asking her to read both papers and tell me what she thought. I didn't tell her the students involved. Immediately, she told me they were identical which meant involving Sr. Alexander. After she read them, she agreed with us about their identical nature and my grading.

Before returning the assignment, I told both girls in question to see me after school. I presented them with their papers. I explained, as always, that they were allowed to work together, but their final work had to be their own. Turning in one paper for both students wasn't allowed.

"But, Mrs. H., you allowed us to work together. That meant we could turn in the same work." Jackie sobbed.

I asked, "When have I ever allowed you to turn in the same work? The assignment was for you to learn about poetry and writing modes of your particular poet, even if you researched the same poet, and then write a poem using his or her writing mode."

I reminded them I never allowed two students to turn in one work to get two grades for that project. "This is a matter of plagiarism, thereby the failing grades." They sobbed as they pleaded with me.

"You can't give us failing grades; think what it will do to our grade points, Mrs. H. Please reconsider."

I told them I had already discussed this with both Mrs. Holland and Sister Alexander and all were in agreement with my grading. They left my room sobbing.

Michelle's mother called me the following morning asking for an afternoon conference. I really felt Michelle had done the work; it was so creative, something Jackie couldn't do on her own. I met with Michelle's mother. I showed her the two papers. She was upset but understood my position. Jackie's father took a totally different approach. He called Sister Alexander and made an appointment to see her, as well as Leah and me, for first thing the following morning.

The frustrated, angry father looked at the papers and unequivocally denied they were identical. He demanded I re-grade them, taking away the failing grade. He threatened legal action if I didn't change her grade to an A or if any of this information got into her school or merit scholarship records. At this point, I looked at Sister for her recommendation. Since she feared the lawsuit, she told me to re-grade the papers as separate works and give them the grades they deserved. That meant two As. I couldn't believe my ears! Two days before, she had agreed with the grades and the plagiarism. Now she had made a complete 180-degree turn to bow to this arrogant, legalistic father so not to have a lawsuit against the school. I took the papers and gave them A's, as that's what they deserved, but my respect for Sister dropped to zero.

One afternoon, just before the seniors left Ladywood's hallowed halls, Jackie left a note on my desk. In it she said she knew she had been a difficult student but she had learned much from me, especially about honesty. I hoped she had, as she would enter the University of Michigan in the fall, and plagiarism wouldn't be tolerated there. They would boot her out without a blink of an eye, even if her father threatened lawsuits. I prayed she had learned a valuable lesson in education and writing and that she would do well at the university.

The final class before my seniors graduated was bittersweet for both them and me. I presented each of them a yellow rosebud. I chose the color of yellow because it meant hope. The rosebud symbolized each of them. I explained that as a rosebud opens up, it reveals all its inner beauty for the whole world to see and marvel at, just as I wanted for them.

"You are all beauties! I only hope and wish for the best life the world has in store for you. Enjoy life, stay steadfast in the Lord in all you do, and let him lead you in whatever you do. Ask for his help and guidance for each step along life's journey. There will be tears, happiness, uncertainty, hope, and joy in all you do. That is God's plan; just rely on and trust in him, as he will see you through everything if you let him."

With my last rosebuds given out, I knew they would soon graduate into the next phase of their lives, as I would begin my new life adventure as well. Graduate school lay before me with all its tests and wonders.

"Thank you, Lord, for always being there for me! Thank you for leading me into your path for my life. Keep me in it and help me along it. Help these young girls keep in your path. Show them the way. Give them courage to do what is best for them. Help them learn from you and have trust in you for all you want for them. Help them stay steadfast in you not only in the hard times, but the easy ones as well. In all things, I ask this in Jesus Christ's name. Amen."

Talk about the strength, perseverance, and help. The Lord gave me all that and more as he helped me finish my master's degree in reading in five straight semesters. I didn't take a break for the spring and the summer semesters. By the time I finished all the classes, research papers, projects, in-depth pupil reading assessments followed by nine- to twelve-week reading sessions with those students, and then final exams, I was mentally and physically wiped out. The reward for all this time and effort was a 3.96 grade point.

On December 16, 1990, dressed in my cap, gown, and new aqua stole signifying my master's degree in reading, I proudly strode down the center aisle and up onto the stage to accept my diploma. What an awesome, breathtaking moment for me! All my hard work and long hours made it all worthwhile, especially when I saw my family cheering as I received my diploma and shook the university's president's hand. I had finished my goal: my MA in reading. I couldn't have been prouder of myself other than the days I was married or gave birth to my two sons. Oh, how glorious!

"Once again, Lord, thank you for seeing me through these past sixteen months. Without you being there for me, leading me, giving me your strength and courage, all this would never have happened. All this glory goes to you, who made it all happen. Thank you, thank you. Amen."

After graduation, I attempted to return to Ladywood High School and my students there, but the new principal had eliminated my position by increasing class sizes. She gave each English teacher five to eight more students in each of their classes. My search for a new position began, but with a master's degree now, many of the school districts wouldn't hire me, as they didn't want to pay a master's degree salary. I applied at two community colleges and was hired by both. At Schoolcraft College, I would teach two basic freshmen English classes, while at Henry Ford Community, I would teach two reading literacy classes and labs. Both positions required master's degrees.

When fall arrived, I was employed and back into a classroom doing my own thing again. "Thank you, Lord, for helping me again."

Good Times Abound for Our Family

"Sing to the Lord a new song."
(Psalm 98:1)

As our family grew older, our sons started dating more seriously. While I spent those many days with Dad on various venues, young Ron had taken a job at Stan's Market. While working there, he met a wonderful young woman, ironically with the same name as me: Nancy. She was and is Nancy Ann, while I am Nancy Lee. Through the years, I have wondered if he loved me so much that he married someone with my name or whether he had issues to work out with me and decided to work them out with her instead of directly with me. I probably will never know the answer to that because he has never answered that question, even though I have posed that question to him. Oh well, maybe I am not supposed to know.

"What do you think, Lord? What do you say or are you not willing to tell me right now?"

Ron and I felt they were in a serious dating mode. One evening not too long after Dad's death, they came and wanted to talk with us. From the looks on their faces, we knew something was up but didn't want to ruin their "news." We talked for a few minutes about various and sundry things. I felt young Ron was biding his time before telling us. After many squirms in his chair, he blurted out, "Mom and Dad, I have asked Nancy to marry me and she has accepted."

We hugged them both and said, "Congratulations." The next instant, I asked, "Have you talked to Nancy's parents about this?"

"Yes," he said.

I asked, "Have you set a wedding date?"

Nancy replied, "We are hoping for a June wedding."

"Oh, what a lovely time for a wedding. The flowers will be out and the weather should be spectacular—not cold and not hot either," I quipped.

"Thank you, Lord, for a wonderful girl for Ron! She is so right for him. Let her be his supportive and caring helpmate. Give them your love, wisdom, and direction in all that lies ahead of them, not only for their wedding but throughout their married life. Be with them always in all they do. I ask this in Jesus Christ's name. Amen."

For the next six months, they filled themselves with plans for the wedding at Nancy's church, the reception at her dad's Knights of Columbus hall, bridal showers, and the usual last-minute hitches that can mess up the perfect day.

Nancy gave me the address of the bridal shop where she had found not only her wedding dress but those of her mother, her attendants, and flower girl. I asked what color her mother had chosen, as I didn't want to wear the same color. Nancy said, "A pretty blue." The bridesmaids would wear pink, and her matron of honor would be in burgundy. I decided to look for a neutral color so not to interfere with the already chosen colors.

A few days later, I drove in my little brown Mustang to the Dearborn Bridal Shop. I chose a full-length, light taupe crepe dress with an overhanging jacket. Taupe isn't a good color on me, but I could dress it up with pearl accessories.

My next task became finding the restaurant for the rehearsal dinner. I checked out the nicer restaurants in Plymouth, but nothing seemed special enough. I remembered Ron and I had had dinner with friends a couple of months earlier in Dearborn. I made an appointment to see its party director during the lunch hour so Ron could be there for our discussion. Suzi Anderson met us at the front desk at Kelley's. We sat and discussed our needs and wants. We wanted a quiet space for fifty or so people.

She said she had a room upstairs that would be perfect for our needs. The room even had an overhang balcony looking over the forest behind the restaurant. We followed her to the room, which was large enough to accommodate our guests. The balcony offered an additional treat for allowing the evening breezes and forest loveliness inside for our special evening. We would serve only red and white wines, beer, and a non-alcoholic punch—no hard liquors. To help the wait staff decipher the beef from the chicken meals of the attendees, I would create individual place cards bearing small burgundy ribbon bows for beef and white ribbons ones for chicken. She needed the final count of dinners on the Wednesday before the Friday night rehearsal.

A month before the wedding, Ron and Nancy signed a year's lease on an apartment close to their workplaces. The apartment filled their needs perfectly, as it had a living room/dining room area, two bedrooms, bathroom, kitchen, and laundry. At various stores they created gift lists for specific items they wanted. They searched furniture stores for a living room sofa, chairs, end tables, lamps, a bedroom set, and a dining room table with four chairs. Once the furniture was delivered the week before the wedding. Ron and Nancy began fixing up their home together. The happiness coming out of them was so exciting to see and be a part of. Within a few days, their home looked wonderful. Nancy put up some curtains and then added some silk plants and collectibles to give the apartment a homey feeling.

After giving Suzi the final tally, making the dinner seating arrangement and place cards, and finalizing everything with the Rons, Nancy, and Suzi, I was free until the night of the dinner.

The afternoon of the rehearsal, I drove to Kelly's. Suzi met me and we walked up to the room to check the table positions. She had one long table against the near wall ready for the wines, beers, and punch bowl. The tables for dinner were set in a large E design. The long table would seat Nancy and Ron and all the parents, the inside table was reserved for the bridesmaids and groomsmen, and the other two end tables were for guests. Using my seating chart, I put each name card in its correct place. Everything looked ready for the evening. I knew Nancy and Ron would be pleased as well.

At five o'clock, all the bridal party met at Divine Savior Catholic Church. Father Carris led us through all the steps we needed to follow for the wedding. After the half-hour tutorial, we left for the dinner at Kelly's, a half hour's drive away. Excitement filled me thinking about how wonderful this evening would be, especially with the open balcony aglow with the setting sun and breezes.

A great time was had by all. Toasts, tears of joy, stories of Ron and Nancy's courtship, and happiness flowed through the whole evening. About ten o'clock, our group started saying their good-byes and see-you-tomorrows. It had been a magical evening.

"Thank you, Lord, for your involvement in this wonderful day and evening, setting off the marriage of our son and soon to be our daughter-in-law with such a happy beginning. See to it both of them have a restful night of sleep readying them for the miracle of tomorrow, when they become one as husband and wife in your presence and love. Be with them always, leading them into your path. All this I ask in Jesus's name. Amen."

Ron's sister, Judy, and her husband, Mitch, had driven in from Philadelphia, meeting us at Kelly's, and would stay with us for the wedding. Eileen and Jim flew in and had booked a room at the nearby Holiday Inn. Judy, Mitch, Ron, and I stayed up and talked, as it had been a while since we had been together. Later, we all ambled up the steps to bed, hoping for a restful sleep before the big day. My night was as restful as possible, with the excitement of the next day surrounding me. Since we didn't have to be at the church until a half hour before the service, we slept in; then I made a leisurely breakfast for us. After the usual primping, we piled into our car and drove off to the church. Everyone was in a thither making sure all was in readiness. The wedding coordinator gave me a corsage of white carnations and baby's breath and accented with pink and burgundy ribbons, representing the bridesmaids' colors.

As I stood in the entry area, the music began calming me until John took my arm. "Mom, it's your turn. I am ready to take you to your seat," he said so gently and lovingly. Taking a huge breath and remembering to place one foot in front of the other, we ambled down the aisle to my place of honor. Within minutes, Nancy's eldest brother escorted her mother, Anne, to her place. Within seconds, the fanfare began with the bridal music. Kelly, Nancy's niece, godchild, and flower girl, along with TJ, Nancy's nephew and ring bearer, followed by pairs of bridesmaids and groomsmen lastly came following behind. Diane, Nancy's sister-in-law, and Ron Sr., serving as Ron's best man, came in just before Nancy. Another flourish announced Nancy and her father, Gene, who started down the long aisle. She was beaming as every bride should be. Ron glowed with pride when he saw her approaching him.

Within minutes, the vows were said, rings exchanged, Anne and I lit the family candles, and then the new couple lit their marriage candle. Afterward, Father Carris pronounced them husband and wife. Ron looked at him, waiting for permission to kiss his bride. Quickly, they strode back down the aisle and out into the bright sunshine that greeted them. We gave the new couple hugs and kisses. They beamed and hugged us back. What a wonderful time. After greeting all their guests, the bride and groom had a myriad of photographs taken of them, the wedding party, and the parents. Once all the picture taking was finished, Ron and Nancy got into their limousine and started off for the reception. No one could miss the fact that they had just been married, what with all the car horns blaring and the "Just Married" signs all over the limousine.

The reception hall filled quickly. Soon the bar opened, followed by a buffet. Once the buffet opened, it looked like a herd of starving turtles rushing for food to survive on. After dinner and the cake cutting, the dancing began. Ron and Nancy danced their ceremonial first dance followed by the attendants. The DJ then asked Gene and Nancy to come to the floor and dance to "Daddy's Little Girl." Then

Ron and I danced to "On Eagle's Wings." I don't believe there was a dry eye in the place.

Later, the kids said their good-byes, and off they went to start their new life together. An hour later, Ron called to ask his dad if he had brought their luggage to the hotel, as the hotel couldn't find it. His dad told him he had dropped them off at the hotel about noon. It wasn't until three in the morning that the hotel found their bags in the wrong room. I am sure their special night wasn't as special as they had wanted. About five hours later, they drove to Mackinaw Island for a week of honeymoon bliss.

"Thank you, Lord, for the blessed day, not only for Ron and Nancy but for all who attended the wedding ceremony. Your love showed through their love for each other, their vows to each other, the giving and receiving of rings, lighting of the family and marriage candles, and the blessing given to their marriage. You are so wonderful to bring these two together, as they are so right for each other. You are all knowing and so awesome in your plans for your children. Bless Ron and Nancy with happiness and health. Watch over their love and marriage, deepening it each day as you have Ron and mine. Thank you for all your blessings and love. In Christ's name I ask. Amen."

Three years later, Ron and I drove to Penn State University to attend John's graduation. What an exciting weekend, although we didn't know how exciting when we started out. Arriving in State College, Ron and I immediately checked into our hotel. Ron had made reservations at the Tavern Restaurant, the traditional place for all celebrations. This definitely was one. Ron and Nancy drove in an hour later.

We walked around downtown and then picked John up at his apartment, which was centrally located to all the university buildings.

After dinner, we all walked back to the hotel. I kept feeling something was on Ron and Nancy's minds. I didn't know what it was but knew in time it would come out. All of a sudden, Ron said they had some news about the future also. "We are going to make you grandparents and an uncle in seven months or so." We were flabbergasted to say the least. Even though they had been married almost three years and both had full-time jobs, we didn't realize they were thinking about starting a family. My husband looked like he had aged fifteen years. Not only was his "baby" boy graduating, but his older son would soon be a father, thereby making him a grandfather. What a weekend this turned out to be! Both sons were starting on new life paths. Boy, did I feel old! I did love the idea of becoming a grandma, though.

"Once again, dear Lord, I come to you with thanks. First, for John's graduation from college. Graduating from the school he loved since we moved there nineteen years before, but it was also his dad's alma mater, which made it an even bigger treat for him. We celebrate his goal knowing you placed him there for your own plan for him. Second, for the announcement of our first grandchild. What an amazing celebration of life that brings. A little one of yours to love and bring up in your love. You are such an awesome God. I can only praise and thank you for all you have done for me and my family. In my Lord Jesus Christ's name. Amen."

Two weeks after graduation, John accepted a position with Madge Computers. What a change! He graduated with a bachelor's degree in economics. Now he would sell mainframes and equipment to companies. He lived with us for a couple of months until he found an affordable place to live.

Those next months seemed to creep along like maple sap in the winter before surging through the tree in the springtime. By the end of December, Nancy had begun showing and preparing for her baby. She had a lot on her mind, as her mother had had abdominal surgery just before Thanksgiving, which had gone badly. She spent most of her free time with her Mother in ICU. Between her work and her mother, Nancy had little time for herself.

"Oh, Lord, here I am again. Please watch over Anne and give the doctors the wisdom to heal her if that is possible. Give Nancy the strength to help her mother in whatever she needs, but help her not overdo it, as she needs rest for herself. Help Nancy celebrate her pregnancy and this child of yours coming into her and Ron's lives. Lord, just be with them through these times and give them your wisdom, love, and path to follow. In all things, I ask these things in Jesus Christ's name. Amen."

By February, I realized Anne wouldn't be out of the hospital any time soon to give Nancy a baby shower. Since I wanted this time to be special for Nancy and the baby coming, I stepped up to the plate.

I asked Nancy if I could do this for her and she quickly said yes.

I said, "I think we should plan it for a month before your due date." This would let Nancy get the baby's room ready before the birth. We chose March nineteenth as the date. I enlisted some friends to create party games while I planned the shower luncheon. Nancy gave me a list of women she wanted at her shower and I added some of my close friends to boot. The number stood at twenty-five.

With the invitations out, party planning hit full gear. I loved picking out the decorations, ordering the cake with squares of pink and blue booties, and choosing the paper plates, cups, and napkins. Nancy continued with her weekly doctor visits. All was going as planned. The acceptances kept coming in—not a single decline.

The night before the shower, our son Ron called.

I said, "Don't tell me you are on your way to the hospital."

"Yes, Mom, Nancy is in labor," was the reply.

I couldn't believe it, but there had been a part of me thinking this might happen. I asked if we could come and just be in the waiting room.

"No, this might be an all-night thing. You have enough to do with the shower. Get a good night's sleep, and we will call when the baby arrives," he told us.

I called my friends to alert them to what had occurred. I couldn't call off the party, as I didn't know how to telephone or contact half the people coming to the shower, so it was on. Knowing all was in readiness, I headed for a long, soothing, hot bath along with a lovely glass of chilled chardonnay. I hoped both would help me get a bit of rest before the events of the next day hit full gear.

Since we hadn't gotten a call by morning, I assumed Nancy had been in false labor. I was wrong. At nine, Ron called, saying they were still at the hospital. Since her water had broken, her obstetrician refused to release her. They had played cards all night, hoping things start moving along. Her doctor had just examined her again and said if Nancy didn't deliver by eleven o'clock, she would induce her. Today would be the day our grandchild was to be born. Ron said he would call with any updates. Well, the party was on without the guest of honor. I immediately sent Ron to pick up the cake, giving him something to do, as well as getting him out of my hair for a few minutes.

At eleven, Ron called to say the obstetrician was inducing Nancy and the baby would be born soon. By eleven thirty, my friends arrived, expecting to hear about the new grandchild in the group. After explaining what was occurring and seeing what a nervous mess I was in, they knew I needed their help. Pat Knudsen, Sandy Rogers, and Marie Hanoian took over, telling me to sit down. "You're in no shape to do this," they chimed in.

"Here I am again praising and thanking you again for having these three wonderful women in my life. They are more than friends; they are sisters to me. They know my needs and do what is needed when I can't. Thank you for seeing to my every need, Lord. Amen."

At one o'clock, the first doorbell rang. I answered and looked at two women I had never met. They asked for Nancy, and I explained she was in the process of delivering the baby. Within a half hour, all twenty-five women were sitting in my family room discussing the situation, which had never happened to any of us.

At two, lunch was served. What a wonderful job my friends did finishing everything and making it look fabulous. The food wasn't bad either.

About two-thirty, the phone rang. I ran to answer it, almost tripping over the step between the family room and the kitchen. Ron was breathless.

"Oh, Mom! We have a little girl. Jennifer Ann is beautiful. She has blonde hair, blue eyes, ten fingers, and ten toes. She was born at 2:24 and weighs six pounds and twelve ounces. She is perfect. Once things started, she came fast. How is the shower going? Nancy is sorry she isn't there, but she was a little preoccupied at the time."

I told him everyone missed not having her here, but they would be delighted to hear about Nancy and our little Jennifer Ann and that all went well. With a cry of joy, I told all in attendance about Jennifer's arrival. It was the first time I had ever been to or given a shower where the mother-to-be delivered her baby so all the attendees learned the particulars during the shower.

A little later, when the kitchen was cleaned up and all the guests had left, Ron and I picked up our brand-new camcorder and drove to Oakwood Hospital to see our first grandchild. I couldn't wait to meet her.

The trip to the hospital seemed to take forever. We must have hit every red light along the fifteen-mile trip. Finally, we arrived. I could have floated to the third floor and room 324. Ron met us at Nancy's door and said, "Would you like to meet your granddaughter?" What do you think our answer was?

"Definitely!" we replied. He walked us around the corner and down the hall to the nursery. There she was! She was naked as a jaybird and under a heating lamp. She would be there for a couple of hours before being put into her cubicle. Oh, how beautiful she was! Tears and more tears flowed down my cheeks as I took in every part of her. She was here and so wonderful. Oh, what a gift from God she was! "Thank you, God!" Ron and I took video of her and just couldn't believe she was here safe and sound, and perfect in every way.

We just stood and admired her until Ron said, "Let's go and say hello to Nancy." Oh, I was so enthralled with Jennifer that I had forgotten Nancy. She glowed in the limelight and happiness of the moment. She was the mother of a beautiful little girl.

She asked about the shower. She felt bad that she wasn't there to be with the relatives and friends that I didn't know.

I said, "Don't worry about it. Things moved along fine."

We only stayed for a half hour, as she needed to rest. We stopped again to see our precious little one before returning home. The next day, we went back to the hospital for another visit. We even held her and I got to feed her. Oh, how warm and cuddly she was. What a wonderful experience it was.

The next months flew by. Jennifer grew, began walking, talking, and was the apple of my life. She was the little girl I never could have. She spent as much time with Ron and me as she did her mom and dad, who worked full-time jobs. Oh, what a blessed time that was. I loved every minute of having her with us.

When she was a year and a half old, we took Nancy, Ron, Jennifer, and John to Disney World for Christmas. Judy, Mitch, Julie, and Jeffrey, their children, had arrived there the week before. We actually had leased a week of their timeshare, which made for a wonderful Christmas with all the family together. The park, as well as the Disney characters, overwhelmed Jennifer. She panicked every time she saw Mickey, Minnie, Pluto, or any of the other characters coming close to her. She sought us out for reassurance.

Toward the end of our week there, John and I talked about his life and his lack of someone in his life. All he saw were couples around him, except for Jennifer. Ron and Nancy, Judy and Mitch, and Ron and I each had someone, making him feel like a fifth wheel. He seemed lost and sad. I suggested instead of flying home with the rest of the family that he drive home with us. He said he couldn't do that, as he had things he had to do, but thanked me for the suggestion. I felt sad for him and prayed that someday he would find someone to share his life with. I had no idea that he was about to find that young lady.

A few weeks later, John called, saying he was flying to Nashville. I assumed it was business related but when I realized he was going on the weekend, this trip seemed strange. He had told me that the previous month, on his birthday, he had been invited out by his longtime friend Mike Grady for a drink and dinner. While having dinner, he saw a young lady who looked familiar to him. He went over and introduced himself and learned that she was Laura Aldrin. Even though they had gone to school together from the sixth grade through their high school graduations, they didn't frequent the same friends or groups.

She told John that although she worked in Nashville, she would like to renew their acquaintance. I believe he was enamored with her, but their schedules didn't synchronize until after Christmas. All during the holiday, I think he thought about her, which only made him lonely. As his trips to Nashville and hers home became more frequent, Ron and I began thinking things between them had become serious. She was perfect for him. Both were professionals with similar career plans. She was beautiful and charming. Judy, Mitch, Julie, and Jeffrey came for Easter that year. John had told me Laura planned to eat with her parents before returning to Nashville and he would eat with us. As I was putting the finishing touches on dinner, I heard the side door close. As I turned around, I found both John and Laura standing there. They both would be having dinner with us, so I set a place for her at our table. Ron and I felt this was serious, as he wanted her to meet his aunt and family.

A few more weekend visits and from what he told me about his hefty telephone and airplane bills, I knew this was serious. In answer to my curiosity, Mother's Day came and Laura was home again. That evening, the two of them walked in and said they had something to tell us. While we sat on the deck drinking chilled glasses of chardonnay, John told us they were getting married. We were thrilled, as we had noticed how happy John was around her and how sad he was with her in Nashville. We asked their wedding plans since both of them lived and held jobs in different states. She had told John she would move here if she could find a job, or he would have to find a job there if that didn't happen. She had already put out her résumé everywhere in the local automotive resale business.

When we asked when they planned to be married, the reply was, "June or July. We know we want to be married, so why wait?" I was skeptical that they could find a place for the wedding and reception in less than three months but didn't say anything.

A week later, Laura had accepted a job with Perfection Company, which suited her to a tee. She came home for an extended weekend so they could begin planning their wedding. They wanted Reverend Robert Clapp, our rector and dear friend, to officiate at their outdoor ceremony at a nearby old inn with the reception also being there. They realized John's apartment was too small for them, so they would look for a starter house.

That Monday, they talked to Father Bob about his marrying them. He was delighted to be a part of this. Later in the day, they signed a contract with Longacre Inn for both the wedding and reception. June through September had been booked, so they chose October eleventh. The Inn gave them the name of its caterer so they could secure his service as well. The only things remaining to do were the band, invitations, dresses, flowers, and honeymoon plans. I couldn't believe they had gotten so much done so quickly. They proved to be efficient planners.

In September, John and Laura found a single-floor house with a living room, kitchen and dinette combination, a screened in Florida room, three bedrooms, and a bath. The third bedroom John would use for his office, and the second bedroom would be for any overnight guests.

"Lord, once again you are watching over our family. You found John a wonderful woman who will share his life and values. She will be as great a support to him as he will to her. Create in them a love and lasting happiness. Watch over them and lead them into the paths you have for them. Let them know and love you as Ron and I do. How wonderful you are! I love you. In all things, I ask this in Jesus Christ's name. Amen."

I began my search for a place for the rehearsal dinner. Laura asked for it to be close to home so people wouldn't have to drive too far after the meal. I remembered having a wonderful meal at an elegant Italian restaurant, Italian Cucina, in Plymouth where Ron and I had dined with another couple. It had a great reputation, and its food was marvelous. When I learned it had a large room in their basement reserved for small parties, I knew we needed to check it out.

One evening, Ron and I sat with their buffet director and discussed our plans and requirements for the special evening. We wanted a simple bar (wine and beer only), appetizers, then dinner and some kind of dessert. They said they would provide a variety of cheeses and crackers, fresh sliced vegetables with dip, and a table for the bar needs. We decided to have a choice of their chicken Frangelico and prime beef for the meal. They would make crème de menthe parfaits for dessert. All sounded wonderful. All I needed was to tell them how many of each dish we would need.

Again, I would make out the seating arrangement and cards with white bows for the chicken and red ones for the beef. We signed the contract then and there. After telling John and Laura our plans, they said the place sounded great. Within days, I had Laura's guest list along with ours. With that done, the invitations were sent.

Early the day of the rehearsal, I took in my table scheme and name cards and drove to the restaurant. Arriving at the restaurant, I went downstairs to check out if everything was ready. They had done exactly as I wanted. After placing the place cards, I left to take a relaxing, hot bath and then dress for the rehearsal.

After Ron came home from work, we drove to Longacre Inn. It was a glorious, crisp fall afternoon! The fading sun shone through the crimson red, mellow yellow, and brilliant orange tree leaves throwing such glory on the scene showing everyone all was right in God's kingdom.

"Oh, Lord, how beautiful this day is. The beginning of new life and family. Be with us all during this rehearsal, dinner, and all through tomorrow's events. Be with John and Laura as they intertwine their lives and love. Make them aware of your presence in the festivities and their new life together. Be their guide and protector. In all things I ask this in Jesus's name. Amen."

With the bridal party assembled, Father Clapp asked them whether they wanted their service to be outside or inside. Quickly they said, "Outside, if the weather holds up, but there should be a quick inside run through, just in case the weather doesn't cooperate tomorrow evening." He said he would do both just to be on the safe side.

After the rehearsal, we all drove to Italian Cucina. Slowly, our guests came and took their places. After the toasts and dinner had finished, I presented Laura and John my wedding gift. I created from each letter of their names a description of who they were separately; then, using their new surname, I described who they were as a couple. Ron couldn't believe I got through reading it without crying, but I did, just barely. After saying our good nights, we left for home.

The sun came out in rare force for the wedding. At four, we left for the inn. As time for the wedding came, the sun lowered itself toward the horizon and the air became quite nippy. Laura and John decided to have the ceremony inside. Since the room had been set up for the reception, it now had to be reset for the wedding and later for the reception and dinner. The dining tables were removed and the chairs placed in rows for the attendees. The staff quickly and efficiently went about their jobs. I was glad both the outside and inside versions of the wedding ceremony had been rehearsed so everyone knew what to do.

At precisely five, Pinky and her Trio played the pre-selected wedding music. Once finished, Ron escorted Ron and me to our places for the ceremony. After their vows and ceremonial kiss, John and Laura went outside for the traditional receiving line. The temperature had fallen considerably, as the sun had settled into the western horizon, giving little light to the festivities. As the newlyweds and their parents stood in the receiving line shaking hands, the inn staff quickly changed the wedding room back into the reception and dinner area.

Once dinner was over, the dancing began. At the stroke of midnight, the newlyweds said good-bye to everyone and left.

"Oh, Lord, be with John and Laura as they begin their marriage. Bless their union and life together. Keep them safe on their honeymoon wherever they go. Make their time beautiful and enjoyable for them. In all things I ask this in Jesus's name. Amen."

After a wonderful week in Key West, our newlyweds returned all aglow.

Many good times were spent with both couples. Many memories of Christmas and Easter were made. Then news came that Ron would be sent to England for a year-and-a-half assignment became reality.

By the end of May 1992, I had finished teaching my winter semester classes and had turned in all my final student grades. Now the time had come to get us ready for our move to England and our new life awaiting us there. What a wonderful experience that would be! A life not many would or could ever live.

Merry Ol' England

> "Until now you have not asked for anything in my name. Ask and you will receive, and your joy will be complete."
>
> (John 16:24)

After endless testing, probing, and immunizations, Ford Motor Company declared us fit for our year-and-a-half assignment in jolly ol' England. England needed a catalytic emissions expert, and Ron had been tapped for the position. By June 1992, Ron and I had been on a rollercoaster ride for better than six months while Ford figured out which side of the pond would pay for our moving, Ron's salary, and benefits.

We sold our home in mid-March and waited for Ford to tell us if and when our transfer would take place. As June fourteenth neared, the day we needed to vacate our home, I still didn't know whether we were going or not. The wrangling over finances still raged between the two Ford international divisions. If we weren't going, I needed to look for a new home and not worry about filling out all those pages of insurance and customs forms for the things we were taking. Not knowing what we were doing, I went into shut-down mode. What was I supposed to do until Ford decided what to do with Ron?

All of a sudden, it was June seventh, the Friday before we had to vacate our home. Ron and I still didn't know whether we were moving abroad. With the movers coming that following Monday, the movers needed to know whether this was a local storage move or an international one so they could figure out what type and number of boxes to bring, the number of trucks and manpower to use for our move(s), and the number of days needed to pack us up for either situation.

Before Ron left for work that Friday, I told him he needed a decision by noon so I could conclude the moving arrangements. Another thing that concerned me was that we didn't have housing in England yet, so I didn't know how much furniture to take with us and how much to store. Remembering Ron and I had taken Dad to visit his British relatives eight years before, I decided to use the smaller cousin's floor plan as a guiding rod for what to take. That was, if we were going!

Noon came and went with no call. At about two thirty, the telephone rang. Ron said we definitely were going to England; the deal between England and the US had been made. Ron said Ford had made arrangements for us to fly to England the following Saturday in order to find housing there.

I alerted Palmer Moving to the international as well as the partial local storage move. The dispatcher said they would be at our home at eight o'clock Monday morning.

We called the kids that evening, relaying the message that we were going. Although they supported our decision, they were sad to see us go for that period of time. I knew we would be able to visit the following summer on a home leave. All of a sudden, I realized I would be leaving Jennifer—how would that be?

"Lord, please help me get through this 'getting through' period of transition that I need to make. Give me the courage and patience to do this. Give me a sense of joy about this new life you have set us on. Help us to blend in with our new neighbors and community. Lead us to the church and help us to become part of their service and congregation. Lord, keep me in your path and loving grace during all this time ahead. I ask all this in your name. Amen."

Ron's sister, Judy, didn't take the news well. She couldn't believe Ron and I would take an assignment in England. This was so opposite from what we had expected. She had always been our support system. This was a complete turnabout for her, one we hadn't expected at all. We hoped by the time we departed for England, she would have reconciled herself to this blip in her life.

With the dawn of Saturday things got frantic for me. I realized I hadn't sorted out what was going to England and what was staying at Palmer Storage. The entire weekend, I worked feverously sorting things and then filling out the needed paperwork.

I remember thinking, *Was that ten oxford shirts for Ron or was it eleven? Oh, how will I ever get this done by eight Monday morning?*

Bright and early Monday morning, Palmer knocked at our front door. The men asked what rooms held what shipment. The ensuing week filled itself with answering the same questions over and over until I was ready to pull my hair out. By Wednesday evening, everything had been boxed and the local things were in their storage warehouse. By Thursday, the sea shipment was crated and ready for the sea containers, which would come Friday morning. The air shipment boxes would leave at the same time.

Friday, the new homeowners checked in with us every hour on the hour to see when they could take charge of their new home. As soon as the movers finished clearing out each room, I followed behind with the sweeper, wash bucket, Pledge, and rags to clean up after them.

By three o'clock, the house was empty and clean. I tearfully said good-bye to our home filled with so many wonderful memories, relinquished our house keys to our Realtor for the anxious new owners, and left for John and Laura's home. The following evening, we would fly to England to find housing for the next year and half.

Saturday evening came, and we boarded British Airways headed for London, England. Sunday morning, we stepped off the plane at Heathrow Airport and into our new life. My body clock told me it was three o'clock in the morning, while British time said it was eight o'clock.

"Ugh. Let's get with it, Nancy," I said to myself, trying to shake off my need for sleep.

Driving in one of London's finest black taxis to Ford's World Headquarters for Europe located in Warley, the jet lag really began to work on me. Since I don't sleep well on planes, I had only at best an hour of nap time before landing at Heathrow. My body was screaming, "Lie down," and I kept saying, "Not yet."

After getting to the security office at Ford's headquarters, Ron filled out the necessary paperwork for our rental car, and then we proceeded to our car. Security had given him a map with directions to our 'home' for our next five days. I opened the car's right door only to notice the steering wheel was on the passenger side. Laughing, we traded sides. Ron started the engine and then realized the accelerator and clutch were on his left side. Oh, all of this newness made both of us nervous. The next situation came when Ron drove out of the car park (parking lot) onto the road. I screamed, "Drive on the left side of the road, not the right!" Thank goodness it was early Sunday morning and there was little traffic on the road, especially on their famous roundabouts.

After a rather hectic drive, we finally found the apartment complex where Ford would put us up for our visit. After looking around, we found George and Barbara Knightsbridge, the apartment manager and his wife, a congenial couple. They showed us our apartment, typically British—a living/dining room combination; small, efficient kitchen; bedroom; and a bath. We unpacked, and I made us a cup of tea to stimulate our bodies, hoping it would keep us awake. International travelers had told us the best way to deal with jet lag was to stay awake until the usual time we went to bed. I wasn't sure I could keep my eyes and body awake that long. I would try.

After a good night's sleep, Ron made his way to headquarters to begin the paperwork required to reinstate the process to acquire his British work permit. The process had been discontinued because of all the Ford infighting about Ron's pay. He signed all the Ford paperwork needed to begin work here as soon as his British work permit came in.

Tuesday, Ron spent the day again at Ford, meeting his supervisor and British coworkers. Many were not too pleased that the position had been filled by an American and not a Brit. While he was at work, I took a walk into Shenfield to get a good look at the shopping and grocery situation. I found two greengrocers, a fish monger, a butchery, two chemist shops, a news shop, two cooperative groceries, two dry cleaners (one with a cobbler), a women's dress shop, a card shop, a travel bureau, a 7–11, a wine shop, and the library. On the end of the town was the British rail station. It was close enough for us to walk to and get a train into London.

After breakfast Wednesday morning, Ron and I waited for Ian Stallworth, Ford's International Housing person, to come and pick us up for the housing part of our trip. The first house was in a dilapidated section of Brentwood, which wouldn't work for us. The second also wouldn't work for us. The third place was a lovely remodeled apartment over one of Shenfield's dry cleaners. The location was great: in the center of town and across from the British rail station. The major drawback was it had no parking space for a car, much less two.

As we started our journey to the fourth place, I made the mistake of asking, "What happens if we don't like that place either?"

His feathers ruffled, and he indignantly said, "Well, then you don't have to come."

I felt I had been hit by a Mack truck. I thought, *How could he talk to me that way? Ron and I are giving up our home, family, friends, and my job to come here and help you with your environmental problem, and you slap me with this?*

"Oh, Lord, don't let me overreact to his indignant behavior and remark. Let me get past this so I can enjoy my time here. Please help me adjust to what is happening to me. I ask this in Christ's name. Amen."

He told me I would love his fourth and final offering. I certainly hoped so after his earlier remark. Was he leading us down the bridle path or to something really good? In a few minutes, he pulled into the front garden (parking area) of a Tudor and brick semi-detached place. *The outside looks good—now let's see what the inside holds.* Stepping inside, I thought he might be right. The entryway was small but sufficient; to the right was a large lounge with sun shining through its front bay windows. Walking down the hall, we passed a half bath and then came to a large dining room with a nice window overlooking the back garden filled with all kinds and colors of blooming azaleas, roses, and shrubbery. The kitchen contained everything a gourmet cook would love to have. It was wonderful! Off to one side of the kitchen was a small room filled with the usual small top-and-bottom refrigerator and freezer, as well as the top-and-bottom washer and dryer.

Upstairs were two and a half bedrooms and a lovely full bathroom.

Going back downstairs and out into the back garden, we found a large stone patio with room enough for some small entertaining. In the back garden there was a shed containing an electric mower, and beyond was a glass greenhouse plus an area for growing all kinds of vegetables and flowers if we wanted.

On our return trip to the headquarters, Ian asked what we thought about the last house and I said, "It's lovely. I really love it." Ron agreed, and he signed the lease papers when he returned to the office. Another task was off our to-do list.

Thursday night, we decided Friday was all ours. We would make a day of it; we would take the British rail train into London. Oh, London! It lived up to its name and reputation. We took the double-decker tour bus around London to see all the sights. We even paused to go in and see the inner workings of Harrods. Oh, what a marvelous city, and to think we would only be twenty-eight minutes away by train.

Saturday morning, we took the taxi back to Heathrow for our flight home. Ford had already organized a furnished apartment for us. We would live there until Ron's British work permit came in and we could actually move to England. The permit, we were told, could take up to six to eight weeks to come in. Ron would continue in his regular position until the move across the pond.

Time passed slowly, until one day in mid-July Ford told Ron his work permit had arrived. Ron would start work August second in England. Our new life was awaiting us. The next week filled me with deep sadness at leaving Jennifer and the families. Saying goodbye for a year was traumatic for me. We flew from Detroit to Philadelphia to visit Judy, hoping she would be happier about our move. That wasn't the result.

The three days we spent with her only left me sadder, as Judy was so upset with our leaving. "How can you leave your family and me for a year or two? That isn't right or fair."

Our time with her was unbearable for me. She only reminded me of all I was giving up–family and especially Jennifer. All I could do was cry.

"Oh, Lord, help me adjust to my new life with Ron. Help me with the pain I am feeling now and relieve it if possible. Please give me your guidance, strength, and courage to leave them and find happiness in my new surroundings. Help Judy with her feelings. I know you can help both of us. Help Ron and I enjoy this new life ahead of us. Let us travel and do things we would never be able to do otherwise. In all things I ask these petitions in Jesus' name. Amen."

Our outbound flight to England seemed to take forever. Having to deal with leaving my family and especially Jennifer was hard, but dealing with Judy's anger, sadness, and tears just added to my feelings of sorrow.

Ron and I moved temporarily back into the Ford apartment since our duplex hadn't been cleaned and revitalized. Not knowing anyone here lay a heavier burden on me as I tried to come to terms with living in England. The realization of now living across the pond away from all I knew and loved hit me with even deeper sadness. I cried at the slightest thing.

"Oh, Lord, let me get a hold of myself and what lies ahead of me. I can't continue this way. It isn't good for me or for Ron. He is beside himself with what to do with me. Help me through this mine field of emotions, dear Lord. I need your help!"

I knew I couldn't return home, as that wasn't the way a marriage worked, especially ours. Heartbroken, I continued to pray for guidance and peace. Little of either came to me. Unfortunately, I heard nothing back from my prayers.

One morning, I heard a knock on the door. Ron had gone to work, and not knowing anyone, I was skeptical about who was on the other side of my door. Opening up the door, I saw what seemed like an angel. She introduced herself as Lorraine Kramp. She said she was part of the Ford group of wives living here and invited me to the Tuesday morning coffee clutch, which was held down the hall. If I wanted to come, she would wait while I dressed; she would take and introduce me there. I couldn't dress fast enough. Maybe I could make friends and lift some of this fog from around me.

After being introduced to the group, they wanted to know about me, my family, where Ron worked, and where we would be living. I met the twenty or so women; later, I went with them to a nearby pub for lunch. I felt I had a beginning. "Thank you, Lord, for this group of women."

Every evening after dinner, Ron and I would walk past our new place to see if it was ready for us. What Ford didn't tell us was they were waiting for our sea shipment to pass through British customs before cleaning our place.

On Monday of our third week in the apartment, Ford let Ron know our shipment passed through British customs. We would be moving into our home on Friday morning. Oh, what joy I felt! Our own place! I was flying high.

Friday came with the moving van parked in our driveway. During the morning, the four men broke open five different wooden crates filled with our furniture and boxes. My job was to "tick" (check off) each thing that came through our front door. At noon, two men returned to the warehouse for the remaining three crates, while the other two men remained to begin the real job of unpacking. At two o'clock, the first two returned with the last crates; they took the furniture and boxes out and placed them in the house. At four o'clock, the leader said they were finished and leaving. I asked if they were coming in the morning to help finish the unpacking, to which he said their job here was done. I was to do the remaining work.

By the time Ron came home from work, I was sitting on the lounge floor surrounded by wrapping papers and opened boxes. One look at me he saw how exhausted I was. He suggested we go to a little restaurant in the nearby village of Brentwood for dinner. That sounded great to me. After reviving myself with food, we returned home. A couple hours later, I found the box containing our sheets. After dressing our bed, I decided to take a leisurely, hot bath before falling into bed for a good night's sleep. I literally did fall into bed, bone-tired and exhausted.

The entire weekend, Ron and I unpacked, placed things in their proper places, and made our new home as cozy as possible. Our life in England had started. Now all I had to do was find something to do with myself daily to get on with life here.

From the Tuesday coffee group, I joined the weekly Wednesday women's Bible study group. I continued attending the Tuesday coffee socials with pub lunches afterward, going on outings with the group, and just traveling into London for shopping or maybe a play in the afternoon. I attempted to find some teaching employment, but with Ron's work permit, that was not available to me. I felt like I was just putting in my days until we could return home.

We kept in touch with our families with Sunday phone calls. I had to keep my guard up so my true feelings didn't show. I told them things were going along fine; whether they believed it or not, I am not sure. Our one-way calls to Judy grew more and more unbearable, as she would either cry continuously through the conversation or just be angry with us. I would write her, as I did the kids, about our travels or what we were doing. Never once did we get a letter from her. The phone calls always went one way from us to her. I tried everything to correct the situation, but how could I when I didn't know what her problem with us was. There was no happy medium with her.

With our assignment extended twice, Judy shocked us with a visit. She was coming for an Alzheimer's conference in Birmingham in the Midlands. She was a director for one of Manor Care's home facilities dealing with Alzheimer patients. She said she would fly in a couple days before the conference and come to visit. My emotions soared.

Oh, how wonderful! Maybe now we can resolve some of this between us, I thought.

We picked her up at Heathrow on the Tuesday. All was light, without any mention of the emotions lying underneath the surface. The following day, I drove her into the Cotswolds so she could visit an installation there to see how they worked with their patients. On the way home, Judy and I stopped in Stratford-on-Avon for a late lunch and a walkabout. Later, we hopped into the car and headed home. On Thursday, I drove her around our area, showing her all the spots of interest and the places where I shopped.

During her stay, I hoped Ron would attempt to sound her out on what was troubling her about our being here. Neither discussed this. I just kept waiting and hoping. Friday came with her repacking her luggage for her taxi ride back into London. Ron had engaged the driver who normally took him to Heathrow or Gatwick for his flights to take her back into London so she could connect with the rest of her conference colleagues and then train to Birmingham.

By lunchtime I knew if anything was going to be said, I had to do it. Ron had said good-bye to her before leaving for work, so I took the bull by the horns and asked her what was bothering her about our move here. She said she didn't have any idea what I was talking about. I told her every time we called she was either in tears or angry with us. I wanted to work out the problem with her. This was so upsetting to Ron and me. She said, "Well, with some people, you have to lower your expectations of them."

"What do you mean? What expectations do you have of us we don't know about?" I asked.

She answered, "I have no expectations of you," and with that, huge tears came in her eyes and she ran up the stairs to her bedroom.

I waited for her to compose herself and come down so we could finish our discussion, but that never happened. She stayed in her room until Steve came to pick her up. She hurried out of her room, only saying good-bye to me as she flew out the door and into the awaiting taxi. Oh, how upset I was. Not only didn't I know what the problem was, but now I realized things were worse than ever. She never even called to let us know she had gotten home safely. I had attempted to rectify what was going on between us, and she wouldn't discuss it.

My sadness lingered; I couldn't shake it. To add to this, Ron's US supervisor asked him to extend for an additional year. Ron said I could make the decision to stay or return home. Ron explained his boss had told him his position in the States had been eliminated and he would have to remain in England until he could find something for him in Dearborn. He and Ford were extremely pleased with his work here and hoped he would stay for an additional year. I told him I wanted to leave and return home to our family.

For the next days, all I got was his cold shoulder wanting to wear me down into submission since he wanted to remain. I relented and said, "Next year we go home." The following year was a repeat performance. Telling the family and Judy was hard. The kids weren't happy but tried to make the best of it. Judy was even more displeased than ever.

During the next year, we learned we were to be grandparents again. John and Laura were expecting. Oh, what bittersweet news. Thrilled by the news, I was saddened I wouldn't be there for this wonderful time. The baby was due on December nineteenth. We made flight reservations home for Christmas. I would fly out first, as Ron had a required meeting in Gratz, Austria, before he could come to Michigan.

Around the first of December, John called. He told me he and Laura were nervous, as her obstetrician thought Laura might have to have a caesarian section a week early, as the baby refused to turn properly.

John asked, "Would it be possible for you to come a week ahead of schedule to help us be calm and see us through all that lies ahead?"

I was overjoyed to be asked. I said, "I'd be more than happy to do that. When do you want me?"

"Is the twelfth too soon?" was his reply.

After changing my flight reservations, I flew to Detroit on December twelfth. Her obstetrician decided to wait out the additional week to see if the baby would turn. We all took the following week as easily as we could. We just had to wait for him or her to make its appearance. The morning of her due date, John, Laura, and I drove to the hospital for her caesarian as the baby had remained breeched. The kids were excited but also quite nervous, which was to be expected. They signed in, and I waited in the waiting room for news of my new grandchild. Laura's parents came about an hour later, then Nancy a little later.

About two thirty, John came out looking upset and exhausted. Christopher James Hurley had been born at 2:24. Both mother and son were doing well. After giving Nancy the phone number where Ron could be reached in Gratz, I went to meet my new grandson. Ron knew today was the day and wanted the news as soon as it happened. He had alerted the hotel where he was conducting his meeting; they were to call him the moment my call came in.

John took Anita, Dick, and me into recovery to see Laura. I knew something was wrong but couldn't put my finger on it. Later, John explained that Christopher had a soft cleft palate problem.

Anita, Dick, Nancy, and I waited to see Christopher. He was wonderful. He looked perfect to me. No one would ever know he had the palate problem. Being able to hold and cuddle him filled me with joy and wonderment.

"Thank you, Lord, for all you accomplished here today. Help them come to terms with his problem. No first-time parents want anything but perfection with their newborn. Help Christopher take in nourishment and not be affected by this in any way physically and emotionally. He is so beautiful. I love him so. I ask all this is Jesus Christ's name. Amen."

Ron flew in the next day. John and I picked him up at the airport and then drove to the hospital for him to make the acquaintance of his first grandson. He instantly fell in love with him. After Laura and Christopher came home from the hospital, we spent Christmas and New Year's with them, Ron, Nancy, Jennifer, and friends.

After New Year's, Ron flew back to England. I stayed on for a while to help Laura regain her strength and help her feed Christopher. Being a soft palate problem, there was no external sign of it, but he had to use specially made bottles and nipples to get the nourishment he needed. When things were stable, I boarded my Northwest flight for England. Oh, how I hated leaving them.

"Oh, Lord, watch over and protect this little family. Help them deal with Christopher and find ways to help him get full nourishment so he can grow into a strong, healthy boy. Keep them in your loving hands. Surround them with your love and warmth. Guide them to the right doctors to get the correct medical attention for Christopher. As always, in all things I pray in Jesus's name. Amen." After uttering this prayer, I heard the Lord say, "I am with them. I will be with them through this. Trust me, Nancy. I have always been there for you and will be there for them as well."

Late in the fall, the call for another extension came from Ron's boss. This time I said no and meant it. I had had all I could take.

I had had enough, and I wasn't taking it any more. I had given five long, hard years to Ford here, and I wasn't giving them any more. Ron again gave me the cold-shoulder silent treatment that had worked three times before, but this time I wasn't caving in to him or Ford Motor Company. I had done my bit for them! Oh, what a joy that was for me. I knew my life in England was closing and my return to family and normalcy was at last at hand.

"Oh, thank you, God, for finally giving me the backbone to tell Ron no." I was determined to return home this time. The relief was overwhelming.

I told Ron he could remain as long as he and his boss wanted, but I was leaving. Once he realized I wouldn't change my mind, he told his boss. Dr. Gandhi required him to finish his fifth-year assignment and train his replacement as soon as he could find one. That might take up to four or five months. Dr. Gandhi would have to find Ron a position in his former group.

When we visited home that Christmas, we chose a lot and signed a contract with Pulte to build a home for us on that lot. By February, Ron had a business trip to Ford; while there, he picked out the outside brick and paint. Our house was a hole in the ground for the foundation. The first of May, Pulte called and said I needed to come and pick out the cabinets, interior wood flooring, and carpet as well as the paint. I flew home for two weeks to do that, as well as visit my family and especially my grandchildren. On August twenty-eighth, we returned home to inspect our new house before closing on it the next day. It was fabulous; a dream come true.

When I returned to England in September, I began getting our home ready for the removers. The move happened mid-October. Ford told us our containers should arrive at our new home toward the end of November. With our English move complete, I flew home in order for Palmer Movers to deliver our things from their storage warehouse. I wanted those things in place before the English shipment arrived.

Later that week, our storage boxes arrived. I went into high gear putting things in their new places.

By mid-November, I had worked through half of the boxes, deciding what I didn't need and could get rid of. One morning as I was working away I got a real shock. Our sea containers had come through US customs and were ready for delivery. They were two weeks early. Palmer asked when they could bring them. As I was only in the middle of my storage packages, I said the first of the following week. The delivery specialist said the trucks would be there first thing on Monday morning. More boxes and unpacking to do! I made a map for the placement of all our furniture to make it easy for the men to know where things went.

After a frenzied weekend of putting things in place, Monday morning came with all the furniture and more boxes. Oh, what a sight! Thank goodness I had my furniture plan in hand for them, or all would have been utter chaos.

For the next two weeks, I sorted and placed things as I could before returning to England for Ron's final two weeks there. People had planned final going-away parties and venues for us to let us know we would be missed and how much we had been a part of their lives. What a wonderful send-off for us.

The night before we flew home, Ron and I transferred from his apartment to the Thistle Hotel in downtown London. We took a taxi through lit up London to the theater to see *Jesus Christ Superstar*. Oh what a wonderful evening that was! I loved the play and especially the music. It was a play I always wanted to see. What a climax to our years in England!

The following morning, Ron and I rose early and hopped into our taxi for Heathrow and our flight home. I couldn't believe I was crying as I took one last glimpse of London, remembering all the wonderful times we had had there and how I would miss that magical city on the Thames.

About four thirty Eastern Standard Time, the wheels of our 474 touched down on Detroit Metro's tarmac. We were home! Our kids and grandchildren met us at the airport. Oh, how joyful that reunion was! We all went to John and Laura's for dinner, and then Ron and I drove to our new home for our first night there together. We had begun our new life back with our family and friends. Home sweet home, or would it be?

"Thank you, Lord, for bringing us home safely to our family. Thank you for the beautiful new home we are going to live in. You are an awesome God! You have watched over us and blessed us with many gifts and joys while helping me through the five years of turmoil and anger at you and Ron for having to be away from my family. We visited many places and met many people, which I realize I would never have been able to do without our time in England. I know I will miss the sights and people, but, Lord, I can't thank you enough for helping me return home to family. In Jesus Christ's name. Amen."

The rest of the week, Ron and I worked together to put our new home in order. That Sunday, we went to church and were welcomed back by our church family. We felt back in sync with life now. We had rejoined our old life, and I was thrilled about that. Unfortunately, Ron missed his life and assignment in England.

The hardest adjustment Ron and I had to make was readjusting to our family and friends. We were on different wavelengths. Friends couldn't reconnect with us because our life experiences had changed us.

Remembering our Ford orientation before going to England, Mr. Blackstone, our moderator, told us, "Going on assignment and living in a foreign land will be hard at first, but returning home will be even harder." At the time, I thought, *What kind of hooey is this*, but he was absolutely correct. The re-entry was twice as tough as the going. How long would this last—as long as it did. I felt like I was caught between two worlds with neither suiting me.

"Lord, here I am again. Help me come to terms with those I love. Create a happy medium for Ron and me with our friends so we can reinstate our relationships and move forward. I don't like this wilderness I am in right now. Put me on the path you want me to follow, guiding my steps onto a solid footing. Thank you, Lord, for all you do for me and us. Amen."

His answer was, "Always remember I am with you in all things. This will work out also. Just trust in me, Nancy. I AM with you."

The one real tragedy in all this remained with Judy. Neither Ron nor I could properly reconnect with her; she still didn't want to discuss it. At one point I called Julie, her daughter, and asked her if she had any idea what the problem was between her mother and us. She said she had never heard that there was a problem; another dead end. On other occasions, I attempted to discuss this with Judy, but all I got was a wall of tears and denials that anything was wrong. Nothing I could do would permeate this wall.

"Lord, I must put this matter in your hands to work out, as I can't do it anymore. My frustration is ongoing, which isn't good for me or her, so I am giving this to you. I hope someday you will work it through, or maybe it isn't supposed to be worked out for whatever reason. All this is in your hands and ballpark now. I ask this in Jesus Christ's name. Amen."

After placing Judy and the situation in God's hands, my Lord gave me something new to focus on. John and Laura were expecting again. Their second child would also be a boy. The idea of two boys in one home was perfect. Now we had something positive in our lives.

Before we knew it, Christopher celebrated his second birthday, his palate had been surgically fixed, Christmas and New Year's were behind us, and the new baby was near. January seventeenth, the day before the baby's due date, came ever so quickly. Laura and John had asked Ron and me to come and watch Christopher when they had to go to the hospital. We told them to just call and we would be there. That morning, I had called Laura to find out how she felt, and she said this might be the day. She planned to have her best friend and husband, Denise and Bob, for dinner that night if all went well. She said they would call when they needed us.

About five o'clock, I called again to see how things were. The weathermen had predicted snow, and it had begun to snow. Laura said Denise and Bob would be leaving soon because of the forecast. She would let me know if we were needed. I worried as the evening moved on and the snow really began to come down, covering everything in sight.

Around ten o'clock, the call came. Ready to go to the hospital, they asked us to come over. We arrived quickly since we lived close by. As we walked in, I knew her labor was active, as she was grabbing onto the kitchen countertop and wincing through the throes of each labor pain. As they readied for their drive, I grabbed a flashlight along with some blankets just in case they didn't make it to the hospital in time. The wind howled while the snow made driving treacherous at best.

"Oh, Lord, watch over John and Laura as they make their way to the hospital. Keep them safe in the snow and away from oncoming cars. Help them get to the hospital in time. Help Laura have a smooth labor and delivery and that their new little one will be delivered safely and be perfect in all ways. In Jesus Christ's name we ask this. Amen."

We waited up for the phone call that never came. At five thirty, John found us asleep on the living room sofa with the television still on. What concerned grandparents we were! They had arrived safely at Oakwood Hospital two hours before the birth, although a couple times John said he almost spun out in the winter storm. He announced Patrick John Hurley made his appearance at 2:24 a.m. He was perfect in every way, and Laura had done beautifully. "Oh, thank you, Lord, for their travel, Laura's safe labor and delivery, and Patrick's birth. Thank you for your gracious help in all this. Amen."

We left for home and a few hours of shut eye. Later that afternoon, we drove to the hospital to see Laura and meet Patrick John. Laura told us she had waited to the last possible moment before going to the hospital. If she arrived after midnight, she could stay an additional twenty-four hours before having to leave the hospital.

When feeding time came, the nurses brought Patrick in. Oh, how beautiful he was: blonde hair and blue eyes. We figured his hair would turn reddish later because of Laura's red hair. What a wonderful sight! Since Laura was quite tired and needed rest, we only stayed a little while. Christopher also needed us to be with him as well. The following day, Laura and Patrick came home.

"Thank you, Lord, for your bounteous gifts of love."

Onto Another New Life: Retirement

"My heart is changed within me."
(Hosea 11:8d)

Returning to Schoolcraft College as an adjunct instructor, I taught two basic freshmen English classes as well as two regular English 101 classes. I loved being back with my students and teaching. I enjoyed teaching them new techniques of writing and ways of expressing themselves in words. I was also asked to become an instructor in their honor's program for gifted students. This intensified program made teachers and students work toward advanced skills. What rewarding work.

Since our return from England, I had been playing with the idea of writing a book about my adventures or encounters in Europe. Slowly it dawned on me that I could combine all my travelogues I had kept on our trips through Europe along with diary notes of things I had done daily, weekly, or yearly, the parties we attended, and how I felt about all of it. The book became a huge undertaking but one that would be a lasting memoir for my children and grandchildren. I wanted to do it.

During the summer months of 1999, I began writing in earnest. It was tough sledding at first. I rewrote each of the travelogues so anyone could see, feel, touch, and smell the sights and sounds of places we visited. Once that task was complete, I did the same with my daily journal entries in order for my readers to understand what living abroad entailed. Lastly, I integrated those two entities into one flowing book.

After teaching the fall semester, I realized I couldn't give my students and classes my full attention and do the writing I needed to do on my book. I decided to take the winter term off so I could write full-time, finish the book, and be able to return for the winter semester.

During those next months, *Close Encounters of the European Kind* was born. I spent the following year, along with my teaching, looking for an editor, agent, or publisher for my creation. Talk about a tough road to travel, as I wasn't a John Grisham or Debbie Macomber.

It wasn't until a dear friend of Ron's and mine died that I found my publisher. During the luncheon after Lyn Knudsen's funeral, I was talking to a friend of his about my book and my inability to find a publisher. Pete Ross told me Lyn had told him of my futile attempt to find a publisher. Pete told me he knew a publisher in Ann Arbor, Michigan, about twenty miles from our home. He would call her and see if he could get her to read my manuscript. After all the other rejections, I assumed this would just be another to chock up on my growing list. He gave me her name and address, and I posted her a few chapters of my book. If this didn't pan out, I had decided to drop the book idea and return to teaching full time.

The following Monday, the telephone rang; it was Hazel Proctor of Proctor Publications. She asked me all kinds of questions about the book's contents, the reason for writing it, and what market I wanted to target. She wanted the entire manuscript so she could read it. I mailed it out to her that afternoon. The following week, she called, telling me she wanted to publish my book. It did need some editing before printing. She had designed the front and back covers and would get a copyright for it, along with an IBSN number. She asked if I had any photos of the places I had written about.

I exclaimed, "Hundreds." She asked me to send her some, as they would make a great front cover.

She told me to do a complete editing of my book then return it to her for hers. Two months later she arranged for a photo shoot for my front and back covers. She wanted me to wear a hot pink hat so to accent the blue background of the covers. I thought, *Where am I going to find a hot pink hat?*

Ironically, I needed some cross-stitch supplies. While walking down one aisle in Michael's Craft Store, I happened upon a brimmed straw hat, giving me a great idea. If I could find some hot pink spray paint, I would have my hat. As I perused the paint aisle, I spotted a can of hot pink paint, just what I needed to create my own prop.

The following week, dressed in my double-breasted navy suit and hot pink hat, I went for my photo shoot at her office. Now I was excited. I was actually going to be a published author. I couldn't believe it! When I arrived for the photo shoot, Hazel showed me what she had done for the front cover. The cover looked fabulous!

After the editing was complete, I paid the printing charges. Once that was done, she sent the manuscript to a Canadian printer, where the printing costs were cheaper. Two months later, the telephone rang. Hazel told me she was holding one of my books in her hand. She wanted me to come and see it. I hurried over, and for the first time I touched my creation in print and binding. It looked unbelievable. Now all I had to do was market five thousand books, which would be a feat in and of itself, especially for an unknown author.

I spent the next six months visiting and writing every book club, bookseller, and library to get my book on their shelves and into consumers' hands. This job was tougher than I ever expected. Next, I sent books to many nationally known talk show hosts: Diane Sawyer, Jay Leno, Kelly Ripa, Oprah, and local television personalities. Still nothing!

Shocking news came that Mother's Day. Ron and Nancy called, saying they had something important to tell us. Our interest was piqued, but we weren't ready for what was coming. First, they wanted both of us on the phone then told us we needed to be sitting down when they told us their news. Their marriage seemed in good shape.

Were they moving back home from Gulfport, Mississippi? We couldn't imagine what was coming. They proceeded to tell us they were expecting a new family member the following February. Floored didn't hit the mark! Jennifer was now thirteen. What a whammy this would be, not only for Ron and Nancy, but especially her.

I asked them how they felt about this news. They said, "We are still trying to digest it. We think we are happy but don't know yet."

Ron and I sank down in our own thoughts. It would be a joy for us to have a new little one to love, but I wondered how this would affect Ron and Nancy. I wanted this to be a blessing for them.

"Oh, Lord, what wonderful news, this new life coming into our family and your world. There must be a reason for this, and only you know what it is. Help them adjust to their new life and child. Keep Nancy and the baby safe until he or she is born into this world. Be there for Jennifer as she adjusts to this new family member, as she has been the only one in Ron and Nancy's life until now. In all things, I ask this in Christ's name. Amen." The answer came: "I will be with them, Nancy."

About the same time, Ron and I had started talking about his retirement plans since Ford was offering buyouts for management level personnel. He had put in his thirty years, and the figures of the early buyout looked good. I told him whether he decided to retire or not, I would support his decision. This was a decision only he could make, as it affected his life more than mine. What would he do in retirement? How would he feel not going to work every day? Did he really want this?

By August, he had virtually made the decision to retire. Now we needed to decide what to do about our home. With retirement, we didn't need the big house, its mortgage payments, and other expenses. I began looking for a condo, which would fit our needs perfectly.

By the last week in August, we had signed the papers for a new condo and our home went on the market. Then September eleventh hit with no housing selling. Now, we had two mortgages instead of one, which we hadn't expected. Knowing our new condo would soon be ready for us to move in, we began taking inventory of what we needed to sell, give away, keep, or just dispose of. The insurance company told us we couldn't vacate our present home to move into our condo, as they wouldn't insure it or us.

We spent our time packing up our things while waiting for a buyer. All of a sudden, the week before Thanksgiving, a couple with three teenage boys came through and loved it. Since their schools were in the area, it made perfect sense for them to buy it. After signing the contract that weekend, we called our friendly moving company. I had them finish packing the breakables before moving us into our new home on the fourteenth of December. The timing couldn't be better. The baby's due date had been pushed ahead to December nineteenth. They wanted us there for the birth. After spending two days unpacking, we readied for our drive to Gulfport, Mississippi.

Early the morning of the seventeenth, Ron and I piled into our car and headed out. After a long, hard day of driving, we called Ron to see how things were. He told us the doctor was thinking of inducing Nancy the next day, as she was showing signs of preeclampsia. Knowing we still had five hundred miles to go, we realized we might not get there in time. Before the sun broke through, we headed straight for them. About two thirty that afternoon, Ron called on our cell phone to tell us Ronald Gene Hurley III had been born. The doctor attempted to induce Nancy, but Ronnie just couldn't handle it, so an emergency c-section quickly took place. Ronald Gene Hurley III arrived at 2:24 p.m. He was tiny—only five pounds—but perfect in every way. Ron gave us directions to the hospital, and within an hour and a half we were there. Oh, how beautiful he was. Nancy was back in her room. She was groggy from the general anesthetic she had been given, but she was alert enough to know we had arrived. Within minutes, I picked Ronnie up for the first time; our third grandson and Ron's namesake. Oh, how precious he was!

Ron and I stayed three weeks, spending Christmas and New Year's with them. I wanted Nancy to be fully able to take care of her family before we left. I loved holding, feeding, and cuddling our newest family member. What a special time! I love taking care of my grandchildren.

"Oh, Lord, what a precious blessing this little one is. I thought there wouldn't be room for loving another little one, but there definitely is. Oh, how I love this child. Help Jennifer adjust to sharing her parents with him. I know this will be hard for her, so please place your blanket of love and peace around her during this getting to know this little one. Help her to love and be there for her little brother. Help Nancy and Ron to have the patience and strength to be new, older parents to this blessing. Keep them all in your hands and guide them through the wrinkles of life as they get to know and love this child. In my Lord and Savior's name, Jesus Christ. Amen."

Leaving them was hard, especially the little one I had become so attached to. It was almost as hard as leaving Jennifer before we moved to England.

Two days later, exhausted from the long drive and helping out with the new baby, we arrived at our new home. When Ron opened our front door, all I saw was the mass of boxes stacked everywhere. All I wanted to do was cry. My nerves and body ached from tiredness. We looked at each other and said, "This can wait until morning."

The Friday after our return to Michigan, Ron's group threw him a retirement party. Almost a hundred of his fellow colleagues, along with some of their spouses, came to wish him well. John, Laura, her friend Denise, Judy, and Mitchell came to help send him off to his new life in retirement. It was a bittersweet night. He felt good about retiring but was sad to be leaving these men he had worked alongside for thirty years.

We both knew we were on a new life path. We had all the time in the world to do the things we wanted, and that felt good.

After another five years, our path took still another turn. We decided to leave the bitter, winter cold and snows for the warmth and sunshine of Sarasota, Florida. Again, we were leaving family, especially our two grandsons, Christopher and Patrick behind, which was tough to do.

A big part of our decision to leave Michigan came from the Lord. In prayer one day as I asked for his direction in my/our life, he said to me, "Your work here is finished. I want you to go to Sarasota. I have work for you to do there. Wait for me to work this through for you. Just follow what I want for you." We have always tried to listen and follow his words in everything, so this was a message we needed to heed. What he had in store for us we didn't know; only that we were to go. Our decision was made; we were off to Sarasota and what he had planned for us.

As we follow his path for us, our main thrust is our work in our church here. Ron enjoys his life as a golfer, and I am writing once again—the evidence of this is this book. I also volunteer my reading services to children who need one-on-one help at a nearby elementary school. I have also joined community activities that give me pleasure and fulfilment. We are content and know this is God's plan for us. We are reaching out to those within our parish, community, and activities to spread the good news and God's light to those in need. I know God is in our lives, as I feel him with me daily in prayer and all I do.

"Thank you, Lord, for your unfailing patience to me/us. You have always been there whenever we have needed you, even through the times we haven't noticed or we denied you were with us. I know you are there. Thank you for leading us to do the things best for us while we attempt to follow your course for us. You are an awesome and gracious God. You are my heavenly Father, and I know you love me because you have blessed not only me but Ron and our family so many times. Continue to guide me as well as Ron so we are never far from you or your principles and path. Thank you, God, for your Son, who lived and died for me taking away my sins on that tree at Calvary. I always want to be one of your children and have Christ as my shepherd protecting, leading, and loving me just as I am; the imperfect human I am. Thank you, Lord. Amen."

Looking Back

What Have I Learned about My Relationship with My Lord?

> "I will say of the Lord, 'He is my refuge and my fortress, my God, in whom I will trust.'"
>
> (Psalm 91:2)

Looking back over the past sixty-eight years, my life has been a real adventure. The Lord has always been with me, even in those times I wasn't aware he was working in my life. From my conception to this very minute, he has been with me at every twist and turn in my life.

He was with me in Mother's womb as he created who I am.

He was with me when Mother left me at the hospital for my tonsillectomy. He watched over me that night as well during my surgery and recovery.

He has protected me from a sexual predator by alerting me something was definitely wrong and had me flee from Mr. Reynolds immediately.

He heard my sobs and wails at Saint Anne's when Mother decided it was in my best interest to be there and wouldn't listen to my pleas not to be there.

He heard my cries of sorrow at my brother's death and the devastation when my sister died.

He has listened through the years of my frustration and anger with Mother as she belittled or criticized me. His patience with me through all my rantings and ravings with her showed me his constant presence in my life, even the times I didn't believe he was with me.

Again, he listened to my cries as I found out Mother had read my letter before her cerebral hemorrhage and subsequent coma, leaving me not knowing what she thought/felt about it. All I knew was she had cried reading it. What did that mean for me? Anger reigned, but he was patient with me. He loved me in spite of it all. He felt my pain.

How could I ever have had the strength and courage to see my dad through those years after Mother's death, and especially his last years on earth? If he hadn't been there with and for me I could never have made it through it all.

He has bent over backward with me as I riled and at times still rile about Judy's denial and indifference to us when we moved to England. We still haven't been able to reconcile that. If it is to be, he will work through that also.

Even through the dark years in England, he stood by me. He has lovingly been there even when I didn't think he was or was thinking he didn't listen or care a thing about me. He remained with me and saw me through those things.

He has been with me through the joyful days as well.

He watched over and protected me through my creation as well as the long, hard hours of labor and delivery of my own birth. He greeted me with love.

He showed his love for me through my wonderful minister grandfather and his loving care and nurturing he expended on me. Grandpa taught me your love and Word through Bible reading and learning.

He laid his rays of love and sunshine on me the day I became confirmed and vowed to be his child.

He found ways to teach me I was capable, successful, and wonderful: class vice-president, photography editor, honor student, and Miss Brigadier.

He brought me to the man he had chosen to be my life-time partner: a loving, understanding, and compassionate man whom I truly love.

As Ron and I vowed to love and be with each other for all time, he showered us with his blessings and love. When we came out of church, his rays of sunshine greeted us, making us know we were to be together for all times. He kept me healthy and safe during each pregnancy from the time of our sons' conceptions through their births into his and our world.

He showed us his love through nature as we grew the crops that sustained us during our years of little money at graduate school. He found the right position for Ron after graduation.

He gave me the strength and courage to obtain my bachelor's and master's degrees. He made me feel confident so I could get through it all successfully.

He chose the two beautiful wives for my sons, giving me the daughters I never was able to have. In that love, Ron and John blessed me with four wonderful grandchildren to love and admire. On top of that, recently he presented me with a beautiful great-granddaughter.

He has been with me every step and word of this book about our relationship!

What would my life have been like if my Lord hadn't always been there with me, guiding and holding my hand and heart all the way? How could I have survived without him there, especially in the hard times? How could I not have praised him for all the blessings he has bestowed on me? I wouldn't be who I am today! He is such an awesome, loving, and forgiving God! I need and want him in every part of my life, as well as those of my families and friends.

Now you might ask, "How can you thank and praise him for all he has done and been in your life?" My answer is this book. In it I reveal who he is, how wonderful, patient, and loving he is. With this book I want to glorify him in all he did and does, not only in my life but our life/lives. He can do the same for you if you only open yourself up to him and let him fill you with his love and presence. This is my thanksgiving to him, to share him with you and to glorify all he does for me and his world if I and we just let him.

"Thank you, God, for being there for me and us. I always want to praise you for all you have done for me. You are my Father, my Lord, my Master, my Shepherd, and my Helpmate in all I do. You also sent your Son to show me your ways and to bring me back to you in a wonderful relationship of love, forgiveness, and redemption. I love you and always want to be in your presence and flock forever. I love you, Lord! Be with me always. Amen.